The

of the Master

How to share your faith simply, effectively, biblically
. . . the way Jesus did

KIRK CAMERON
and
RAY COMFORT

TYNDALE HOUSE PUBLISHERS, INC., WHEATON, ILLINOIS

Visit Tyndale's exciting Web site at www.tyndale.com

The Way of the Master: How to Share Your Faith Simply, Effectively, Biblically . . . the Way Jesus Did

Edited by Dave Lindstedt

The material in this book has been revised and expanded from *Revival's Golden Key: Unlocking the Door to Revival,* edited by Lynn Copeland, published by Bridge-Logos Publishers, 2002; previously titled *God Has a Wonderful Plan for Your Life: The Myth of the Modern Message,* published by Living Waters Publications, 2000.

Library of Congress Cataloging-in-Publication Data

Comfort, Ray.
    The way of the Master : how to share your faith simply, effectively, biblically—the way Jesus did / Ray Comfort, Kirk Cameron.
        p. cm.
Includes bibliographical references.
    ISBN 1-4143-0061-1 (pbk.)
    1. Witness bearing (Christianity)   I. Cameron, Kirk, date.   II. Title.
BV4520.C638 2004
248'.5—dc22   2003026185

Printed in the United States of America

08   07   06   05
7   6

Woe to you lawyers! For you have taken away the key of knowledge. You did not enter in yourselves, and those who were entering in you hindered. LUKE 11:52

CONTENTS

SPECIAL THANKS TO

Joc and Walter Greeman, Mark Cahill,
Jay and Margie Grosfeld, Larry and Carol Ells,
Jeff and Melissa Loritz, Barbara Cameron,
Anna and Dale Jackson, Felicia Woodson,
"Scotty" and Carol Scott, Larry Taggart,
Lynn Copeland, Dan Arnold, Rick Hart,
Tammy Hays, and Ashley and Larry Lee
for their faithful support of our ministry,
and to Dave Lindstedt for his
invaluable editorial work.

FOREWORD

When I became a Christian at the age of eighteen, I was a successful young actor who had attained riches and fame. But a faithful pastor helped me to realize that my wealth and Hollywood charm wouldn't help me on Judgment Day. I learned that because God is holy and just, He cannot be bribed. Despite the fact that I was admired by my fans and considered myself to be a good person, I came to understand that I had grievously sinned against God and needed His forgiveness. I learned about God's love and mercy shown through Jesus' death on the cross, and it overwhelmed me. I wholeheartedly turned away from my sin, trusted God to forgive me, and asked Him to make me the man He wanted me to be. Someone gave me a Bible, which I began to read, and I fell in love with the One who first loved me and gave His own life for me.

I can honestly say that nothing in all my life compares with the joy of knowing Jesus Christ as Savior and Lord. But after learning the principles of biblical evangelism—the principles contained in this book—I fell to my knees with a deeper sense of brokenness and gratitude for the Cross than ever before. I now understand why the apostle Paul felt indebted to all men and compelled to preach the gospel to every creature. Because I now know God's will for my life and better understand God's call to every believer, I too can say, "Woe is me if I do not preach the gospel!" (1 Corinthians 9:16). These foundation-shaking principles have opened my eyes to the destiny of the unsaved, taught me how to share my faith effectively, and shattered my lukewarm concern for my unsaved family members and friends.

Who do you know who isn't saved? Your mother or father? A sibling? A good friend? Your spouse? Your child? Think of their terrible fate if they die without Christ. I'm sure you want to share your faith, but perhaps you're afraid, or maybe you don't feel equipped. This book will help you overcome your fears and give you the tools you need. With Ray Comfort's powerful and biblically sound text, together with my commentaries and real-life stories of sharing my faith, I know this publication will be a great blessing to you. My prayer is that God would do within you what He did within me. May you, too, be given a fresh and deeper understanding of the true gospel, and may it ignite a fire in you to compassionately share your faith with those you know and love. Please don't let anything distract you as you read *The Way of the Master*. May God richly bless you.

Kirk Cameron

PREFACE

The roots of this book go way back to an experience I had in the early 1980s as I waited to take off in an airplane. I noticed that someone had left a small scrap of paper sitting precariously at the top of the seat pocket. As I leaned forward and took hold of the two-inch-square piece of paper, I mumbled in semi-jest, "Could be a word from the Lord." I turned it over and my eyes widened as I read, "I have yet many things to say unto you, but ye cannot bear them now (John 16:12, KJV)." I remember being mystified by the words "ye cannot bear them now."

One year later, I entered into the deepest, darkest, most frightening time of my life as I began to suffer ongoing episodes of irrational fear. These panic attacks left me so broken that for more than a year I couldn't even muster enough courage to eat a meal with my family. It took five long years to recover from these experiences.[1] I now understand what the verb *to bear* means. In its various usages it can mean "to endure," "to bring forth," and "to disseminate." That terrible time left me with a broken spirit, yet it brought me to a point where I could endure the attacks and bring forth and disseminate the many things I had learned. This book is about those "many things."

In October 2001, when I met Kirk Cameron, one of the first things he said was, "How can we get this teaching out there?"[2] We decided that one way was for him to lend his name to this book and to add his personal comments in the places that stirred his heart. (Kirk's comments and additions are marked by an arrow: ➤.)

The purpose of this book is simply to equip you to share the gospel biblically. After you read it, I suspect you will want to learn more, so I have compiled another publication called *The Evidence Bible,* a "munitions resource" for soldiers of Christ that is designed to help you hone your evangelistic skills to hit your target with precision and power. *The Evidence Bible* was a finalist for the Evangelical Christian Publishers Association (ECPA) 2002 Gold Medallion Book Award, and it has been commended by Franklin Graham, Josh McDowell, Dr. D. James Kennedy, and many other Christian leaders.

Other resources to help you share the gospel simply, effectively, and biblically—the way Jesus did—include our online School of Biblical Evangelism and our television series, *The Way of the Master.* You will find more information about these resources on our Web site: www.wayofthemaster.com. While you're there, sign up for the free newsletter, and together let's reach the world for Jesus Christ while there is still time.

1 | DERELICTION OF DUTY

Do you enjoy worshiping God? Most people in the Church would say they do. Every Sunday all across the country, auditoriums are filled with hand-raising, God-loving Christians singing their praises to God. That's understandable, because when the Holy Spirit dwells within us, it's not hard to worship our glorious and worthy Creator. It's as natural for Christians to worship the Lord as it is for flowers to open their petals in the warm sunlight.

On the other hand, demonstrating our love for God through our obedience to His will (John 14:15) doesn't happen quite as naturally. It takes a concerted effort to obey the Great Commission and follow in Christ's footsteps, seeking to save the lost. Nevertheless, our professed love and worship of God should show itself in a determined devotion to do His will.

May I ask you a personal question? When was the last time you shared your faith with an unsaved person? When did you last meditate on the fact that all who die in their sins will be cast into a lake of fire? In his book *The Coming Revival,* Dr. Bill Bright notes that only 2 percent of American churchgoers share their faith with others.[1] That is tragic. If the love of God dwells in us, how can we not be horrified by the fate of the lost? Yet, many professing Christians today are so locked into worship (with the volume turned high) that they seem to give little or no thought to the fate of the ungodly.

To make a very important point, I would like for you to consider the following scenario:

> *An experienced big-city firefighter was charged yesterday with grave neglect of duty. Prosecutors maintain that he abandoned his responsibility and betrayed the people of the city when he failed to release rescue equipment during a recent fire, resulting in the needless and tragic deaths of a family of five.*
>
> *The lead prosecuting attorney said that for more than three minutes after arriving at the scene, the firefighter sat in his vehicle, wearing earphones and listening to a CD, while a family of five screamed to be rescued from the sixth floor of the burning building. Horrified bystanders reported that, as flames licked at the mother's clothing, she cried out in terror and fell to her death, still clutching an infant in her arms.*
>
> *The distraught onlookers also said that the father held two terrified children as he was engulfed by the massive flames. This terrifying drama took place in full view of the firefighter as he remained seated in the fire truck listening to the CD.*
>
> *Eyewitnesses were sickened when they discovered that the reason the firefighter had remained in the locked emergency vehicle was simply to test a new high-tech CD player that he had purchased as a gift for the fire chief.*
>
> *The chief immediately distanced himself from the defendant and dishonorably discharged him from the fire department. In a prepared statement, the chief said that there were no words to describe such a betrayal of those the firefighter was sworn to protect.*
>
> *At the trial, the defense pleaded "no contest," but added that the defendant had gone to great personal sacrifice to purchase the expensive gift for the chief, and he hoped that the judge would take that into account when passing sentence.*

What do you think would be a fitting punishment for this firefighter's serious crime—probation? Two years in jail? Twenty years? Life? Death? What sentence would you give the negligent firefighter?

Perhaps you're saying, "That's ridiculous. A firefighter would never do that." Allow me to apply the parable: If you and I are not seeking to save the lost "with fear, pulling them out of the fire, hating even the garment defiled by the flesh" (Jude 1:23), are we not, in effect, negligent firefighters? That's a sobering question, isn't it?

Am I saying that if we don't evangelize we're not saved? Of course not. But if we would expect a firefighter to make saving lives a priority, are we honest enough to judge ourselves by the same standard? Are we doing all we can to rescue the lost, or are we sitting passively in the pews while people perish?

I recognize that these questions are shocking—and perhaps you're feeling a bit put off at this point. But I urge you to stay with me. My purpose is not to offend, but it is to get your attention and to present things as they really are. After all, what the Bible tells us about the fate of the lost (Revelation 20:15) is pretty shocking.

In Revelation 3:1-3, Jesus says to the church at Sardis, "I know your works, that you have a name that you are alive, but you are dead. Be watchful, and strengthen the things which remain, that are ready to die, for I have not found your works perfect before God. Remember therefore how you have received and heard; hold fast and repent. Therefore if you will not watch, I will come upon you as a thief, and you will not know what hour I will come upon you."

Oswald J. Smith said, "Oh, my friends, we are loaded down with countless church activities, while the real work of the Church, that of evangelizing and winning the lost, is almost entirely neglected." We have been gazing to the heavens while sinners are sinking into hell.

Worship is the highest calling of the Christian, and we can see in the book of Revelation that the Church will one day be consumed in worship before the throne of the Almighty. But when we look back at the book of Acts, we don't find the Church consumed with worship. Instead, we find that those Christians were devoted to reaching the lost, to the point that they willingly gave their lives to preach the gospel.

Time is short. Let us not sit passively by during these crucial days of opportunity, drowning out the cries of a dying humanity with the sweet sounds of worship. Let us reevaluate our priorities, take off the earphones, unlock the doors, become equipped, and demonstrate the depth of our love for God by rescuing those who are about to perish.

I wonder if you have been praying for revival. Many are, and that's good. But if we make revival sovereign and don't share our faith with the lost, in effect this is what we are saying: "Lord, I know that you have commanded us to go into all the world and preach the gospel to every creature. But we will stay here and pray. We know that you have chosen the 'foolishness' of preaching to save them that believe. But we will stay here and pray. And we know that the Bible asks us, 'How will they hear without a preacher?' But we will stay here and pray, because it sure is easier to talk to God about people than it is to talk to people about God."

C. T. Studd said: "We Christians too often substitute prayer for playing the game. Prayer is good; but when used as a substitute for obedience, it is nothing but a blatant hypocrisy, a despicable Pharisaism.... To your knees, man! And to your Bible! Decide at once! Don't hedge! Time flies! Cease your insults to God. Quit consulting flesh and blood. Stop your lame, lying, and cowardly excuses."

A. W. Tozer hit the nail on the head: "Have you noticed how much praying for revival has been going on of late—and how little revival has resulted? I believe the problem is that we have been trying to substitute praying for obeying, and it simply will not work. To pray for revival while ignoring the plain precept laid down in Scripture is to waste a lot of words and get nothing for our trouble. Prayer will become effective when we stop using it as a substitute for obedience."

God has given the Church the ability (under His hand) to govern the tides of revival. A. W. Pink writes, "It is true that [many] are praying for world-wide revival. But ... it would be more timely, and more scriptural, for prayer to be made to the Lord of the Harvest that He would raise up and thrust forth laborers who would fearlessly and faithfully preach those truths which are calculated to bring about a revival."

That is the purpose of this book—to put into your hands "truths which are calculated to bring about a revival."

PHENOMENAL GROWTH . . . BUT WHERE HAS IT GONE?

We live in exciting times. All around us we are seeing signs of the end of the age. Nation is rising against nation. There are wars, earthquakes, famines, and violence. The Jews are back in Jerusalem and the city has become a "burdensome stone" to the nations (Zechariah 12:3, KJV). Jesus said that iniquity (or lawlessness) would abound (Matthew 24:12), and it certainly has. At the same time, we have seen the phenomenal rise of megachurches with congregations in the tens of thousands; we have heard of millions in Russia, China, and Africa coming to the Savior; and pockets of revival have sprung up in the United States and other parts of the world. These are indeed exciting times.

Yet, with all the excitement, it seems that many Christians in the United States have overlooked a few statistical inconsistencies. In 1996, for example, a survey conducted by the Alan Guttmacher Institute in New York found that "18 percent of abortion patients describe themselves as born-again or evangelical Christians."[1] That is, of all those who murdered their own children, nearly one in five professed faith in Jesus Christ. That is difficult to reconcile with the fact that Christians are supposed to love God and love others as much as they love themselves.

In 1994, the Barna Research Group found further evidence that all is not well in the contemporary Church. A survey revealed that one in four American adults who said they were born again also believed that Jesus sinned while He was on the earth. Think for a moment of the implications of such a theology. Here we have millions of "believers" who supposedly confess that Jesus is Lord, and yet they think He sinned. They either don't know what the Bible teaches about Jesus or they believe it is inaccurate when it says that Jesus "knew no sin" (2 Corinthians 5:21), that He was "in all points tempted as we are, yet without sin" (Hebrews 4:15), and that He "committed no sin, nor was deceit found in His mouth" (1 Peter 2:22). Furthermore, if Jesus sinned, it would mean that He wasn't the spotless Lamb of God the Scriptures say He was (1 Peter 1:19); that His sacrifice wasn't perfect; and that when God accepted Jesus' death as an atonement for our sins, He sanctioned a "contaminated payment" and is therefore corrupt by nature. Sadly, the multitudes who profess faith in Jesus yet deny His sinless perfection appear to be strangers to true regeneration.

Some years ago, the Barna Research Group revealed that 62 percent of Americans claim to have "a relationship with Jesus Christ that is meaningful to them." Yet a Gallup poll taken around the same time found that, of those Americans who say they have a relationship with the Savior, only 10 percent (approximately) were what the Gallup researchers called "a breed apart": "They are more tolerant of people of diverse backgrounds. They are involved in charitable activities. They are involved in practical Christianity. They are absolutely committed to prayer."

That sounds like normal, biblical Christianity, but if it applies to only 10 percent of the Church, it means there are great masses of people who say that Jesus Christ is meaningful to them but who are not "a breed apart." They are not involved in good works, nor are they tolerant of others. Neither are they involved in practical Christianity or committed to prayer. In other words, there are millions of people in America who insinuate that they belong to Jesus Christ, but their lives don't match their claims. Another Gallup poll found "very little difference in the behavior of the churched and unchurched on a wide range of items including lying, cheating, and stealing." These surveys were taken during the 1990s, but is there any reason to believe the situation has improved since then?

According to the book *The Day America Told the Truth*, 91 percent of Americans lie regularly at work or at home, 86 percent lie regularly to parents, and 75 percent lie regularly to friends. A staggering 92 percent own a

Bible, but only 11 percent read it daily. Other surveys have found that 90 percent of Americans pray, but 87 percent do not believe in all of the Ten Commandments. To top it off, 61 percent, according to a Roper Center poll, believe that premarital sex is not morally wrong.

A more recent Barna poll, reported in the October 24, 2003, edition of the *Los Angeles Times*, noted that "one out of ten born-again Christians—those who believe entry into heaven is solely based on confession of sins and faith in Jesus Christ—also believe in reincarnation, which violates Christian tenets … *and half believe a person can earn salvation based on good deeds even without accepting Christ as the way to eternal life*" (emphasis added). Read the last part of that quote again.

When I travel, I often channel surf in my hotel room in an effort to find something wholesome to watch on television. This often means crossing the polluted and shark-infested waters of MTV. If anything epitomizes today's foul-mouthed, sexually perverted, depraved, blasphemous, and rebellious generation, it is MTV. Nevertheless, a surprising number of Christian teenagers watch MTV, according to an article in the December 1995 issue of *Youth Leader* magazine: "More Christian teens watch MTV each week (42 percent) than non-Christians (33 percent), according to a Barna Research Group survey of evangelical teens."

The article went on to quote Barna surveys showing that of these same teens, 65 percent said they prayed daily. An amazing 72 percent believed the Bible. However, 66 percent confessed that they had lied to a parent or teacher in the last three months, 55 percent had had sex, 55 percent had cheated on an exam, and 20 percent had either gotten drunk or used illegal drugs.

In an interview on a popular national radio program, a Christian youth leader spoke with great concern about how young people were "leaving the Church in droves." He had taken a survey to find out why these teenagers were turning their backs on God, and he cited the number one reason as "a lack of opportunity in the Church," implying that the Church should get its act together and give young people more opportunities.

Ask any pastor if there are opportunities to serve within his church and he will no doubt tell you of the lack of people willing to teach Sunday school, visit the sick and the elderly, go out with the evangelism team, clean the church building, etc.

Perhaps there is another reason why young people are leaving the Church in droves. Today there are many who name the name of Christ but who never "depart from iniquity" (2 Timothy 2:19). They are false converts who "ask Jesus into their heart" but are actually unconverted because they have never truly repented. The truth is that if someone's heart is still in the world—if he is a "Judas" at heart—he will find *any* excuse to stay there. It is important that we examine ourselves to see if we are in the faith (2 Corinthians 13:5). Those who allow sin in their lives are actually opening themselves up to demonic influence, just as Judas did.

If Judas had been given a survey form to fill out, he would likely have had many justifications for his betrayal of the Savior and his falling away:

- He was publicly humiliated by Jesus when he suggested giving funds to the poor.
- He felt a deep sense of rejection because he was not part of the "inner circle."
- He needed the money.
- The chief priests made him do it.
- The devil made him do it.
- The responsibility of looking after the finances became too much for him.
- He was abused as a child.
- He had a betrayal syndrome.
- He lacked a father figure.
- He didn't think his actions would have the grisly repercussions they had.

There are some who believe that Judas had never even been a believer. There is a good reason for this, because Jesus said of him, "One of you is a devil" (John 6:70). That's not something Jesus would likely say about one of His true followers.

The Parabolic Key

In Mark 4:3-8, Jesus taught the crowd the well-known parable of the sower:

> *Listen! Behold, a sower went out to sow. And it happened, as he sowed, that some seed fell by the wayside; and the birds of the air came and devoured it. Some fell on stony ground, where it did not have much earth; and immediately it sprang up because it had no depth of earth. But when*

the sun was up it was scorched, and because it had no root it withered away. And some seed fell among thorns; and the thorns grew up and choked it, and it yielded no crop. But other seed fell on good ground and yielded a crop that sprang up, increased and produced: some thirtyfold, some sixty, and some a hundred.

When Jesus told His disciples the parable of the sower, they did not understand what it meant. When they asked Him about it later, He said, "Do you not understand this parable? How then will you understand all the parables?" (Mark 4:13). In other words, if they could understand the parable of the sower, they would hold the key to unlocking the mysteries of all the other parables.

If there is one message that comes from the parable about the stony ground, the thorny ground, and the good ground, it is this: *When the gospel is preached, there will be true and false conversions.*

Judas, for example, was a false convert. He was a hypocrite—a *pretender*—whose desire (it seems) for riches and power choked out his affection for Christ. In terms of the parable, we would say that he was a thorny-ground hearer, in whom "the cares of this world, the deceitfulness of riches, and the desires for other things entering in choke the word, and it becomes unfruitful" (Mark 4:19).

Judas had no idea who Jesus really was. When a woman anointed Jesus with an expensive ointment in an act of sacrificial worship, Judas complained that the ointment should have been sold and the money given to the poor (John 12:3-6). In his estimation, Jesus of Nazareth wasn't worth such extravagance—He was only worth about thirty pieces of silver. Moreover, the Bible tells us that Judas was lying when he said that he cared for the poor. He was actually a thief who so lacked a healthy fear of God that he was stealing money from the collection bag (John 12:6). Nevertheless, to all outward appearances, Judas was a follower and disciple of Christ.

Once the premise has been established that there will be true and false conversions when the gospel is preached, then the light of revelation begins to dawn on the rest of what Jesus taught in parables about the kingdom of God. If one grasps the principle that true and false converts will be *alongside each other* in the Church, then the other parabolic teachings also make sense: the wheat and tares (Matthew 13:24-30), the wise virgins and the foolish virgins (Matthew 25:1-13), and the sheep and goats (Matthew 25:31-46). Take, for example, the parable of the dragnet:

> *"Again, the kingdom of heaven is like a dragnet that was cast into the sea and gathered some of every kind, which, when it was full, they drew to shore; and they sat down and gathered the good into vessels, but threw the bad away. So it will be at the end of the age. The angels will come forth, separate the wicked from among the just, and cast them into the furnace of fire. There will be wailing and gnashing of teeth." Jesus said to them, "Have you understood all these things?" They said to Him, "Yes, Lord." (Matthew 13:47-51)*

Notice that the good fish and the bad fish were in the net *together.* Notice also that *unbelievers* are not caught in the dragnet of the kingdom of heaven; they remain in the world. The "fish" that are caught are those who hear and respond to the gospel—the evangelistic "catch." They remain together, the true and the false, until the Day of Judgment.

False converts *do* have a measure of spirituality. Judas certainly did. He had apparently convinced the other disciples that he truly cared for the poor. And he *seemed* so trustworthy that he was the one who looked after the finances. When Jesus said, "One of you will betray me," the disciples didn't point the finger at Judas; instead, they suspected themselves, saying, "Is it I, Lord?" That's why it's not surprising that so few within the body of Christ today would suspect that we are surrounded by those who fall into the "Judas" category. However, alarms should go off when we look at statistics such as those cited in this chapter. A warning should sound when the Church, which ought to have tremendous clout in society, sadly lacks influence. Despite the millions of professed believers in the United States, we can't even outlaw the killing of the unborn. Something is *radically* wrong. However, before we look at the remedy, we must consider the cause.

THE WAY OUT
OF PROBLEMS?

In light of the alarming statistics cited in the previous chapter, few would deny that the Church as a whole has fallen short of the powerful, disciplined, sanctified Church we see in the book of Acts. This has happened because the enemy has very subtly diverted our attention away from our core message. Instead of preaching the Good News that sinners can be made *righteous* in Christ and escape the wrath to come, we have settled for a "gospel" that implies that God's primary purpose in saving us is to unfold a "wonderful plan" for our lives: to solve our problems, make us happy in Christ, and rescue us from the hassles of this life.

> ➤ Read this sentence again: Instead of preaching the Good News that sinners can be made righteous in Christ and escape the wrath to come, we have settled for a "gospel" that implies that God's primary purpose in saving us is to unfold a "wonderful plan" for our lives: to solve our problems, make us happy in Christ, and rescue us from the hassles of this life. Make sure you understand the difference. —KC

One of America's largest Christian publishers produces a full-color tract that epitomizes the promise of a hassle-free life. Titled *Is There Any Way Out?* it reads:

Everyone is looking for a way out of their problems. . . . There's no easy way out. You won't get respect by joining a gang. You won't find love on the backseat of a car. You'll never find success by dropping out of school. And the chances are about one million to one that you'll win the lottery. If you're really serious about making your life better, then try God's way. God gets right to the source of most of our problems: **sin.**

It may sound admirable—and even biblical—to imply to sinners that Christianity promises to make their lives better, but it's just not true.

It seems that some are so entrenched in the "wonderful plan" message that they don't equate *real life* with the message they preach. I know from many years of itinerant ministry that it is no exaggeration to say that the following scenario is commonplace in many pulpits each Sunday morning:

God loves you and has a wonderful plan for your life. He wants to give you true happiness and to fill the God-shaped vacuum in your heart that you've been trying to fill with sex, drugs, alcohol, and money. Jesus said, "I have come that [you might] have life, and . . . have it more abundantly." So come forward now and give your life to Jesus, so that you can experience this wonderful new life in Christ.

While they are coming, let's pray for the Smiths, who lost their two children in a car accident this week. Brother Jones has been diagnosed with cancer. Remember to uphold the whole family. His wife had another miscarriage on Tuesday, and both of their other children are chronic asthmatics. Sister Bryant fell and broke her hip. She's such a dear saint—she's had trial after trial in her life, especially since the death of her husband, Ernie. Elder Chambers lost his job this week. That will make things difficult for the Chambers family, especially with his upcoming triple-bypass operation. Sister Lancing died of kidney failure on Monday night. Keep the Lancing family in prayer, because it's their third tragedy this year.

How many of you this morning need prayer for sickness or have problems with depression? That many? You had better stay in your seats and we will have a corporate prayer.

This makes no sense. The preacher promises a bed of roses for those who come to Christ, but those who are in Christ are evidently sitting on a painful bed of thorns. He promises a smooth flight, but those who are already on board are suffering terrible turbulence—and no one seems to notice the paradox.

Let me tell you about a few of my Christian friends who live in the real world. One went with his wife to a meeting. Their teenage son drove there alone. On the way home, my friend came across an accident, so he stopped to help. When he looked in the vehicle, he saw his beloved teenage son, dead—impaled on the steering wheel.

The senior pastor of a church where I was on staff was roused from his bed at three o'clock one morning to counsel a man who had come to his door and was waiting in the living room. As the pastor stepped into the room, the man began to slash him with a machete. The pastor almost died, and was irrevocably scarred both physically and mentally, so much so that he was unable to minister and required twenty-four-hour care.

Another pastor friend learned that his wife had multiple sclerosis. Her crippling disease left him as the only one in the family able to take care of their three young boys. Then he was diagnosed with cancer.

One of my friends, a graphic artist, married a woman whose Christian husband had died of cancer, leaving her to raise five kids. The marriage seemed fine until she ran off with another man. She left my friend with the one child that was his. Some time after that, someone broke into his home and beat him to a pulp. He had to be rushed to the emergency room for treatment.

On June 19, 2000, five trainees with New Tribes Mission pitched a tent during a violent storm in Mississippi. Jenny Knapp, an attractive twenty-year-old, noticed that rain was causing the roof to cave in, so she lifted the tent pole to raise the height of the roof. Suddenly, a bolt of lightning struck the pole and tore through her body, giving her second-degree burns on her face, arm, and back. Her friends resuscitated her lifeless body and rushed her to the hospital where she was placed in the intensive care unit. The young missionary recovered, but she is terribly scarred and partially blind. It is a sad fact of life, but in the real world, lightning strikes the just and the unjust.

At least one church I know of may have noticed the paradox. They were called The Happy Church but recently decided, for some reason, to change their name.

If we still want to cling to the message that "God loves you and has a wonderful plan for your life," we had better hide *Foxe's Book of Martyrs* from the eyes of non-Christians. Speaking of martyrdom, have you ever pondered what it would be like to be huddling together as a family in a Roman arena as hungry and ferocious lions rush in? Have you ever considered what it would be like to be eaten by lions? I have. My fertile imagination runs wild. What do you give the lion to eat first—your arm? How long would you remain conscious as he gnawed on it?

Can you imagine the feelings you would have if you had led your loved ones in the sinner's prayer using the *wonderful plan* hook? Suppose you had read to them from a booklet by a well-known and respected man of God in which he writes, "Everyone is seeking happiness. Why, then, are more people not experiencing this happiness? According to the Bible, true happiness can be found only through God's way." What would you tell your beloved family as you looked into their terrified eyes? How could you reconcile the words *wonderful* and *happiness* with having the fierce teeth of a lion rip you apart, limb from limb?

These are terrible thoughts, but they are not merely my fantasies. Multitudes of martyrs have suffered unspeakable torture for the name of Jesus Christ. It should not have been a surprise to the early Church when persecution hit them. Jesus warned them that they may have to give their lives for His name's sake. He even said, "Brother will deliver up brother to death, and a father his child; and children will rise up against parents and cause them to be put to death. And you will be hated by all for My name's sake" (Matthew 10:21-22).

Church tradition tells us the fate of several apostles and early evangelists:

- Philip: Crucified, Phrygia, AD 54
- Matthew: Beheaded, Ethiopia, AD 60
- Barnabas: Burned to death, Cyprus, AD 64
- Mark: Dragged to death, Alexandria, AD 64
- James (the Less): Clubbed to death, Jerusalem, AD 66
- Paul: Beheaded, Rome, AD 66

- Peter: Crucified, Rome, AD 69
- Andrew: Crucified, Achaia, AD 70
- Thomas: Speared to death, Calamina, AD 70
- Luke: Hanged, Athens, AD 93

Persecution has always been the portion of the godly. According to Scripture, "Others were tortured. . . . Still others had trial of mockings and scourgings, yes, and of chains and imprisonment. They were stoned, they were sawn in two, were tempted, were slain with the sword. They wandered about in sheepskins and goatskins, being destitute, afflicted, tormented—of whom the world was not worthy. They wandered in deserts and mountains, in dens and caves of the earth" (Hebrews 11:35-38).

The "wonderful plan" message is evident in almost every corner of Christendom. If you train yourself to keep an eye out for it, you will see it everywhere. Years ago I purchased a yellow VW Beetle. Before I made the purchase, I hardly saw a Beetle anywhere. After I had my own, they seemed to be almost everywhere I looked. This wasn't because there had been a sudden increase in sales of VWs; it was because I now had an eye to look for them.

The same applies to the message of the contemporary church. Search the Web sites of respected evangelistic organizations and local churches and you will see the "God has a wonderful plan for your life" message in their gospel presentations. It is in the lyrics of popular songs, ingrained in Christian books, tracts, tapes, CDs, and videos. You will regularly find it tagged on at the conclusion of radio and television Bible teaching. Let's look at a few examples:[1]

- "God loves you and offers a wonderful plan for your life . . . the reward is eternal life. God had a plan when He created the world in which we live. He also had a plan when He made you. The most wonderful experience that can happen to you is to discover and participate in God's plan for your life." (From the Web site of a well-known music group)
- In an article titled "That Wonderful Plan for Your Life," a respected Bible teacher writes, "I am amazed at the variety of things that are offered to us every day to help us find the secret of successful living. Magazine articles by the dozens tell us how to cope with various problems; TV commercials—dozens to a program it seems—bombard

us, telling us how to be successful in life, or at least how to look successful even if we really are not; health clubs offer us saunas and whirlpool baths to relax us so we can face life with equanimity; while various kinds of drugs are available to turn us on, turn us off, take us out, or whatever. All this is evidence of the universal search for the secret of enjoyment of life. Billions of dollars are spent every day on this quest. Many of us are familiar with Bill Bright's Four Spiritual Laws, the first of which is, "God loves you and has a wonderful plan for your life." When talking to someone about his relationship with God, that is an appropriate place to begin."

o   "Bridge to Life," a well-known and much used gospel presentation by a very well respected Christian organization begins as follows:

"Step 1—God's Love and His plan. God created us in His own image to be His friend and to experience a full life assured of His love, abundant and eternal.

"Jesus said, ' . . . I have come that they may have life, and have it to the full.' (John 10:10b)

"' . . . we have peace with God through our Lord Jesus Christ.' (Romans 5:1)

"Since God planned for us to have peace and abundant life right now, why are most people not having this experience?"

o   What about the popular "Roman Road" method of sharing the gospel?* Ironically, a typical presentation doesn't even mention the principle of using the Law to reach the lost, even though a key element of Paul's message in the book of Romans is about the purpose of God's Law. When the Roman Road leaves out the "stones" of the Law, those who travel its path become bogged down in the muddy methods of modern evangelism. If we would simply put the stones of the Law into the road, it would become a first-class evangelistic highway to heaven.

The "God has a wonderful plan for your life" message often comes in other, more subtle forms. Listen to the message of the popular preachers of our day. Unless you are familiar with the "whole counsel of God" (Acts 20:26-27), you may not even notice what's missing. Do they faithfully preach

---

* The "Roman Road" is a systematic presentation of the gospel, based on the following verses: Romans 1:20-21, Romans 3:23, Romans 5:8, Romans 6:23, Romans 10:9-10, Romans 10:13, and Romans 11:36.

against sin? Do they preach righteousness and judgment (as Jesus did)? Do they speak about true repentance (not simply a "change of mind"), and warn about the reality of hell (as Jesus did)?

> If you have an ear to hear, you will find that many of today's preachers fill their churches by teaching legitimate life-changing principles. However, although these principals are helpful for daily living, they fail to unmask the villians of sin and self-righteousness that keep vast numbers of false converts sitting in a fool's paradise, comfortable in the pews, thinking they are friends with God when they are still His enemies.

Psalm 53:2-3 tells us that "God looks down from heaven upon the children of men, to see if there are any who understand, who seek God. Every one of them has turned aside; they have together become corrupt; there is none who does good, no, not one." If the Bible tells us that no man naturally seeks after God, what then is the typical "seeker" seeking? No doubt most are seeking after peace, joy, happiness, and fulfillment (a wonderful plan for their lives). Not surprisingly, that is precisely what the modern gospel message offers them. This method of evangelism is also known as "felt needs" evangelism.* Find out where a sinner hurts, and tell him Jesus will make it better. Remember the old advertising principal: "Scratch 'em where they itch"? Well, the modern gospel does it. The problem is that sinners aren't itching to crucify their flesh. They aren't hungering and thirsting for righteousness. They're itching for a more enjoyable life and thirsting for sin. The Bible says they drink it in like water (Job 15:16). What unregenerate sinners really seek is a life change that brings positive results, won't cramp their style, and won't cost too much. Does that not sum up the promise of much of contemporary American Christianity? No wonder some churches are so full they're bursting at the seams. —KC

---

* Should we not address the legitimate "felt needs" of the lost? To answer that important question, let's look at an analogy: A child who was running through a wooded area fell onto a sharp stick and cut his jugular vein. His father immediately swooped him up and pressed his thumb to the boy's neck in an effort to stop the gushing blood while he rushed him to the hospital. In the emergency room, when the surgeon arrived, the child showed him a small splinter he had received in his thumb when he fell. He wanted the surgeon to remove it. Of course, the surgeon ignored the child's plea, and began work to stop the life-threatening injury to the boy's neck. Modern evangelism preaches a message that calls sinners to come to God for their "splinters" rather than for that which is life-threatening. It tells the world that God will heal marriages, drug problems, alcohol problems, etc., when the real reason they should come to the Savior is that their life's blood

Again, if you don't know what *should be there* in the gospel message, you won't know what's missing. However, if you know what to look for, you'll find the teaching of the Law, hell, and judgment conspicuous by their absence. In essence, these preachers are saying that the patient will swallow the medicine far easier if it is watered down a little. If they leave out the parts that taste bitter to the world, people will come and fill their churches. The problem is that the bitter medicine they are watering down loses it curative properties. To keep a patient comfortable at night and then find him dead in the morning is not successful medicine by anyone's definition.

In the following story, Pat (not her real name), a mother of four, seems to be trying to reconcile the "wonderful plan" message with the reality of her life experience:

> *Have you ever heard, or said to someone you're witnessing to, that God has a wonderful plan for your life? What happens when that wonderful plan is not one you would have designed for yourself? It was almost Christmas, 1993. As my husband, Charlie, and I left the mall, I threw him the keys and settled into the passenger seat. I reached for the seat belt, then laid it back down, thinking that I would just recline and be comfortable for the ninety-minute trip home.*
>
> *The next thing I remember is waking to Charlie's terrified screams. I looked ahead and only saw grass and darkness. Soon I awoke in inten-sive care, strapped to a rotating bed. My legs were badly bruised and my teeth broken, but worst of all, my back was broken in three places and I was paralyzed from the waist down. These injuries have had a physical, emotional, and financial impact on my family. I never really thought about something like this happening. I didn't worry about it because things like this always happen to "the other guy," not to me.*

> ➢ Do you see how the "God has a wonderful plan for your life" hook can be misleading? Do you see how it can cause a woman like this to conclude that the promise of Christianity is only wishful thinking and doesn't hold up in the real world? Can you see how a sinner

is gushing from their throat. They are in debt to eternal justice. It's like a devious criminal saying to a judge, "I know I'm guilty of rape and murder, but I have an important personal problem that I think the courts should deal with first." God's priority is to deal first with the fatal wound of sin before He even looks at the splinters of our personal problems. We are to seek first the kingdom of God and His righteousness (Matthew 6:33). Biblical evangelism deals with the eternal issues first; all else is temporal.

who only trusts God for a "wonderful plan" may feel terribly disillusioned when tragedy strikes, and may feel bitter toward God and those who gave her the so-called good news?—KC

Now look at this excerpt from an article titled "Is There Happiness without Jesus?" by Merle Hertzler. This article reveals the common and bitter fruit of preaching the "happiness" gospel:

> *Much of the Bible is false. God never visited this world as a man. We are on our own in this world, without direct intervention from God. So it would seem to me.*
>
> *How do you react to those statements? Does it make you feel sad to think that someone would write them? Perhaps to you, Christ is the only hope in this world. Your life is centered on him. He is your purpose in life, your Lord, and your Redeemer. I understand. I have been there. I accepted Jesus Christ as my personal savior many years ago. I have read the Bible from cover to cover six times—every chapter, every verse, and every line.... I have been there and done that.... I know the excitement of doing God's work all day Sunday. And I also know the emptiness that would come on Monday.*
>
> *I am no longer a Christian. I am no longer marching behind the cross. I have found something different. Life without Christ can be far more fulfilling than anything that I had ever found in Christianity. And there are hundreds of others who testify to the same thing.*
>
> *Have you found joy in Christ? I am glad that you are happy.*
>
> *But tell me something—why do so many Christians struggle to find that joy? Where is their peace? Why are they so discouraged? You may wonder why I think many Christians are sad. Here is one way that I know—fire up your search engine and search for "sad and depressed Christians." What do you find? As I write this I find 1510 sites. Sure, some are not relevant, but most of the top sites on the list are. Look at them. They are written by Christians to help sad, depressed Christians. Why are all of these people trying to help discouraged Christians? It seems that there is a problem....*
>
> *Non-Christians are told that they need to accept Christ to have peace and joy in their life. Yet many believers are missing peace and joy, and*

many Christians recommend that these turn to therapies such as cognitive therapy, a treatment that was developed in the secular world. Is this consistent? If cognitive therapy is the cure for the troubled mind, why do evangelists tell us that Jesus is the cure?

Do you need to give yourself pep talks to avoid depression? Do you have a daily struggle trying to find peace and joy? If you are not happy, then you cannot be sure that what you have gives happiness, can you? And you cannot tell me that I need what you have to be happy, can you?

Perhaps you have indeed found genuine happiness in Christ. I am glad for you. I hope you understand that others have found happiness elsewhere. You may not need what I have to be happy, and I may not need what you have.

In reference to a popular Christian song that includes the words "every day with Jesus is sweeter than the day before," John Piper writes:

Christian Hedonism is very much aware that every day with Jesus is not "sweeter than the day before." Some days with Jesus our disposition is as sour as raw persimmons. Some days with Jesus we are so sad we feel our heart will break open. Some days with Jesus fear turns us into a knot of nerve ends. Some days with Jesus we are so depressed and discouraged that between the garage and the house we just want to sit down on the grass and cry. Every day with Jesus is not sweeter than the day before. We know it from experience and we know it from scripture.[2]

Perhaps some would argue that the Christian life is a wonderful plan because God works all things out for the good of those who love Him (Romans 8:28). That fact is wonderful in the truest sense of the word. No matter what happens to us as Christians, we can rejoice because of that promise. But the promise does not guarantee that our lives will be without suffering and trial and pain.

In 1413, John Huss was summoned to appear before the Roman church council in Constance. When he was thrown into a prison for nineteen months awaiting trial for his faith and then sentenced to death, he no doubt knew that God would work things out for his good. When he was burned alive at the stake and his charred, lifeless body fell among the ashes, the wonderful promise that God would work out for his good such an unspeakable horror remained unwavering.

In 1995, in Mainland China when Li De Xian was arrested for his faith, he no doubt knew that God would work all things together for his good. When he was beaten with a heavy club, kicked in the groin and stomach until he vomited blood, then beaten in the face with his Bible and left bleeding on the floor, the promise remained steadfast.

When Muslims burst into churches in Rwanda in the late 1990s and hacked men, women, and children to death with razor-sharp machetes, if the many who bled to death loved God and were called according to His purpose, they too could claim this incredible promise.

According to a Regent University study, in 1998 there were approximately 156,000 Christian martyrs throughout the world. The promise of Romans 8:28 was also true for each and every one of these children of God.

If indeed our Creator works all things out for good—if He brings ultimate good out of every agony suffered by His children—why then shouldn't we use that truth as bait when fishing for men? Simply because it's not biblical to do so. Go through the book of Acts and see if you can find any of the disciples telling sinners that God loved them and had a wonderful plan for their lives.

Instead, they confronted their hearers as guilty criminals—enemies of God who desperately needed righteousness. The disciples in Acts didn't merely seek to enhance their hearers' lives with God's wonderful plan. The word *wonderful* has positive connotations; it doesn't typically evoke negative images of machetes, hatred, persecution, beatings, and martyrdom. If non-Christians respond to the gospel message only to improve their lives, they will be disillusioned when persecution comes, and they may fall away from the faith. This is because many respond *experimentally,* simply to see if the "wonderful life" is as good as Christians make it out to be.

Jesus didn't shield the newly converted Saul of Tarsus from what was in store for him as a Christian. Instead, He said that He would "show him *how many things he must suffer* for My name's sake" (Acts 9:16, emphasis added). Stephen was cruelly stoned to death for his faith. James was murdered with a sword. John the Baptist also felt the sharp steel of persecution. Down through the ages, Christians have been hated, persecuted, thrown to lions, and—like John Huss—even burned at the stake for the sake of the gospel.

In light of the fact that in February 2000, Christians in central Africa were being burned to death for their faith, and Christians in Indonesia and China are yet today suffering persecution for their faith, perhaps the message that "God has a wonderful plan for your life" applies only to the United States. One might have offered that argument until the shooting death of Cassie Bernall and other Christians in Littleton, Colorado, on April 20, 1999. Cassie was shot in the head when she answered "yes" to the question, "Do you believe in God?"

If you still want to hold on to the modern approach to evangelism, let me try one other thought that should convince you that the "wonderful plan" message is erroneous and misleading.

Imagine that you have been supernaturally taken back to September 10, 2001. You have been asked to address the people who work in Tower One of the World Trade Center. Your topic is "The Benefits of the Christian Life." What an incredible opportunity you have to reach the lost!

You look at the sea of faces in front of you. There are mothers and fathers, husbands and wives, sons and daughters. Many have already made retirement plans. Others have made plans to be with their families for Christmas. Just like you, they have hopes, dreams, and fears.

What are you going to tell these people? Are you going to tell them what a wonderful plan God has for them? How could you? You know that within twenty-four hours *many of your hearers will die in unspeakably horrible ways.* In an instant, some will become human torches as jet fuel saturates them and their bodies ignite and burn to ashes. Others will be horribly suffocated in a huge ball of fiery, poisonous gases as their burning and heaving lungs gasp for breath. Rather than face the horror of burning to death, some will jump more than one hundred stories in inconceivable terror to their deaths on the unforgiving sidewalks of New York City. Those who manage to stay alive on the upper floors will eventually come crashing down, along with the earthshaking weight of twisted metal and concrete, their bodies so horribly mangled and ripped apart that they will be unidentifiable. Many others, working in the lower stories, will be crushed like helpless spiders as the building collapses.

Again, what will you tell them? Can you in good conscience say, "God has a wonderful plan for your life"?

You may be saying, "Hold on. God *does* has a wonderful plan for their lives—*for their eternity*." You know that if they repent and give their lives to Christ they will go to heaven after they have been burned to death or smashed on the sidewalk. But sinners don't equate the promise of a "wonderful plan for your life" with *eternity*. They think of the here and now.

If the "God has a wonderful plan" message isn't appropriate for the people who worked in the World Trade Center, who is it for? The only logical answer is that the message isn't biblical.

Perhaps you are thinking, "This guy is destroying my gospel presentation. Now what am I going to tell sinners? What would bring someone to the Savior if not the promise of a wonderful new life in Christ?" If that is what you are thinking, please be patient with me. We will answer these questions in the next chapter.

> ➤ At this point, some readers may feel angry. "Why would anyone tell us not to tell sinners that God has a wonderful plan for their lives? If this is what you feel, don't stop now. Press on and read the next few chapters. Your anger will turn to joy! —KC

4 | A LIFESTYLE WITHOUT A LIFE

If those who say that "God has a wonderful plan for your life" were "converted" under the same gospel they propagate, and they did not repent, then there may be some truth in what they are saying. If they continue to live in lawlessness, they will not have a struggle with the world, the flesh, and the devil. If they are friends with the world, they will flow *with* it rather than against it, and therefore will not have tribulation in it. If they don't "live godly in Christ Jesus," they won't "suffer persecution" (2 Timothy 3:12), and they will not be hated for His name's sake, because their lives will be no different from those who are of the world. If they continue to live according to the flesh, they won't have to struggle to deny fleshly desires. Neither will they wrestle against the devil. In fact, Satan will be pleased with what he sees.

Those who have come to Christ seeking happiness have "found religion" and think that by going to church on Sunday morning they are all right with God, thereby assuaging their nagging consciences. They may have joined the fellowship of the church—enjoying the music, the social activities, the friendship, and the many other benefits of modern American Christianity, including what they think is the assurance of everlasting life. And they may have actually found *happiness* in their new lifestyle—but they haven't found new life in Christ.

And here's the double tragedy. When the Church declares the message that "Jesus solves problems" or "Jesus provides happiness," it restricts the field of evangelistic endeavor to those in society who are unhappy and caught up in their problems.

These "problem" people don't hear the message of sin, righteousness, and judgment with the command to repent and flee from the wrath to come. Instead, they hear that Jesus is the answer to their alcohol, drug, marriage, personal, or financial problems, and that He is the one who can fill the God-shaped vacuum in their lives. Many, therefore, come only to have their problems solved.

If they don't repent of their sin, however, they will have a false conversion (Mark 4:16-17) and they won't become new creatures in Christ. They may "[name] the name of Christ," but they won't "depart from iniquity" (2 Timothy 2:19). Rather, they will bring their sins *and* their problems into the local church. This has the following unfortunate effects on the body of Christ:

1. *Wearing out the pastors. Instead of being able to give themselves fully to feeding the flock of God in the capacity of shepherd, pastors find themselves forever counseling those who are only hearers of the Word and not doers.*
2. *Tying up the laborers (who are already few in number) in the functions of being counselors and propping people up, when what these "problem" people need is repentance.*

After addressing the many problems plaguing the modern Church, J. I. Packer offers these insightful words:

> This is a complex phenomenon, to which many factors have contributed; but, if we go to the root of the matter, we shall find that these perplexities are all ultimately due to our having lost our grip on the biblical gospel. Without realizing it, we have during the past century bartered that gospel for a substitute product which, though it looks similar enough in points of detail, is as a whole a decidedly different thing. Hence our troubles.[1]

In a publication titled *What Do You Want from Life?* the conclusion is drawn that we all want to be happy. Despite the list of things cited—sex, money, friends, fame, love, and so on—the question is posed: Can we be truly and continually happy? The answer provided is, of course, that knowing Jesus produces "ultra happiness ... your happiest moment magnified a million times over."

Not many would see that there is anything wrong with this publication. However, the call of the gospel is universal and is not confined to the unhappy, "hurting" world, as it is so often promoted. The gospel is a promise of righteousness, not a promise of happiness, and it therefore may also be offered to those who are enjoying the "pleasures of sin for a season." Before my conversion, I was very happy, content, satisfied, cheerful, thankful, and joyful. I was loving life and living it to the fullest. Therefore, I was not a candidate for the modern gospel. However, when I was confronted by the spirituality of God's Law and understood that "riches do not profit in the day of wrath, but righteousness delivers from death" (Proverbs 11:4), I saw my need of the Savior.

Let me repeat: Because of the belief that the chief end of the gospel is happiness on earth rather than righteousness, many fail to see its God-given intention. They think the gospel is only for those who lack money, those who are brokenhearted by life's difficulties, those who are the problem people in society. The belief is further perpetuated through popular worship choruses that have splendid melodies but carry this message: "Heartaches, broken people, ruined lives are why Christ died on Calvary." Before I became a Christian, my life, like the lives of many others, was not "ruined." At the age of twenty I was a successful businessman with my own house, a beautiful wife, a car, money, and, being self-employed, the freedom to enjoy it to the fullest.

The Competition

If you search the Internet using the keywords "true happiness," you will find that Jesus is offered as a solution. Among many other Christian sites selling books and tapes, etc, you will find www.amazingjoy.com, which presents the message that "Jesus Is the Source of All True Love, Joy, Peace, and Hope.... God is intensely interested in you. You are special to Him. He wants you to be happy and fulfilled. To learn more about this amazing God who loves you and cares for you so personally, read on."

You will find other Christian Web sites offering variations on the idea that "if you want to be really happy, if you want to experience true satisfaction in your life," you will find it only in relationship with Jesus Christ.

Here's the dilemma: The idea that "Jesus gives true happiness" has some competition. There are more than 100,000,000 other results to the keywords "true happiness," many of which refer to self-help strategies, such as that proposed by author Martin E. P. Seligman in *Authentic Happiness: Using the New Positive Psychology to Realize Your Potential for Lasting Fulfillment.*[2]

The Jehovah's Witnesses ask, "Would You Welcome a Visit? Even in this troubled world, you can gain happiness from accurate Bible knowledge of God, his Kingdom, and his wonderful purpose for mankind."[3]

Hinduism offers the same thing: "Without remembering the name of God, even the sovereign King of the World, would be unhappy.... By dwelling on the Name of God, he can obtain true happiness. Hence, Realization of God is the key that unlocks the doors to unending happiness, eternal peace of mind and unimaginable bliss."[4]

So does Islam. In a lecture delivered in Washington, his eminence Maulana Shah Muhammad Abdul Aleem Siddiqui al Qaderi expounded on "The Quest for True Happiness." He said, "Here I shall state some basic facts, and the principles pertaining thereto, so that if anyone practices them, he or she may attain peace of mind, comfort of the soul and true happiness."[5]

In April 2003, *USA Today* conducted a survey asking Americans if they were satisfied with their lives. Fifty-seven percent said that they were very satisfied. Another 34 percent said that they were "fairly satisfied." So the modern gospel has some competition—many people in the United States already have a wonderful plan, and they are quite happy as they are.

If Jesus gives true happiness, as the modern gospel message maintains, then it follows that the happiness that the world gives must be false—or at the very least, shallow. Consequently, the evangelist sees his job as one of unmasking the world's promise of happiness and contrasting it with the true and lasting happiness that Jesus gives. From there arises the "Jesus is better than beer" mentality. This is demeaning to the name of Jesus, and totally unnecessary. There's no contest between Jesus and beer, because happiness isn't the issue.

> In Hollywood I work with hundreds of people who are very success-
ful and are having an enormous amount of fun. If ever there was a
group of people who need the Lord, this is it. But if we limit the
focus of the gospel to improving the lives of those who have been
broken by life's circumstances, it doesn't apply to many of my col-
leagues. However, if we preach the gospel of righteousness in
Christ through repentance from sin, it applies to *everyone*. —KC

Evangelistic outreaches are often billed as "taking the Good News to the
hurting and the needy." Again, the gospel is not confined to the hurting people with ruined lives and heartaches. Both hurting and happy people need
to be shown their sinful state before God so they will seek after the righteousness that is in Christ.

Let me further illustrate this common misunderstanding by quoting
from another modern publication:

> *You will desire to be where the Lord is. And He spends His time with*
> *those who hurt. At the beginning of His ministry, Jesus quoted Isaiah to*
> *describe the work He was called to do: "The Spirit of the Lord is upon Me,*
> *because He has anointed Me to preach the gospel to the poor; He has*
> *sent Me to heal the brokenhearted, to proclaim liberty to the captives,*
> *and recovery of sight to the blind, to set at liberty those who are*
> *oppressed; to proclaim the acceptable year of the Lord" (Luke 4:18-*
> *19). . . . Thus the more you go after God, the deeper you will move into a*
> *world filled with hurting people.*

I am in no way questioning the sincerity of the author, but I believe he per-
petuates a common misunderstanding of what Jesus intended to communicate when he quoted from Isaiah 61:1-2. We live in a "therapeutic" culture
that places a high value on feeling good, self-esteem, and self-actualization.
Consequently, when we see words like *poor, brokenhearted,* and *oppressed,*
we think of people who are beset by life's circumstances, whether it's poverty, divorce, addiction, or disease. Jesus, however, is speaking primarily in
terms of spiritual poverty and spiritual brokenness, bondage, blindness, and
oppression. In other words, He is offering freedom to those who recognize
their sinful state and are broken by the realization that their spiritual

poverty and bondage separates them from a just and holy God. That isn't to say that He did not minister to those who were beset by life's circumstances—but His message was not *only* for those people, and the freedom He offered was not freedom from the hardships of life.

In Luke 4:18-19, Jesus gives a summation of whom the gospel is for:

o The poor
o The brokenhearted
o The captives
o The blind
o The oppressed

When Jesus speaks of "the poor," He is not necessarily referring to those who lack financial resources. Instead, He's referring to the "poor in spirit" (Matthew 5:3)—those who are meek, humble, lowly. These are the blessed ones to whom the kingdom of God belongs: those who know that they are destitute of righteousness. In his commentary on Luke 4:14-30, Matthew Henry writes: "Observe . . . to *whom* He was to preach: to the *poor;* to those that were *poor in the world*; whom the Jewish doctors disdained to undertake the teaching of and spoke of with contempt; to those that were *poor in spirit,* to the meek and humble, and to those that were truly sorrowful for sin" (emphasis in the original).[6]

When Jesus speaks of the brokenhearted, He doesn't mean those unhappy people whose hearts are aching because they have been jilted by a sweetheart, but those who, like Peter and Isaiah, are contrite and sorrowing for their sin. In the words of Matthew Henry, "[Christ] was sent to *heal the broken-hearted, . . .* to give peace to those that were troubled and humbled for sins, . . . and to bring them to rest who were weary and heavy-laden, under the burden of guilt and corruption."[7]

The captives are those "taken captive by [the devil] to do his will" (2 Timothy 2:26). The blind are those whom "the god of this age has blinded . . . [to] the light of the gospel of the glory of Christ" (2 Corinthians 4:4). The oppressed are those who are "oppressed by the devil" (Acts 10:38).

The gospel of grace is for the humble, not the proud. "God resists the proud, but gives grace to the humble" (James 4:6). The Scriptures tell us, "Everyone proud in heart is an abomination to the Lord" (Proverbs 16:5);

"He has put down the mighty from their thrones, and exalted the lowly" (Luke 1:52); God looks on the one who "is poor and of a contrite spirit, and who trembles at [His] word" (Isaiah 66:2). Only the sick need a physician, and only those who are convinced of the disease of sin will appreciate and appropriate the cure of the gospel.

The Abundant Life

Still, the question may arise, why not use the fact that Jesus said He had come to bring us an abundant life (John 10:10) to draw unregenerate sinners to the Savior? True, the Christian life is full. Consider the life of Paul. Read 2 Corinthians 11:23-28 and see if you think he was bored while being stoned (once), shipwrecked (three times), beaten (three times), and whipped (five times). His life was full. There were also times when he wasn't happy. In fact, at one point he was in such despair that he wanted to die (2 Corinthians 1:8).

The apostle gives the carnal-minded Corinthians a glimpse of the abundant life. He told them that he had been condemned to death. He was hungry and thirsty. He lacked clothing. He was beaten and had nowhere to live. Even with his established ministry, he was forced to work with his hands. He was reviled, persecuted, slandered, and treated as the filth of the world. What a terrible, uninviting path Paul walked down. One would think that he would put up a sign saying "Don't enter here." However, he did the opposite. He told the Corinthians to imitate him (1 Corinthians 4:9-16).

Where Is God's Love?

How was it, then, that the apostle Paul knew God loved him? As we have seen, he faced countless trials and tribulations, was mocked and hated, imprisoned for years, and finally martyred. What did he look to for assurance of God's love for him?

He didn't look to his lifestyle, because to the untrained eye, it didn't exactly speak of God's caring hand for him. His "abundant" life was certainly full, but it wasn't full of what we might think it should have been if God loved him.

Picture Paul, lying half-naked on a cold dungeon floor, chained to hardened Roman guards. You look at his bloody back and his bruised, swollen face and you say, "Paul, you've been beaten again. Where are your friends?

Demas and the others have forsaken you. Where is your expensive chariot and your successful building program? Where is the evidence of God's blessing, Paul? What's that? What did you say? Did I hear you mumble through swollen lips that God loves you?"

Now picture Paul slowly lifting his head. His blackened, bruised eyes look deeply into yours. They sparkle as he says two words: "The Cross!" He painfully reaches into his blood-soaked tunic and carefully pulls out a letter he had been writing. His trembling and bloodstained finger points to one sentence. You strain your eyes in the dim light and read, "I have been crucified with Christ; it is no longer I who live, but Christ lives in me; and the life which I now live in the flesh I live by faith in the Son of God, *who loved me and gave Himself for me*" (Galatians 2:20, emphasis added).

Christ's sacrifice was the source of Paul's joy and thus his strength: "God forbid that I should boast except in the cross of our Lord Jesus Christ" (Galatians 6:14). Those who come to faith through the door of seeking happiness in Christ will think that their happiness is evidence of God's love. They may even think that God has forsaken them when trials come and their happiness leaves. But those who look to the Cross as a token of God's love will never doubt His steadfast devotion to them.

If the "abundant" life is different from the "happy" life, who is going to listen if we are blatantly honest about the persecution promised for all who "live godly in Christ Jesus" (2 Timothy 3:12)? Certainly not as many as are attracted by the talk of a wonderful plan. What, then, is the answer to this dilemma?

> ➤ The following chapter contains principles that liberated me from something that had frustrated me for years. The Bible paints such a different picture of the Christian life than the one we try to paint in our churches today. No one in the Bible ever used the "wonderful plan" hook to attract sinners to Jesus. Instead, they employed what Charles Spurgeon called "our ablest auxiliary"—that is, our most powerful weapon. Read on . . . —KC

5 THE PURPOSE OF THE LAW

In recent years it has become popular in some sectors of the Church to ask the question "What would Jesus do?" And as often happens with catchphrases, it has been taken to extremes—everything from "What would Jesus eat?" to "What kind of SUV would Jesus drive?" At first glance it might seem worthwhile to ask what Jesus would do in a particular circumstance, but the question has an inherent flaw: it opens the door to speculation. The answer becomes open-ended so that people can make up whatever "Jesus" they want to fit anything they would like to do: "What would Jesus do? I'll tell you what He *wouldn't* do. He wouldn't condemn people because they want an abortion, and He wouldn't go around ramming religion down people's throats!" Or "Surely Jesus wouldn't condemn me for being weak—or for *that* little sin." The better question to ask is "What *did* Jesus do?" This confines our answers to the safe and reliable boundaries of the Bible.

What did Jesus do when He confronted sinners? As we see from Scripture, He made the issue one of righteousness rather than happiness (Matthew 5:20). He used the Ten Commandments to show sinners the righteous standard of God (Matthew 5:17-37).

In Mark 10:17-21, a man came running to Jesus, knelt before Him, and asked how he could obtain everlasting life. It would seem that his earnest and humble heart made him a prime candidate as a potential convert. Yet

Jesus didn't give him the message of God's grace. He didn't even mention the love of God. Neither did He tell him of an abundant, wonderful new life. Instead, Jesus used the Law of God to expose the man's hidden sin. This man was a transgressor of the first of the Ten Commandments. His money was his god, and one cannot serve both God and money. Then the Scriptures reveal that it was *love* that motivated Jesus to speak in this way to this rich young man.

Every time we witness to someone, we should examine our motives. Do we love the sinner enough to make sure his conversion is genuine? If Jesus had accepted at face value the rich young man's profession of righteousness, He might have led him into a false conversion. Instead, Jesus used the Moral Law to reveal the man's hidden sin—his love of money above all else. Why did Jesus use the Ten Commandments? His method seems a bit archaic compared to the quick and easy modern methods of making instant converts. Dr. Martyn Lloyd-Jones gives us the answer:

> *A gospel which merely says "Come to Jesus," and offers Him as a Friend, and offers a marvelous new life, without convincing of sin, is not New Testament evangelism. (The essence of evangelism is to start by preaching the Law; and it is because the Law has not been preached that we have had so much superficial evangelism.) True evangelism . . . must always start by preaching the Law.*

> ➢ What planet is this guy from? "Evangelism must always start by preaching the Law"? Could that be true? Is it biblical? It's what Jesus did. Keep reading to find out why. —KC

When you use the Law* to show lost sinners their true state, be prepared for them to thank you. For the first time in their lives, they will see the Christian message as expressing love and concern for their eternal welfare rather than merely proselytizing for a better lifestyle while on this earth. They will begin to understand why they should be *concerned* about their eternal salvation. The Law shows them that they are condemned by God. It even makes

---

* Throughout the book we will be using the term "the Law" to refer to the Moral Law of God or the Ten Commandments. This is consistent with how Jesus referred to "the law" or "the law and the prophets" in His teaching (Matthew 5:17, 7:12, 22:40, 23:23; Luke 10:26, 16:16; John 7:19-23). When the apostle Paul speaks of "the law" in Romans 2:20-23 and 13:8-9, he quotes a number of the Ten Commandments, making it clear he is referring to the Moral Law. This is also the case with other writers of Scripture, including James (2:10-11).

them a little fearful—and "the fear of the Lord is the beginning of wisdom" (Psalm 111:10; Proverbs 9:10).

Look at how John Wesley reconciled the use of the Law to produce the fear of God with love:

> *The second use [of the Law] is to bring him unto life, unto Christ that he may live. It is true, in performing both these offices, it acts the part of a severe schoolmaster.* It drives us by force, rather than draws us by love. And yet love is the spring of all. *It is the spirit of love which, by this painful means, tears away our confidence in the flesh, which leaves us no broken reed whereon to trust, and so constrains the sinner, stripped of all to cry out in the bitterness of his soul or groan in the depth of his heart, "I give up every plea beside, Lord, I am damned; but thou hast died."* (emphasis added)

Perhaps you are tempted to say that we should *never* condemn sinners. However, Scripture tells us that they are *already condemned* (John 3:18). All the Law does is show them their true state. If you dust a table in your living room and think it is dust-free, try pulling back the curtains and letting in the early morning sunlight. You will more than likely see dust still sitting on the table. The sunlight didn't create the dust, *it merely exposed it.* When we take the time to draw back the high and heavy curtains of the Holy of Holies and let the light of God's Law shine upon the sinner's heart, the Law merely shows him his true state before God. Proverbs 6:23 tells us that "the commandment is a lamp, and the law a light."

> ➤ You may be familiar with the idea that we should befriend sinners and address their "felt needs" before speaking to them about salvation. However, it may take weeks, months, or even years before we get around to talking to them about the subject of sin. On the other hand, if we understand sin in its true light as enmity with God, and we grasp the urgency of the situation—that our unregenerate friend could die tonight and face God's righteous judgment—would we not be motivated to show our friend her depravity in relationship to the Law, and to use the Law to appeal to her conscience in order to bring her to repentance and salvation?

Let's see how a "felt needs" approach would work in a court of law with a child molester. Take for instance the man who kidnapped a seven-year-old girl from her southern California home in 2002. He sexually molested her, strangled her to death, set her little body on fire and left her in the desert. Imagine the following courtroom scenario when this man is brought to trial:

The judge says, "All the evidence is in. You are guilty. However, I don't want to deal with your guilt at the moment. I want to first address your felt needs. Are you happy? Do you have an emptiness inside?"

Such talk would be absurd. Any judge who asked such things would be thrown off the bench. The criminal is in court because he has committed a serious offense, and that is the *only* subject that should be addressed. Justice must be served. The man must be punished for his terrible crime. His felt needs have nothing to do with the issue.

We may not think that sin is terrible, but God certainly does—and the only way to understand sin from His perspective is to view it through the eyes of the Law. Sin is so serious in His sight that He calls for the death sentence. Therefore, the issue we should address is the sinner's guilt. You may say, "But we can't convince him of his guilt. Only the Holy Spirit can do that!" That's true; all we need to do is shine the light of the Law on the sinner's heart. —KC

It was the wrath of the Law that showed the adulterous woman in John 8:3-11 that she was condemned. She literally found herself between a rock and a hard place. Without those heavy rocks waiting to pound her sinful flesh, she may have died in her sins and gone to hell. I doubt if she would have fallen at the feet of Jesus without the terror of the Law having driven her there. Thank God that it awakened her and caused her to flee to the Savior.

Most people believe they are rich in virtue, but the Law shows them they are morally bankrupt. If they do not declare bankruptcy, the Law will mercilessly call for their last drop of blood.

> ➤ See for yourself whether this is true. Ask anyone if he considers himself to be a good person. The vast majority of people will say that they are. To really get to the bottom of what sinners think of them-

selves, ask if they believe that they're morally bankrupt like the Bible says (Romans 3:10-12, 23; Jeremiah 17:9). Ninety-nine percent of the people you ask (especially church-goers) will emphatically answer, "No!" —KC

What about Legalism?

One evening when I had taken a team to Santa Monica to preach the gospel open-air, it began raining. It not only rained, but the heavens flashed with lightning. Thunder seemed to shake the earth in an unusually severe thunderstorm for southern California. As a consolation for our team, we purchased two large pizzas to snack on as we took shelter from the pelting rain under a movie theater veranda.

As most of the thirty-member team munched on pepperoni pizza, I noticed the heartwarming sight of an elderly homeless woman having a fight with a ten-inch piece of cheese. It looked like a stretched rubber band as she pulled at it with her few remaining teeth. After she had downed the large slice of pizza, I offered her another one. Surprisingly, she declined. A few minutes later, however, she was battling a second piece. The scene was truly heartwarming.

Just then, the police arrived. The theater manager had called them to remove the homeless woman from in front of the theater. There were thirty of us sheltering from the rain, yet he had singled out a poor, hungry, homeless woman. I heard the officers protesting that the woman was just sheltering from the rain, but the manager was adamant: the woman had to move on.

At that moment I remembered that my pocket was bulging with a bundle of one-dollar bills. Each Friday night I would attract a crowd by asking trivia questions and giving dollar bills to those who answered correctly. Once the crowd felt comfortable, I would transition to talking about spiritual matters and preach the gospel. As the police officers reluctantly began to move the old woman on, I stepped forward and grabbed her hand. She flinched and turned her fear-filled eyes toward mine, probably thinking that she was being handcuffed. Then she noticed that I had stuffed a wad of bills in her hand, and in a second her fear changed to joy.[1]

The Bible tells us in 1 Timothy 1:8 (AMP), "Now we recognize and know that the Law is good if anyone uses it lawfully [for the purpose for which it was designed]." Just as the theater manager used the local municipal law for something for which it was never designed—turning an elderly homeless woman out into the rain—so there are those who would use God's Law for something for which it was never designed.

For what purpose was God's Law designed? The following verse tells us: "The Law is not made for a righteous person, but . . . for sinners" (1 Timothy 1:9). It even lists the sinners for us: the disobedient, the ungodly, murderers, fornicators, homosexuals, kidnappers, liars, etc. The Law's main design is not for the saved but for the unsaved. It was given as a "schoolmaster" to bring us to Christ (Galatians 3:24, KJV). It was designed primarily as an evangelistic tool. D. L. Moody said, "The Law can only chase a man to Calvary, no further."

It is an *unlawful* use of the Law to use it for justification. No one will make it to heaven by keeping the Ten Commandments. The Scriptures make that very clear: "A man is not justified by the works of the law but by faith in Jesus Christ . . . ; for by the works of the law no flesh shall be justified" (Galatians 2:16). The Law's rightful purpose is simply to act as a mirror to show us that we need cleansing. Those who seek to be justified by the Law are taking the mirror off the wall and trying to wash themselves with it.

Neither should the Law be used to produce legalism. We are given incredible liberty in Christ (Galatians 5:1), and there are those who would seek to steal that liberty by placing the Law on the backs of Christians. Obviously, Christians refrain from lawlessness. They don't lie, steal, kill, commit adultery, etc. If they fall into sin (as opposed to *diving* into sin), they confess and forsake it, because they know that "without holiness no one will see the Lord (Hebrews 12:14, NIV). However, a Christian's motivation for holy living isn't one of legalism, imposed on them by the Law. Why do they refrain from sin? To gain God's favor? No. They already have that in Christ. Instead, Christians live lives that are pleasing to God *because they want to do all they can to show God gratitude for the incredible mercy they have received through the gospel.* Their gratitude isn't driven by guilt—to somehow try to pay God back for the Cross. No, their motive is pure. It's like the one leper who, when he saw that he was healed, was overwhelmed with gratitude. He turned back to Jesus and "with a loud voice glorified God, and fell down on his face at His feet" (Luke 17:15). The motive for gratitude is love, not legalism.

Why then would any Christian stray into legalism? Why would they begin telling other believers what they can and cannot do in Christ? This happens simply because the Law hasn't been used lawfully in the first place. Let me try to explain. If the spiritual nature of the Law is used in evangelism, it will once and for all rid new believers of any thought of legalism. The Law reveals to them that there is no way they can please God outside of faith in Jesus. As they stand before the ground-shaking thunder and vivid lightning of Mount Sinai, it dawns on them that a holy Creator sees their wicked thoughts. They cringe as they begin to understand that God sees lust as adultery and hatred as murder. Guilty sinners see that they are "by nature children of wrath" (Ephesians 2:3) and therefore flee to shelter in Christ from the rain of God's indignation. They know that grace, and grace alone, saves them. In the words of the hymn "Rock of Ages," nothing in their hands they bring, simply to the Cross they cling.

True believers are saved knowing that *nothing* commends them to God. After a lifetime of good works, of reading the Word, of prayer and seeking the lost, they are still saved by grace and grace alone. They are "unprofitable servants" who merely do what they should.

However, people who make a commitment to Christ without the Law may do so because they are seeking true inner peace and lasting fulfillment. They come to fill a "God-shaped vacuum" in their lives. There is no trembling. There is no fleeing from wrath. There is no fear. To them, God is a benevolent, fatherly figure, not a holy God of wrath. Without the Law, they haven't been stripped of self-righteousness. They don't truly believe that their just reward is eternal damnation. Therefore, even as professing Christians, they think they are basically good.

Because of this faulty foundation, these converts are likely to think that they are pleasing God by reading the Bible, praying, fasting, and doing good works. They are susceptible to being deceived into thinking that somehow their good works commend them to God, and they are therefore liable to stray into legalistic standards such as "do not touch, do not taste, do not handle" (Colossians 2:21).

The Law, when expounded before grace is presented, liberates from legalism those who come to Christ. However, if the Law is neglected before the message of the Cross is presented, those who profess faith in Christ are prone to go astray, falling into legalism and imposing demands on other believers, stealing from them the great liberty they have in Christ.

Look at the function of the Law from the great classic *The Pilgrim's Progress* by John Bunyan:

> Christian: *"It was he [the Law] who did bind my heavy burden upon me."*
>
> Faithful: *"Aye. Had it not been for him, we had both of us stayed in the City of Destruction."*
>
> Christian: *"Then he did us a favor."*
>
> [Faithful then shows how the Law alarms us]: *"Aye. Albeit, he did it none too gently."*
>
> Christian: *"Well, at least he played the part of a schoolmaster and showed us our need. It was he who drove us to the cross."*

There are many wonderful references to the work of the Ten Commandments hidden within the pages of God's Word. We will unveil some of these in the next chapter.

OUR BROKEN BACKBONE

There are two reasons why the Church might seem to be full of people whose lives don't live up to what they profess. As we have seen, the modern gospel has degenerated into a means of happiness rather than one of righteousness. Second, we have failed to show sinners that they are lawbreakers, that they have violated the Law of a holy God.

Perhaps one the greatest errors made by modern preachers is to assume that sinners know that they are sinners and therefore don't need to be confronted with the fact. They say that unsaved people only need to realize that God loves them and can forgive them. This is just not true, either biblically or experientially. The Bible says that most people think they are good (Proverbs 20:6), and even the apostle Paul said that he had no idea what sin was until the Law gave him understanding about its true nature (Romans 7:7). Despite America's mountain of sin, most think it's a tiny molehill in God's eyes, and they look forward to the reward of heaven. Consider this article by K. Connie Kang in the *Los Angeles Times:* "Next Stop, the Pearly Gates ... or Hell?"

> *An overwhelming majority of Americans continue to believe that there is life after death and that heaven and hell exist, according to a new study. What's more, nearly two-thirds think they are heaven-bound.*
>
> *On the other hand, only one-half of one percent said they were hell-*

bound, according to a national poll by the Oxnard-based Barna Research Group, an independent marketing research firm that has tracked trends related to beliefs, values and behaviors since 1984. . . .

The survey, released this week, found that 76 percent of Americans believe in heaven and 71 percent in hell—the same as a decade ago, and that 64 percent believe they're heaven-bound.[1]

They think they are going to heaven because as the Bible says, they are deceived into thinking that they are morally good. They, like Paul, have no idea what sin is until the Law gives them that knowledge. Look now at what an internationally known evangelist believes, and look at where he obtained his information to form those beliefs:

Over the years [he] has softened his message. Where he once sounded strident about sin and repentance, he now talks of "emptiness, loneli-ness, lost-ness" and concentrates on the "good news" of Jesus and for-giveness.

He changed his approach after talking to psychologists on several continents. . . . [T]hey say the vast majority of their patients suffer from "unresolved guilt."

"When I get up to speak, I am convinced that everyone in front of me feels a burden of guilt, even when they deny that there is such a thing as guilt," [he] said. "I prefer to tell them the good news, which is what the gospel really means."[2]

When I emphasize the importance of using the Law in evangelism, I do not mean merely making casual reference to it. Rather, the Law should be the backbone of our gospel presentation because its function is to prepare the heart for grace. Martin Luther said of the Law, "In its true and proper work and purpose it humbles a man and prepares him—if he uses the Law cor-rectly—to yearn and seek for grace." The Law is the rod and staff of the shepherd to guide the sheep to himself. It is the net of the fisherman, the plow of the farmer. It is the ten golden trumpets that prepare the way for the king. The Law makes the sinner thirst for righteousness, that he might live. Its holy light reveals the dust of sin on the table of the human heart, so that the gospel in the hand of the Spirit can wipe it perfectly clean.

The Law should be esteemed by the Church because of its wonderful work in preparing a sinner's heart for grace. In Joshua 3:14-17, God cut off the flow of the Jordan River when the feet of the priests, who were carrying the ark of the covenant, touched its waters. Do you remember what the ark contained? It was the two tablets of God's Law. Do you think that God would have opened the waters for the priests if they had complained that the two stone tablets were too heavy and had tipped them into the dirt to lighten their load? The Law is the embodiment of this gospel we carry, but many have "neglected the weightier matters of the Law" and counted them as worthless (Matthew 23:23). They have emptied the Law out of the ark, stripping the gospel of its power.

J. C. Ryle said of God's Law, "But never, never let us despise it. It is the symptom of an ignorant ministry, and unhealthy state of religion, when the Law is lightly esteemed. The true Christian 'delights in God's Law' (Romans 7:22)."[3] The Ten Commandments are like the ten camels that carried Abraham's servant in search of a bride for his only begotten son, Isaac (Genesis 24:10-20). When the servant arrived at the city of Nahor, he had his ten camels kneel down outside the city before the well at the time the women go out to draw water. He prayed that the bride-to-be would be evidenced by the fact that she would have consideration for the camels. When Rebekah saw the camels, she *ran* to the well to get water for them.

God the Father sent His Spirit to search for a bride for His only begotten Son. He has chosen the Ten Commandments to carry this special message.

Although we may not be able to clearly distinguish the bride of Christ from the rest of this world, the Holy Spirit knows that the primary reason the bride draws water from the well of salvation is to satisfy the ten thirsting camels of a holy and just Law. If the Law didn't demand death for sin, we wouldn't need a Savior. The true convert comes to the Savior simply to satisfy the demands of a holy Law. The espoused virgin has respect for the commandments of God. She loves God's Law because of what it is (an expression of His holy nature) and what it does (shows us our need for mercy). She is not a worker of lawlessness. Like Paul, she delights in the Law and says with the psalmist, "I will run the course of Your commandments" (Psalm 119:32). The true convert is not like Adam, who ran from God in the Garden. Instead, he delights to do God's will because God's Law is within his heart (Psalm 40:7-9).

The Law is like Aaron's rod that budded (Numbers 17:8). It looks like hard and dead wood, but from it issues the life of the gospel. In Acts 7:44, Stephen refers to "the tabernacle of witness in the wilderness." That's what the Church is—a tabernacle of witness in the wilderness of this world. If you are not sure whether the use of the Law is right, incorporate it into your tabernacle of witness and see if it buds.

In Numbers 21:6-9, God sent fiery serpents among the Israelites, which caused them to admit they had sinned. When the people turned to God in repentance, He instructed Moses to craft a bronze serpent and place it on a pole where the people could see it. Those who had been bitten and were doomed to die could look at the bronze serpent and live. In John 3:14, Jesus specifically cites this Old Testament passage in reference to His impending sacrifice on the cross to purchase our salvation from sin. The Ten Commandments are like ten biting serpents that carry with them the venomous curse of the Law. It drives sinners to look to the One lifted up on the cross. If the Law of Moses did not demand death for sin, Jesus would not have had to die. The Messiah became a curse for us and redeemed us from the curse of the Law.

The Old Testament said of the Messiah that He would "magnify the law, and make it honourable" (Isaiah 42:21, KJV). The religious leaders had dishonored the Law. By their tradition, they had twisted God's Law, rendering it ineffectual (Matthew 15:6). They even hindered others from entering God's kingdom. This is what Jesus said to them: "Woe to you lawyers! For you have taken away the key of knowledge. You did not enter in yourselves, and those who were entering in you hindered" (Luke 11:52).

The lawyers were professing to be experts in God's Law. But because they didn't use the "key of knowledge" to bring sinners to the Savior, they hindered the work of the Law as a "groundbreaking" instrument in people's hearts.

Discerning the Difference

God's Law prepares the heart of the sinner for the good news of the gospel. Without this preparatory work, his heart is hardened, and he therefore becomes a candidate for a false conversion. Now and then we can catch a glimpse of the difference between the true and false converts. In 1 Kings 3:16-28 we read of two women, both claiming to be the mother of one child.

Solomon, in his wisdom, commanded that the baby be cut in half and thus revealed the true mother.

Let's look at some of the parallels:

Just as both of these women dwelt in the same house, the true and false converts dwell together in the house of the Lord.

Both women called Solomon "lord," and both the true and false converts call Jesus "Lord."

It takes the wisdom of Solomon to discern which woman is the true mother. At the "end of the age," God will send His angels to separate true and false converts in the Church (Matthew 13:39, 49). In the meantime, these false converts are in fellowship with God's people. They are tares among the wheat, foolish virgins among the wise, bad fish among the good. They look and play the part of a Christian. They sing the right songs and say the right words, but their hearts are not right with God. They call Jesus "Lord" but don't do the things that He tells them to do (Luke 6:46). Because they are false converts (not truly converted), their agenda is self-centered. They have never cried, "Not my will but Yours be done." They have no real concern for the lost.

What was it that showed Solomon the real mother? It was her expression of true love. She would rather lose her child to the other woman than see him cut in two with a sword.

Again, it is difficult to discern between true and false converts, but they are often revealed when they don't get their own way. In Acts 20:30, the Scriptures warn, "Also from among yourselves men will rise up, speaking perverse things, to draw away the disciples after themselves." They divide rather than striving to unify the body of Christ. They will make a stand on a pet issue and bring the sword of division. However, true converts have the "wisdom from above." This wisdom is first peaceable, and open to reason. They would rather back down from their own agenda than to see the body of Christ divided. Their love for God and for the agenda of the Great Commission to reach the lost is their primary concern.

Jesus said that the world would recognize His followers by their love for one another (John 13:35). He also said, "Greater love has no one than this, than to lay down one's life for his friends. You are My friends if you do whatever I command you" (John 15:13-14). In the next chapter, we will look further at what Jesus commanded us to do.

7 | WHAT DID JESUS DO?

Right from the beginning of His ministry, Jesus made it clear that His supreme mandate was to reach lost humanity with the gospel. He said, "Follow Me, and I will make you fishers of men" (Matthew 4:19). That's why He called His disciples—because He wanted to teach them how to "catch" men and women. In Matthew 5:17-20, Jesus declares His divine commission—to magnify the Law and make it honorable:

> *Do not think that I came to destroy the Law or the Prophets. I did not come to destroy but to fulfill. For assuredly, I say to you, till heaven and earth pass away, one jot or one tittle will by no means pass from the law till all is fulfilled. Whoever therefore breaks one of the least of these commandments, and teaches men so, shall be called least in the kingdom of heaven; but whoever does and teaches them, he shall be called great in the kingdom of heaven. For I say to you, that unless your righteousness exceeds the righteousness of the scribes and Pharisees, you will by no means enter the kingdom of heaven.*

The religious leaders had demeaned and dishonored God's Law. They had warped its holy precepts and twisted its ordinances. They had nullified the Law's power to accomplish its purpose: bringing people to a knowledge of their sinfulness and their need for repentance and salvation. They had "neglected the weightier matters of the Law," limiting the scope of its precepts to mere outward piety (Matthew 23:23). Jesus called them "blind guides, who strain out a gnat and swallow a camel!" (Matthew 23:24).

First, Jesus straightened out what the religious leaders had bent, and He magnified what they had demeaned. He also established the permanency of the Law—which God Himself had written in stone and which wasn't going to change. Not one jot or tittle would pass away. It was the stony hearts of people that had to change—and if they didn't, a greater stone would fall upon them and grind them to powder (Matthew 21:44; Luke 20:18).

Next, Jesus opened up the spiritual nature of the Law, showing how God "desire[s] truth in the inward parts" (Psalm 51:6). Notice how He magnifies its precepts:

> *"You have heard that it was said to those of old, 'You shall not murder, and whoever murders will be in danger of the judgment.' But I say to you that whoever is angry with his brother without a cause shall be in danger of the judgment. And whoever says to his brother, 'Raca!' shall be in danger of the council. But whoever says, 'You fool!' shall be in danger of hell fire.... You have heard that it was said to those of old, 'You shall not commit adultery.' But I say to you that whoever looks at a woman to lust for her has already committed adultery with her in his heart."* (Matthew 5:21-22, 27-28)

Later in this same discourse, Jesus, the master teacher, magnified the Law further by opening up the ninth commandment:

> *"Again you have heard that it was said to those of old, 'You shall not swear falsely, but shall perform your oaths to the Lord.' But I say to you, do not swear at all: neither by heaven, for it is God's throne; nor by the earth, for it is His footstool; nor by Jerusalem, for it is the city of the great King. Nor shall you swear by your head, because you cannot make one hair white or black. But let your 'Yes' be 'Yes,' and your 'No,' 'No.' For whatever is more than these is from the evil one."* (Matthew 5:33-37)

Jesus concluded this part of his teaching by saying, "Be perfect, just as your Father in heaven is perfect" (Matthew 5:48). This statement must have left His hearers speechless—which is likely what Jesus intended, because the function of the Law is "that every mouth may be stopped, and all the world may become guilty before God" (Romans 3:19).

Who can justify themselves in God's sight if we are commanded to be perfect? *No one.* Our mouths are stopped and we see our guilt. Some Bible commentators have suggested that Jesus didn't really mean *perfect,* because that would require that we be "without defect, flawless." Instead, they contend that He was telling us to be *mature.* However, if that were true, then Jesus would be saying, "Therefore you are to be mature, as your heavenly Father is mature." Calling God "mature" would imply that He was once *immature.* Such a thought is clearly contrary to Scripture. God never changes (Malachi 3:6). He has always been perfect and doesn't need to mature. His Law is also perfect, and if we are not perfect in accordance with the Law, we will perish on the Day of Judgment. That's why the apostle Paul says that we are to "[warn] every man and [teach] every man in all wisdom, that we may present every man *perfect*" (Colossians 1:28, emphasis added).

Jesus continually used the perfect standard of God's Law and its spiritual nature to call sinners to repentance.* He emphasized the reality of future punishment and was not afraid to *alarm* His hearers. He said, "Serpents, brood of vipers! How can you escape the condemnation of hell?" (Matthew 23:33). He never softened words like *sin* or *repentance.* He wasn't afraid to call hell by its name. In fact, He went so far as to describe it in terrible detail: "the fire that shall never be quenched—where 'their worm does not die, and the fire is not quenched'" (Mark 9:43-44).

Neither did he entice His hearers with talk of a "wonderful new life" or compromise His words when it came to the "weightier matters of the law." When He spoke to the rich young man in Matthew 19:16-22, He didn't try to develop a nonconfrontational, no-strings-attached relationship. He was not a "seeker-friendly" Savior.

Free from Their Blood

Down through the ages, there have been many prominent preachers and evangelists who have taken to heart God's admonition in Ezekiel 3:17-19:

---

* Matthew 22:36-40; Mark 7:9-13; Mark 10:11-12, Mark 10:17-22; Mark 12:29-31; Luke 10:26; Luke 16:16-17; Luke 18:18-23; John 4:18; John 5:46-47; John 7:19.

"Son of man, I have made you a watchman for the house of Israel; there-fore hear a word from My mouth, and give them warning from Me: When I say to the wicked, 'You shall surely die,' and you give him no warning, nor speak to warn the wicked from his wicked way, to save his life, that same wicked man shall die in his iniquity; but his blood I will require at your hand. Yet, if you warn the wicked, and he does not turn from his wickedness, nor from his wicked way, he shall die in his iniquity; but you have delivered your soul."

Although labor in preaching the gospel was often slow and arduous, these preachers knew if they preached *according to the pattern of God's Word*, that with His help they would eventually deliver sinners from death and hell. If they sowed in tears, they would reap in joy. They wanted, above all things, to be true and faithful witnesses. If they preached the whole counsel of God, they would be free from the blood of all men. These ministers—men such as Wesley, Wycliffe, Whitefield, Spurgeon, and many others—were greatly effective in reaching the lost. *The key was in the careful and thorough use of the Law to prepare the way for the gospel.*

As time went by and the reality of hell, judgment, and sin fell out of favor in an increasingly pluralistic and secular society, some in the Church began to alter their gospel message to focus primarily on God's love or God's grace instead of continuing to use the Law as their primary means of bringing sin-ners to repentance. Unfortunately, these new methods had a number of problems.

1. The methods are unbiblical.

The methods are unbiblical because they don't follow the scriptural exam-ple of balancing Law and grace as Jesus did. He always preached Law to the proud and arrogant and grace to the meek and the humble (Luke 10:25-26; 18:18-20; John 3:1-17). Never once did the Son of God give the Good News (the message of the Cross, grace, and mercy) to the proud, the arrogant, or the self-righteous. He followed His Father's example: He resisted the proud and gave grace to the humble (James 4:6). Paul did the same, as seen at Ath-ens, when he used the essence of the first and second commandments to reprove the Athenians' idolatry (Acts 17:15-34), and on other occasions (Romans 2:22-23). Biblical evangelism always proclaims the Law to the proud but grace to the humble. With the Law, we should break hardened hearts, and with the gospel we should heal broken hearts.

Martin Luther, commenting on the right use of the Law, said, "Wherefore this is the proper and absolute use of the Law, by lightning, by tempest and by the sound of the trumpet (as in Mount Sinai) to terrify, and by thundering to beat down and rend in pieces that beast which is called the opinion of righteousness."

Without the Law, there can be no knowledge of sin: "What shall we say then? Is the law sin? Certainly not! On the contrary, *I would not have known sin except through the law.* ... For apart from the law sin was dead. I was alive once without the law, but when the commandment came, sin revived and I died" (Romans 7:7-9, emphasis added).

The Law is the instrument by which the old nature is put to death. It ensures that sinners are truly born again, that our Adamic nature is dealt with by nailing it to the cross. Repentance that comes by conviction under the Law makes certain that the convert is a new creature in Christ.

According to Romans 7:7, the Law of God—specifically as expressed in the Ten Commandments—is the biblical means of awakening sinners. John Wesley writes, "The very first end of the Law [is], namely, convicting men of sin; awakening those who are still asleep on the brink of hell. ... The ordinary method of God is to convict sinners by the law, and that only. The gospel is not the means which God hath ordained, or which our Lord himself used, for this end."[1]

A. W. Pink writes, "The unsaved are in no condition today for the Gospel till the Law be applied to their hearts, for 'by the Law is the knowledge of sin.' It is a waste of time to sow seed on ground which has never been ploughed or spaded! To present the vicarious sacrifice of Christ to those whose dominant passion is to take fill of sin is to give that which is holy to the dogs."[2]

Charles Spurgeon, in speaking of preparing the soil of the heart with the plow of the Law, stated:

> *One other reason why this soil was so uncongenial was that it was totally unprepared for the seed. There had been no plowing before the seed was sown, and no harrowing afterwards. He that sows without a plow may reap without a sickle. He who preaches the gospel without preaching the*

Law may hold all the results of it in his hand, and there will be little for him to hold.

Robbie Flockhart, when he preached in the streets of Edinburgh, used to say,

You must preach the Law, for the gospel is a silken thread, and you cannot get it into the hearts of men unless you have made a way for it with a sharp needle; the sharp needle of the Law will pull the silken thread of the gospel after it.

There must be plowing before there is sowing if there is to be reaping after the sowing.

> ➤ This makes so much sense. I can't believe that I didn't see it before! Because the gospel is all about grace, I had wrongly believed that there was no longer any use for the Law today. But the Law is still the plow that breaks up the soil of the stony heart, and the needle that makes a way for the thread of the gospel. Without the plow, the soil is not prepared and the seed cannot take root. Without the needle, the thread cannot penetrate. —KC

What was Jesus referring to when He said, "Do not give what is holy to the dogs"? What was He pointing to when He said don't "cast your pearls before swine, lest they trample them under their feet, and turn and tear you in pieces" (Matthew 7:6)? The most precious pearl the Church has is "Christ crucified." When the Cross is preached to the proud, and a decision is "won" using modern evangelistic methods, what happens next is very predictable. It's not long until the new converts fall away from the faith and trample the blood of the Savior under their feet. Those who regularly share their faith with the unsaved know what it's like to speak to someone we call a backslider. They usually have their own testimony as to why they turned away from God, and it's often accompanied by bitter and colorful language. They know how to talk the talk because they think they walked the walk, and because of this they know how to do damage to the kingdom of God. Take the time to look into the backgrounds of occult rock musicians and listen to their anti-Christian venom. Dig a little, and often you will find some sort of Christian profession. Bitter backsliders (those who proved to be false converts) verbally tear to pieces those who had anything to do with their "religious experience." The proselyte becomes a twofold child of hell.

Those who make a profession of faith without first coming to a knowledge and understanding of their complete depravity and sinfulness before a holy and righteous God (which the Law produces), and who haven't therefore truly repented of their sin, are liable to fall back into their former way of life, experiencing what Peter describes in 2 Peter 2:22: "According to the true proverb: 'A dog returns to his own vomit,' and, 'a sow, having washed, to her wallowing in the mire.'" This is the tragic result of casting pearls of the gospel of grace to the proud, whom the Bible calls "dogs" and "swine."

False converts have never "crucified the flesh with its passions and desires" (Galatians 5:24). Therefore, like the pig, their natural inclination is to go back to wallowing in the mire. Pigs *need* to wallow in mire because they crave the mud to cool their flesh. So it is with false converts. Because they never truly repented, their flesh is not dead with Christ. Instead, it is still burning with unlawful desire. The heat of lust is too much for a sinful heart; thus the sinner must go back to the filth.

The new, modern methods of evangelism that are based on a message of God's love and His plan for our lives forsake the Law and its power to humble the proud heart and convert the soul. They do, however, sometimes speed the process of evangelism, making it much easier to get "commitments." Also, they often stir up less opposition and appear to get results. However, if the "converts" end up backsliding or falling away, of what benefit is the supposed conversion? According to Peter, "the latter end is worse for them than the beginning" (2 Peter 2:20).

2. The new evangelistic methods often fail to mention the fact of Judgment Day.

The Bible presents the great and terrible Day of the Lord as *the very reason* to repent and trust the Savior: "Truly, these times of ignorance God overlooked, but now commands all men everywhere to repent, *because He has appointed a day on which He will judge the world in righteousness*" (Acts 17:30-31, emphasis added). The new evangelistic methods are not faithful to God if they don't even give a hint of Judgment Day's approach. The reason Jesus died on the cross was to save us from the wrath to come (1 Thessalonians

1:10). That is the essential message of the gospel, but in many contemporary gospel presentations there isn't even a mention of hell's existence. General William Booth, founder of the Salvation Army, warned that in the twentieth century a gospel would be preached that promised heaven without mentioning hell. Modern evangelistic methods do just that. Take the time to study closely the contents of today's popular tracts and see the critical flaws:

o No mention of Judgment Day
o Not a hint of hell
o No use of the Law of God to bring the knowledge of personal sin
o The gospel put forth as a means of happiness rather than a means of righteousness

It is a perfect recipe for a false conversion when the "seed" falls on the hearts of "stony ground" hearers. They receive the Word with joy and gladness, but in times of tribulation, temptation, or persecution, they fall away.

False converts are nothing new. George Whitefield said of his day, "That is the reason we have so many 'mushroom' converts, because their stony ground is not plowed up; they have not got a conviction of the Law; they are stony-ground hearers."

A great preacher once said, "Evermore the Law must prepare the way for the gospel. To overlook this in instructing souls is almost certain to result in false hope, the introduction of a false standard of Christian experience, and to fill the Church with false converts.... Time will make this plain."

I hesitate to be critical of the authors of modern evangelistic literature. They are sincere, earnest, loving, godly brethren, but their zeal for the lost lacks knowledge of the importance of using God's Law to bring true repentance. The results are a devastation that cannot be ignored.

After discovering the rampant hypocrisy among professing believers, the late Dr. Bill Bright, founder of Campus Crusade for Christ, wrote, "A belief that Christians are entitled to the 'good life' can result in demoralized church members. Expecting the Christian life to be a bed of roses can be very discouraging to a new Christian—and to more mature ones as well—when they are jostled by the storms of life."[3]

In the same book, this godly author weeps at the evident sin in the contemporary Church.

3. The modern methods often gloss over sin.

When the definition of sin is separated from the standard of the Law, it can become merely an abstract concept in the minds of sinners. When sin is mentioned in modern evangelism, a typical reference given is Romans 3:23: "For all have sinned and fall short of the glory of God." If I were not a Christian, my first two questions about this verse would be, "What is sin?" and "What is God's glory?"

Perhaps you've heard about how in ancient times, the word *sin* was shouted during archery competitions to let the archer know that the arrow had fallen short of the target. But when it comes to sin, what is the target? If I have fallen short of a mark, I would at least want to know what and where the target is, *to measure how far I have fallen short,* to know whether I should give up or try another shot.

If the target is God's glory, what does that mean? The Greek word used for *glory* in Romans 3:23 is *doxa,* which literally means "honor, worship, praise." Humanity has fallen short of God's mark by failing to give our Creator the honor, worship, and praise due to Him. We have failed to love God with all of our heart, mind, soul, and strength, which is the essence of the Law (Mark 12:30-31). In fact, the statement that "all have sinned" comes in the context of Paul saying that *the Law* has left the whole world guilty before God (Romans 3:19). In other words, the Law is the target, the standard by which our "best shots" will be measured. If we call out "Sin!" to unregenerate sinners but fail to tell them anything about the mark for which they are aiming, we leave them believing that they can simply "grab another arrow" and give it their best shot. However, when we display the high standard of the Law, we show sinners the utter hopelessness of their ever coming near the mark, so that their only hope will be in the Savior. Convicted sinners are left with a pressing dilemma: "What now? If my life depends on hitting the target, but I can never hit the target, what hope is there for me?" Only then are they ready to hear and receive the gospel message of salvation through Jesus Christ, because only then do they realize how lost and "off the mark" they truly are.

Check the Soil

Here is the problem with contemporary evangelistic methods: Up to 90 percent of the evangelistic crop is failing. They wither and die as soon as the sunlight of tribulation, persecution, and temptation shines on them. We encourage them to be watered by the Word. We give them the "fertilizer" of counsel and support. We follow up thoroughly, but all to no avail.

Perhaps we need to check the soil. If before we plant the seed of the gospel we take the time to turn the soil of the heart thoroughly with the Law, upon repentance the effect will be the removal of the stones of sin.

God has given us insight into the area in which we are planting. The ground of the human heart is very hard. The Scriptures call it a "heart of stone" (Ezekiel 36:26).

I have heard a number of well-known preachers say that it is normal to see 75 percent of those coming to Christ fall away. This thought is based on the parable of the sower, which shows that only 25 percent of the seed fell on good soil and produced a harvestable crop (Mark 4:1-20). But I don't think Jesus gave us this parable as consolation for disappointing evangelistic results. I think He gave it for our instruction, so that we wouldn't settle for a subpar yield.

When we study the parable of the sower closely, we see that the good-soil hearer, the *genuine* convert, had some things the other hearers didn't have. He had *understanding* (Matthew 13:23) and he had *"a noble and good heart"* (Luke 8:15, emphasis added). Does that mean that there are only certain people who somehow have understanding and a noble and good heart, and we have to keep on sowing until we find them? No. Scripture makes it clear that there is *no one* who understands (Romans 3:11) and that the heart of man is not good, but deceitful and desperately wicked (Jeremiah 17:9).

How then did the good-soil hearers obtain these necessary virtues? It is clear that something from *outside* themselves must have given them understanding and brought them to a point of having a noble and good heart. The plow—that is, the Law—turned the soil of their hearts, exposing their wickedness and breaking loose the stones of sin. When the stones were removed through repentance, it left the good soil of understanding and a heart that was ready to receive the seed of the gospel.

An old movie has a scene where an officer of the law enters an illegal casino. The manager of the casino says to him, "Are you going to speak to the people *before* you arrest them? They must have the law spelled out to them so they will know that what they are doing is wrong." Doesn't that make sense? How on earth are the gamblers going to come peacefully if they don't realize they have broken the law? Likewise, how can sinners be brought to true repentance—and thus true salvation—if they don't realize they've broken the Law of God? If we continue to disregard the importance of the Law in bringing people to salvation, we will continue to witness the devastating results revealed in the next chapter.

8 | MANGLED BODIES

Imagine that someone invented a parachute that was 100 percent trustworthy. It made no difference whether the user was large or small—the chute opened *every time* and got him safely to the ground. The key was in the way the parachute was folded. Every part had to be carefully and painstakingly placed in certain positions, following the instructions given by the manufacturer. True, it was somewhat arduous, but it was well worth the effort. It had the effect of ensuring that the life of every precious human being who trusted the parachute would be preserved.

Now imagine that a group of young men known as "fast-folders" entered the packing room. These men so influenced the other workers with their new "fast-and-easy" method of folding parachutes that soon everyone began to ignore the instruction book supplied by the manufacturer. Production increased greatly and everyone rejoiced that so much time and effort could now be saved.

As time passed, however, it gradually became evident that something was radically wrong. A small group of investigators who went to where the parachutes were being used discovered, to their horror, that *nine out of every ten people who jumped using the "fast-folded" parachutes fell to their deaths!*

The horrible sight of so many torn and mangled bodies strewn all over the ground sickened the investigators. Those who had tragically died weren't just faceless customers. They were husbands, wives, fathers, mothers, sons, and daughters—cherished human beings who had plunged to a needless and terrifying death.

The news was quickly relayed to the fast-folders. Many were heartbroken and immediately went back to the instruction book and corrected their mistakes. With great sobriety and care, they began painstakingly folding each parachute exactly as the manual instructed. Their knowledge of the tragedies motivated them to make sure that they did their job with uncompromising conviction.

Despite the evident tragedy, there was resistance from a few of the fast folders. Even though they knew that so many lives were being lost, they still refused to follow the instruction book. Unbelievably, they ignored the mass of mangled bodies for which their methods were responsible. Instead, they pointed to those who had survived as justification for their technique.

Likewise, there are some in the body of Christ who say, "Yes, we hear what you are saying about using the Law. We can see that it's biblical and that it's what Jesus did . . . but we have our own way of doing evangelism, and it's working. Just look at all the decisions we're getting and how our churches are growing. So, you do it your way, and we'll do it ours."*

Look at this testimony to the effectiveness of the "fast-folder" method from a prolific writer for *Christianity Today*:

> *I broke in this innovative system on an easy target—my little sis (aged 15). I hoodwinked her into meeting me on the swing set, and then I laid out God's blueprint:*
> *—God loves you and offers a wonderful plan for your life.*
> *—Man is sinful and separated from God, thus cannot know and experience God's love and plan.*
> *—Jesus Christ is God's only provision for man's sin.*
> *—We must individually receive Jesus as Savior and Lord.*

---

* Let me be clear about the application of this allegory. I'm not saying that evangelism based on presenting the Law is one hundred percent effective. It isn't the method that is trustworthy, but the Savior. Christ is the parachute, the One who "is able to keep you from falling and to present you before his glorious presence without fault and with great joy" (Jude 1:24, NIV). The method isn't one hundred percent sure, but the work of God's grace—the conversion experience—is. When there is genuine conversion, the Christian puts his hand to the plow and doesn't look back (Luke 9:62). The instrument of genuine conversion is genuine repentance, and as we've seen, the purpose of the Law is to bring hardened hearts to repentance. So it does matter how sinners are "folded" into the body of Christ.

Got it? Without hesitation she told me she wanted to "receive Christ" and "pray the prayer." I read the prayer from the booklet; she echoed. She cried; I cried. I thought, This is easy.

The "God has a wonderful plan" method seems more desirable to some because, at first glance, the use of the Law seems confrontational or judgmental, and therefore they are afraid to use it. But they shouldn't be.

Those who preach grace without first preaching the Law to prepare the sinner's heart, point to the many thousands of converts remaining in fellowship as evidence to justify their way of presenting the gospel. But let's take a closer look at the tragic and sobering results of contemporary methods of evangelism that neglect to use the Law as the primary means of bringing sinners to repentance.

> ➤ Please don't skip these next pages or read them lightly. Go through the information thoughtfully and reflectively, as you would walk through a holocaust museum. These statistics are a testimony to an unspeakable human tragedy, affecting not just the body but the soul. —KC

- At a 1990 crusade in the United States, 600 "decisions for Christ" were obtained. No doubt there was much rejoicing. However, ninety days later, follow-up workers *couldn't find even one* who was continuing in his or her faith. That crusade created 600 backsliders— or, to be more scriptural, *false converts.*
- In Cleveland, Ohio, an inner-city outreach brought 400 decisions. The rejoicing no doubt tapered off when workers involved in a follow-up campaign couldn't find a single one of the 400 who had supposedly made a decision.
- In 1985, a four-day crusade obtained 217 decisions. However, according to a member of the organizing committee, 92 percent fell away.
- Charles E. Hackett, the division of home missions national director for the Assemblies of God in the United States, said, "A soul at the altar does not generate much excitement in some circles because we realize approximately ninety-five out of every hundred will not

become integrated into the church. In fact, most of them will not return for a second visit."

o In his book *Today's Evangelism,* Ernest C. Reisinger said of one outreach event, "It lasted eight days, and there were sixty-eight supposed conversions." A month later, not one of the "converts" could be found.

o In 1991, organizers of a Salt Lake City concert encouraged follow-up. They said, "Less than 5 percent of those who respond to an altar call during a public crusade . . . are living a Christian life one year later." In other words, *more than 95 percent* proved to be false converts.

o A pastor in Boulder, Colorado, sent a team to Russia in 1991 and obtained 2,500 decisions. The next year, the team found only thirty continuing in their faith. That's a retention rate of 1.2 percent.

o In Leeds, England, a visiting American speaker acquired 400 decisions for a local church. Six weeks later, only two were still committed and they eventually fell away.

o In November 1970, a number of churches combined for a convention in Fort Worth, Texas, and secured 30,000 decisions. Six months later, the follow-up committee could find only *thirty* still continuing in their faith.

o A mass crusade reported 18,000 decisions—yet, according to *Church Growth* magazine, 94 percent failed to become incorporated into a local church.

o In Sacramento, California, a combined crusade yielded more than 2,000 commitments. One church followed up on fifty-two of those decisions and couldn't find one true convert.

o A leading U.S. denomination reported that during 1995 they secured 384,057 decisions but retained only 22,983 in fellowship. They couldn't account for 361,074 supposed conversions. That's a 94 percent fall-away rate.

o In Omaha, Nebraska, a pastor of a large church said he was involved with a crusade where 1,300 decisions were made, yet not even one "convert" continued in his or her faith.

o Pastor Dennis Grenell from Auckland, New Zealand, who has traveled to India every year since 1980, reported that he saw 80,000 decision cards stacked in a hut in the city of Rajamundry, the "results" of past evangelistic crusades. But he maintained that one would be fortunate to find even eighty Christians in the entire city.

o In the March/April 1993 issue of *American Horizon,* the national director of home missions of a major U.S. denomination disclosed that in 1991, 11,500 churches had obtained 294,784 decisions for Christ. Unfortunately, they could find only 14,337 in fellowship. That means that despite the usual intense follow-up, they couldn't account for approximately 280,000 of their "converts."

o A major Christian television network broadcast an interview with a Russian Christian leader on July 5, 1996. The interviewer said of Russian converts, "Many thousands have received salvation and healing . . . but because of there not being many leaders, not many stayed with their faith."

Notice where the blame is laid with the Russian professions of faith. They fell away because they needed more leaders. In light of the fact that God "is able to keep you from falling, and to present you faultless before the presence of his glory with exceeding joy" (Jude 1:24, KJV), either He wasn't able to keep them, or His hand wasn't in their profession of faith in the first place.

Statistics such as these are very hard to find. What organizing committee is going to shout from the housetops that after a mass of pre-crusade prayer, hundreds of thousands of dollars of expenditure, preaching by a big-name evangelist, and truckloads of follow-up, the wonderful results that initially seemed apparent have all but disappeared? Not only would such news be utterly disheartening for all who put so much time and effort into the crusade, *but the committee has no reasonable explanation as to why the massive catch has disappeared.* The statistics are therefore hushed up and swept under the carpet of "discretion."

A southern California newspaper bravely printed the following article in July 1993: " 'Crusades don't do as much for nonbelievers as some might think,' said Peter Wagner, professor of church growth at Fuller Theological Seminary in Pasadena. Three percent to sixteen percent of those who make decisions at crusades end up responsible members of a church, he said. 'That's not counting Christians who recommit their lives.' "

In October 2002, Pastor Ted Haggard of New Life Church in Colorado

Springs had a similar finding: "Only three to six percent of those who respond in a crusade end up in a local church—that's a problem.... I was recently in a city that had a large crusade eighteen months earlier, and I asked them how many people saved in the crusade ended up in local churches. Not one person who gave his heart to Christ in that crusade ended up in the local church."

These statistics of an 84 to 97 percent fall-away rate are not confined to crusades but are typical throughout local church evangelism. In his book *Fresh Wind, Fresh Fire,* Jim Cymbala notes the lack of growth in the Church: "Despite all the Christian broadcasting and high-profile campaigns, the Christian population is not growing in numbers nationally. In fact, church attendance in a given week during 1996 was down to 37 percent of the population, a ten-year low ... even though 82 percent of Americans claim to be Christians."[1] The problem is not with the crusades, but with the methods and message of modern evangelism.

Sadly, these are not isolated cases. I received the following letter from a pastor in Florida:

> *We have seen over a thousand led to the Lord on the streets. Not many of these teens are at church. I've been analyzing this, and last month, for example, I preached face-to-face on the streets the whole gospel (death, burial, and resurrection) with a focus on repentance and remission to 155 people. Seventy made commitments to Christ. I know my preaching is correct, but I know I need better follow-up; any recommendations?*

His dilemma was that he was preaching the light of the gospel (Christ's death, burial, and resurrection) without using the Law to awaken his hearers. Like many others who have seen this enigma, this pastor thought that his converts needed more follow-up. Another respected minister, whose evangelism program has exploded across the world, said that his evangelism course attempts to get at the heart of the fall-away rate of new converts "by placing great stress on the follow-up." However, "following up" with a false convert is like putting a stillborn baby into intensive care. Neither approach solves the problem.

Author Gordon Miller writes of his deep concern about the number of professed converts who stay in the Church but continue in sin:

> A few months ago, a senior minister of a large, growing church rang me about a new situation in their church.... An increasing number of converts bring their old ways into their Christian lives and do things that shock their leaders. Here, after further reflection, is an extended version of my response.
>
> The first thing to note is that this church and its ministers haven't diluted the gospel or lowered their standards. The church is one of the best in the country with gifted, godly leaders. They fearlessly preach a no-compromise gospel and are even better at nurture than they were years ago. Yet an increasing number of their numerous converts fail to show evidence of moral change in their lives.[2]

Again, even a "no-compromise gospel" will not awaken sinners. That's not its function.

Perhaps you are thinking, "But I didn't have the Law preached to me when I came to Christ." Let me ask you a few questions. When you came to the Savior, did you have a knowledge of sin? You must have, or you would not have repented. He who repents turns from sin, and "sin is the transgression of the law" (1 John 3:4, KJV).

What then was your sin? Was it lust, adultery, or fornication? If so, then your sin was that you transgressed the seventh commandment. Did you steal (eighth), hate (sixth), lie (ninth), or blaspheme (third)? Were you covetous (tenth)? Were you selfish or ungrateful to God? Did you realize that God should be first in your life (first, fourth)? Or maybe you suddenly discerned that God was nothing like you thought He was (second). Did you feel bad about your attitude toward your parents (fifth)? How did you know that you had sinned against God? Wasn't it because you knew of the Ten Commandments? Someone, somewhere, somehow must have said to you: "You shall not kill, you shall not steal," etc., and your conscience bore witness with the Law. Like Paul, you too can say, "I would not have known sin except through the law" (Romans 7:7).

Impersonal Statistics

One Saturday in 1998 near Davis, California, a female student from Sacramento and a skydiving instructor (a veteran of about two thousand jumps) leaped from a plane at ten thousand feet. Both were in their twenties. Tragically, their parachute failed to open and their reserve became tangled in the main chute. Witnesses reported that they heard the young woman screaming for help and they felt the impact from a distance of two football fields away. It was the woman's first—and last—jump. And though the instructor had jumped many times before, his past success couldn't save him.

I have related this true story to bring a personal note to the horror of seeing people entrust their lives to a faulty parachute. The cold statistic that one in 100,000 jumps ends in death somehow doesn't communicate the reality, but the tragic death of a particular young man and woman is heartrending. One would never forget the sound of the terrified young woman's screams, nor the experience of feeling the earth shake as her fragile body hit the ground. Nevertheless, when we speak of the hundreds of thousands who fall away from the faith, we can lose sight of the reality that we are speaking about the salvation of *individual* human beings.

I can't put into words the heartbreak of seeing so many spurious converts who have left the Church, and the multitudes of false converts who stay within the Church. A. W. Tozer writes, "It is my opinion that tens of thousands of people, if not millions, have been brought into some kind of religious experience by accepting Christ, and they have not been saved."

We are not talking about mere statistics but the salvation of men and women from death and eternal damnation in hell. We must put a quick end to the fast-and-easy methods of contemporary evangelism, even though they eliminate the reproach of the gospel and seem to be filling our churches.

Please don't be tempted to ignore the devastating results and point to those *comparatively few* who are continuing in their faith as justification for the method. Remember, for every one thousand genuine converts, there are as many as nine thousand who fall away to destruction because the soil of their hardened hearts was never properly prepared by the quick and easy methods of modern evangelism.

MAKING GRACE AMAZING

After reporting that 280,000 converts from an evangelistic crusade couldn't be accounted for several months later, one editorial writer concluded by saying, "Something is wrong." Yes, and something has been wrong for nearly one hundred years of modern evangelism, since the Church began to neglect the key to the sinner's heart. As we have seen, when we set aside the Law of God and its designed function to convert the soul (Psalm 19:7), we remove the very means by which sinners are able to see their need of God's forgiveness.

Romans 5:20 explains the purpose of God's Law: "Moreover the law entered that the offense might abound. But where sin abounded, grace abounded much more." When sin abounds, grace abounds *much more;* and according to Scripture, the thing that makes sin abound is the Law.

We can see the work of God's Law illustrated in civil law. Watch what often happens on a freeway when there is no visible sign of the law. See how motorists exceed the speed limit. It would seem that each speeder says to himself that the law has forgotten to patrol this part of the freeway. He is transgressing the law by only fifteen miles an hour—and besides, he isn't the only one doing it.

Notice, however, what happens when the law enters the fast lane with red lights flashing. The speeder's heart misses a beat. He is no longer secure in the fact that other motorists are also speeding. He knows that he is *personally* guilty, and *he* could be the one the officer pulls over. Suddenly, his "mere" fifteen-mile-an-hour transgression doesn't seem such a small thing after all; it seems to abound.

Now look at the freeway of sin. The whole world naturally goes with the flow. Who hasn't had a lustful thought at one time or another? Who in today's society doesn't tell the occasional "white" lie? Who hasn't taken something that belongs to someone else, even if it's just a "white-collar" crime? They know they are doing wrong, but their security lies in the fact that so many others are just as guilty, if not more so. It seems that God has forgotten all about sin and the Ten Commandments. The wicked person "has said in his heart, 'God has forgotten; He hides His face; He will never see'" (Psalm 10:11).

Now watch the Law enter with red lights flashing. The sinner's heart is stopped. He places his hand on his mouth. He examines the speedometer of his conscience. Suddenly, it shows him the measure of his guilt in a new light—the light of the Law. His sense of security in the fact that there are multitudes doing the same thing becomes irrelevant because every man will give an account of *himself* to God. Sin not only becomes personal, it seems to "abound." His mere lust becomes *adultery of the heart* (Matthew 5:27-28); his white lies become *false witness*; his own way becomes *rebellion*; his hatred becomes *murder* (1 John 3:15); his "sticky fingers" make him *a thief*. "Moreover the law entered that the offense might abound." Without introduction of the Law, sin is neither personal, nor is it veritable: "For without the Law sin is dead [the sense of it is inactive and a lifeless thing]" (Romans 7:8, AMP).

> ➢ When asked about being a thief, many people will deny stealing *anything*. The label "thief" sounds too harsh for their crimes. But remind them that stealing also includes cheating on taxes, neglecting to return library books, taking items from work, fudging on an expense report, etc. "Petty" theft is still theft in God's sight. —KC

It was the commandment that showed Paul sin in its true light, that it is "exceedingly sinful" (Romans 7:13). Paul spoke from his own experience, because he sat at the feet of Gamaliel, the great teacher of the Law, and therefore saw sin in its vivid colors.

The Offense and the Foolishness of the Cross

According to Scripture, "[the real function of] the Law is to make men recognize and be conscious of sin [not mere perception, but an acquaintance with sin which works toward repentance]" (Romans 3:20, AMP).

To illustrate this point, imagine if I said to you, "I have some good news for you. *Someone has just paid a $25,000 speeding fine on your behalf!*" You would probably answer me with some cynicism in your voice, "What are you talking about? *I don't have* a $25,000 speeding fine!" Your reaction would be quite understandable. If you don't know that you have broken the law in the first place, the good news of someone paying a fine for you won't be good news; it will be foolishness to you. My insinuation that you are guilty of unlawful activity will even be offensive to you.

But if I were to put it this way it may make more sense: "Today, a law enforcement officer clocked you traveling fifty-five miles an hour in an area designated for a blind children's convention. You totally ignored ten clear warning signs that indicated the maximum speed was fifteen miles an hour. What you did was extremely dangerous. The penalty is a twenty-five thousand dollar fine or imprisonment."

As the shock and horror of your transgression and your guilt begin to sink in and you consider the consequences of your actions, I add, "The law was about to take its course when someone you don't even know stepped in and paid the fine for you. *You are very fortunate.*"

Can you see that telling you the good news of the fine being paid, without first telling you that you have broken the law, will leave you thinking that the "good news" is nothing but nonsense? However, clearly making known your transgression gives *sense* to the good news. An unclouded explanation of the law, *so that you can plainly see your violation,* helps you understand and appreciate the news that your penalty has been paid.

In the same way, simply telling someone the good news that Jesus died on the cross for his sins makes no sense to him: "For the message of the cross is foolishness to those who are perishing" (1 Corinthians 1:18). Therefore, it is also quite understandable for him to say, "What are you talking about? I haven't got any 'sins.' I try to live a good life," etc. Your insinuation that he is a sinner, when he doesn't think he is, will be offensive to him.

But those who take the time to follow in the footsteps of Jesus and open up the spirituality of the Law, carefully explaining the meaning of the Ten Commandments, will see sinners becoming *"convicted by the law as transgressors"* (James 2:9, emphasis added). Once they understand their transgression, the good news will be neither offensive nor foolish, but the power of God to salvation.*

What "Sin" Are You Talking About?

When David sinned with Bathsheba, he broke every one of the Ten Commandments. He coveted his neighbor's wife, lived a lie, stole her, committed adultery, murdered her husband, dishonored his parents, and thus broke the remaining four commandments in reference to his relationship with God. So the Lord sent Nathan the prophet to reprove him (2 Samuel 12:1-13).

There is great significance in the order in which the reproof came. Nathan gave David, the shepherd of Israel, a parable about something that he could understand—sheep. He began with the natural realm rather than immediately exposing the king's sin. He told a story about a rich man who, instead of taking a sheep from his own flock, killed a poor man's pet lamb to feed a stranger.

David was indignant and sat up on his high throne of self-righteousness. He revealed his knowledge of the Law by saying that the guilty party would restore fourfold for the lamb and would die for his crime. Nathan then exposed the king's sin of taking another man's "lamb," saying, "You are the man!... Why have you despised the commandment of the Lord, to do evil in His sight?" When David cried, "I have sinned against the Lord," the prophet *then* gave him grace and said, "The Lord also has put away your sin; you shall not die."

---

* The devil hates God's Law because of what it does. That's why there has been such a concerted effort to rid America of the restrictions of the Ten Commandments. However, every church in America should take up a collection and send it to the headquarters of the American Civil Liberties Union as a token of appreciation for their efforts on behalf of the Ten Commandments in our nation. For more than thirty years, the Ten Commandments were largely hidden from the eyes of a generation. Until 2002, many young people didn't even know what the Ten Commandments were. That's no longer the case, thanks to the ACLU and their efforts to remove a monument displaying the Ten Commandments from an Alabama state judiciary building. As part of the media coverage of the controversy, ABC, CBS, NBC and other major television networks scrolled through the Ten Commandments on their nightly news programs. As a result, millions of

Imagine if Nathan, *fearful of rejection,* had changed things around a little, and instead told David, "God loves you and has a wonderful plan for your life. However, there is something that is keeping you from enjoying this wonderful plan; it is called sin."

Imagine if he had glossed over the *personal nature* of David's sin with a general reference to *all* men having sinned and fallen short of the glory of God. David's reaction might have been, "What *sin* are you talking about?" rather than to admit his terrible transgression. Think of it. Why should he say, *"I have sinned against the Lord"* at the sound of *that* message? Instead, in a sincere desire to experience this "wonderful plan," he might have admitted that he, like all men, had sinned and fallen short of the glory of God.

If David had not been made to *tremble* under the wrath of the Law, the prophet would have removed the very means of producing godly sorrow, which was so necessary for David's repentance. It is "godly sorrow" that produces repentance (2 Corinthians 7:10). It was the weight of David's guilt that caused him to say, *"I have sinned against the Lord."* The Law caused him to labor and become heavy laden; it made him hunger and thirst for righteousness. It enlightened him as to the *serious* nature of sin as far as God was concerned.

I received the following letter from a man who had listened to my teaching online and then tried using the Law in his preaching. He writes: "I visited the Lebanon, Tennessee, prison system and witnessed to around thirty hard-core criminals in the maximum security area. I have never seen grown men cry like that!"

Another letter came from someone in Colorado: "God introduced me to your [teaching].[1] New power and anointing came my way, and in preaching the Law over the last nine months or so, I have seen the fruit falling! Grown men crying, teens falling to their knees in front of their peers, and skeptics taking a new look."

viewers saw close-ups of "Thou shalt not commit adultery," "Thou shalt not steal," "Thou shalt not bear false witness," etc. A nation lying in moral darkness was shown the light of God's Law via secular television. The Church couldn't have done a better job if it had embarked on a multimillion-dollar advertising campaign. Not only were the commandments displayed on television, but they were also the subject of articles in newspapers, letters to the editor, talk shows, radio news, magazines, and Internet sites. Although many Christians perceived the 2003 removal of the Ten Commandments monument from the Alabama courthouse as a negative outcome, it was actually very positive. The ACLU did our groundwork. Now it's just a matter of the Church doing what it should, by opening up the commandments to a sinful world, just as Jesus did. When unregenerate sinners across the nation understand the perfection required by God's Law, they will

Sin is like an onion. Its outer wrapper is a dry and crusty self-righteousness. It is only when its external casing is peeled away that it brings tears to the human eye. The Law peels the onion and allows contrition.

The Vase

A child broke his father's antique vase. It was one that he was forbidden to touch, worth $25,000. However, the child thought the vase was worth only $2, so he wasn't very concerned. He thought he could easily replace it. It was only when he discovered its true value that he saw the seriousness of his transgression and felt sorrow of heart. It was only the knowledge of the grave nature of his transgression (breaking an expensive antique that he knew he was wrong to have touched) that enabled him to feel sorrow. If he had been left in ignorance of the value of the vase, he wouldn't have been truly sorry. Would you be upset if you had broken a vase you could easily replace?

The Law-less message that "God loves you and has a wonderful plan for your life" doesn't cause sinners to tremble. It doesn't show them the utterly serious nature of their transgression; consequently, they don't experience godly sorrow that produces repentance.

How true are these words spoken by Charles Spurgeon, the Prince of Preachers: "The Law serves a most necessary purpose." He said of sinners, "They will *never* accept grace until they tremble before a just and holy Law." Those who see the role of the Law will be Sons of Thunder *before* they are the Sons of Consolation. They know that the shoes of human pride must be removed before sinners can approach the burning bush of the gospel.

It is important to realize that we *can* evoke a tearful response from sinners by telling them that God loves them. The message is more appealing to both the Christian and the sinner. It is certainly easier to speak of love than to speak of sin. Many years ago, before I understood the function of God's Law, I told a prostitute of God's love and was delighted that she immediately began weeping. Unbeknown to me, her tears were not tears of godly sorrow for sin, but merely an emotional response to the need of a father's love. In my

flee to the safety of the Savior. God's ways are certainly not the same as ours. Throughout history, God has used seemingly negative circumstances, such as a den of lions, a pharaoh's stubbornness, a fiery furnace, the impassable Red Sea, and the workings of anti-God organizations to achieve His own positive results. When God decides to fulfill His wonderful purposes, no evil device will thwart Him.

ignorance, I joyfully led her in the sinner's prayer. However, I was disappointed some time later when she fell away, and her tender heart became *very* callous toward the things of God.

Music can also evoke a tear-filled response. However, I believe that when it comes to reaching out to the lost, it is a great mistake to use music to stir the emotions of the human heart. Music can produce fear, peace, joy, tension, etc., and can easily bring us to tears. Think of it like this: A little child has broken something precious that I told him not to touch. I soberly challenge him by saying, *"I told you not to touch that. Are you sorry for what you have done?* Before you say anything, let me put on some gentle music to help you make up your mind." Why would I do that? It would stir his emotions, when instead I should be appealing to his will and conscience. Paradoxical as it may seem, the Law makes grace abound, in the same way that darkness makes light shine. It was John Newton, the writer of "Amazing Grace," who said that a wrong understanding of the harmony between Law and grace would produce "error on the left and the right hand." I don't know whether any of us could claim to have a better understanding of grace than the one who penned such a hymn.

The question arises, Should a sinner be moved by Law or grace, by fear or love, when it comes to his salvation? We'll look at this question in the next chapter.

10 | FROM WHAT DID THEY FLEE?

In 1993, the Washington, D.C., traffic authorities found themselves in a public dilemma. Members of a foreign embassy had been issued numerous parking tickets for breaking the law, but because their diplomatic status made them immune to any form of prosecution, they felt no obligation to pay for their violations. To that date, they owed the city six million dollars in unpaid fines.

How could that be? They simply had no respect for the law or for the agency of the law, *because there was no fear of future punishment.* Consequently, they became bold in their lawlessness.

In an effort to force these scofflaws to pay their debts, the authorities amended the law so that vehicles that were driven by traffic violators could not be registered. The violators would therefore be unable to drive their cars.

A similar thing has happened with the Church. Because it has failed to preach future punishment for violation of God's Law, sinners have become bold in their lawlessness. They have lost respect both for the Law and for its agency, the Church.

In San Diego, a strip club has a large sign that reads "We didn't create sin, we just perfected it." One TV channel boasted of their adult programming: "Guaranteed to break more commandments than any other lineup." A magazine cover in the Los Angeles airport was headlined "Teenage Sex Romps.

Stuff so bad, it's good. We're *so* ashamed." The secular world has become devoid of the fear of God; but how can they be expected to fear the Lord when much of the Church is offended by the concept? Instead, sinners are daily clocking up debt to the Law, unbeknownst to them, living as if they will never have to pay the bill. They are storing up wrath that will be revealed in the day of wrath (Romans 2:5). If on that day they are found in debt, they will pay for it with their souls in hell. Unless they are *convinced* that the day of reckoning is coming, that God will bring to light and will judge every secret thing, whether it is good or evil, they will continue to believe that God will not hold them accountable.

Not Moved by Fear

L. E. Maxwell, Bible teacher and principal at the Prairie Bible Institute in Alberta, Canada, wrote of how students came to a knowledge of salvation. Some were "moved by fear" and others were "moved by love." He noted that between 1931 and 1949, of the 2,507 students, nearly 65 percent were moved by fear, and only 6 percent were moved by love. The remaining 29 percent came with another motive or couldn't remember why they came to the Savior.

> ➤ This is an extremely important point. It deals with the wrath of God—an issue I seriously wrestled with when I first encountered this teaching. —KC

This side of Judgment Day, one can only surmise how those not moved by fear ever found a place of repentance. This thought provokes the following inquiries:

○ When they found a place of repentance, of what did they repent? It *must* have been sin.
○ When they understood that they had *sinned against God,* did they not fear at all? Didn't they have enough reverence for God to produce the fear of the Lord, which is the beginning of wisdom?
○ When they turned from sin, how did they "flee from the wrath to come" without fear?
○ If they were "moved by the love of God," seen in the sacrifice of the

Cross, were they not provoked to fear by the extreme measures that God undertook to redeem them because of their sin?

As Christians, have they yet come to a point of fearing God? What do they think when they read that God killed a husband and wife because they broke the ninth commandment (Acts 5:1-10)? Do they conclude that the psalmist was misguided when he wrote, "My flesh trembles for fear of You, and I am afraid of Your judgments" (Psalm 119:120)? Have they obeyed the command of Jesus: "I will show you whom you should fear: Fear Him who, after He has killed, has power to cast into hell; yes, I say to you, fear Him!" (Luke 12:5)? God provides a promise for those who fear Him: "Blessed is every one who fears the Lord, who walks in His ways" (Psalm 128:1). Psalm 2:11 commands, "Serve the Lord with fear, and rejoice with trembling." The early Church did just that; they walked "in the fear of the Lord" (Acts 9:31).

Scripture makes it very clear what it is that causes men to flee from sin. It's the "fear of the Lord" (Proverbs 16:6). Understandably, Maxwell's conclusion was not a concern that so many had fled to Christ in fear, *but that some hadn't*. When F. B. Meyer questioned four hundred Christian workers about why they had come to Christ, "an overwhelming number testified that it was because of some message or influence of the terror of the Lord." The renowned Bible teacher then said, "Oh, this is more than interesting and astonishing, especially in these days when we are rebuked often for not preaching more of the love of God!" R. C. Sproul said, "Jesus doesn't save us *to* God. He saves us *from* God." He also stated, "There's probably no concept in theology more repugnant to modern America than the idea of divine wrath."

> ➢ If we minimize sin by downplaying it to sinners, we paint God as barbaric when we say that hell is the punishment for sin. This leads many believers to gloss over the mention of hell. Jesus, on the other hand, did the opposite. He took the time to open up the moral Law and show the sinner that the depth of his sin is "exceedingly sinful." By using the moral Law to appeal to a man's conscience, Jesus made the sentence of eternal punishment reasonable and right in the eyes of the guilty party, thereby shining light upon his darkened mind. This gives the sinner a clear reason to repent and seek forgiveness through the mercy of the Cross. —KC

Over the years that I have shared my concerns about contemporary evangelism, I have been careful never to name names. However, many have guessed that on occasion I have been referring to the incredibly popular tract *The Four Spiritual Laws,* penned by the late Dr. Bill Bright of Campus Crusade for Christ. More than a billion copies have been distributed in all the major languages of the world, and his approach has become the model for the modern gospel presentation.

In July 2002, Kirk and I were invited to Orlando, Florida, to join Dr. Bright at his home for breakfast. After breakfast, we sat down in his living room and heard this warm, humble, sincere man of God (then eighty-one) confess that he had been in error. Let me use his own words from his book *Heaven and Hell* (published the same year) to tell you what he said to us:

> *In His approximately 42 months of public ministry, there are 33 recorded instances of Jesus speaking about hell. No doubt He warned of hell thousands of times. The Bible refers to hell a total of 167 times. I wonder with what frequency this eternal subject is found in today's pulpits. I confess I have failed in my ministry to declare the reality of hell as often as I have the love of God and the benefits of a personal relationship with Christ. But Jesus spent more of His time warning His listeners of the impending judgment of hell than speaking of the joys of heaven. . . . I have never felt the need to focus on telling people about hell. However, as a result of a steady decline in morals and spiritual vitality in today's culture and a growing indifference to the afterlife, I have come to realize the need for greater discussion of hell. . . . I have thus come to see that silence, or even benign neglect on these subjects, is disobedience on my part. To be silent on the eternal destinations of souls is to be like a sentry failing to warn his fellow soldiers of impending attack.[1]*

Dr. Bright even took the time to use the Law lawfully, by quoting every one of the Ten Commandments, then expounding the Law by saying, "Breaking these commandments will take us to hell without the intervening grace and mercy of Jesus Christ."[2] By admitting that "benign neglect on these subjects is disobedience on my part," Dr. Bright revealed his honest humility and his genuine love of the truth.

Please, follow Dr. Bright's example and examine your evangelism methods in light of God's Word. At stake is the eternal salvation of millions of people. You don't need to throw away *The Four Spiritual Laws*. Simply make four important changes. First, don't tell sinners that Jesus will improve their lives with a wonderful plan. Second, don't make the unbiblical mistake of giving the cure before you've convinced them of the disease. Third, take the time to follow in the way of the Master by "opening up" (or explaining) the Ten Commandments. And fourth, faithfully remember to include the terrible realities of Judgment Day and hell.

> ➤ When I became a Christian, I was deeply touched by the love of God. Although I had sinned against God, He sent His Son to die for my sins and wanted a personal relationship with me! I thought about these things and came to the realization that if I were to die that night, I wouldn't go to heaven. I had ignored God my whole life. I not only hadn't trusted Him, I had denied His very existence. There *was* an element of fear, but as I reflect on it now, it was simply a fear that I wouldn't go to heaven.
>
> The tragedy was that I had never shined the light of the Ten Commandments into the dark well of my heart and seen how deep the sinful waters were. I hadn't seen my own heart as "desperately wicked" and "deceitful above all things" (Jeremiah 17:9), so it never dawned on me that God was angry with me—that I was actually an *enemy* of God because I had so greatly offended Him. The result of my shallow understanding of sin and hell paralyzed me from courageously reaching out to the lost—the very thing Jesus was most passionate about.
>
> Those who come through the door of fear and trembling are made to perceive how ugly and offensive their sin really is to God. Therefore, they understand why God is angry with them and why hell is what they deserve. When people realize that God is offering salvation from His terrible wrath, gratitude for the Savior is infinitely deeper. The depth of their gratitude is in direct proportion to their perception of their sin. Shallow sorrow equals shallow gratitude.
>
> Having a clear picture of hell has become a very effective motivator for me to run to the unsaved, snatch them from the fire, and bring them to the shelter of the Cross.

Shortly after meeting Ray and understanding the reality of hell—
that no matter how good or kind a person perceives himself to be,
he is headed for a place of eternal torment—I began to lose sleep. I
had to do something. So I started talking about the things of God
with more urgency and regularity. I'd think to myself, *What about
the nice waitress in the restaurant? How can I in good conscience enjoy
my meal, offer her a tip, and not even mention the dreadful fate she's
heading toward unless she turns to Jesus?* I was sleepless over
thoughts of people dying that very night, after I had told them to
have a nice day but failed to give them the message that could
have saved their eternal soul. I wanted to race back to the restaurant and write on a napkin the way of eternal life, and ask the wait-
ers and waitresses to read it before they went home that night. I
then realized that I would simply be writing my own gospel tract!

Maybe, like me, you have thought that passing out gospel tracts
might do more harm than good. I used to see "freaks" out on street
corners handing out "Jesus junk" to everyone who passed by, shov-
ing their religious propaganda into people's faces. But now I recognize that there are also sane Christians who are passionate to reach
the lost. I came to realize that tracts are a good thing. However,
there are thoughtful, honest, effective tracts, and there are obnox-
ious, offensive, annoying tracts. I prefer those that reflect the heartfelt concern I have for people who don't know Jesus. Now I hand
out tracts as often as I can and say, "This is for you. I'd really appreciate it if you'd take the time to read it. It has a gospel message
inside." It may not be as good as a personal conversation, but at
least it allows me to share the gospel with gentleness and respect.

I was recently enjoying a day at the beach in southern California.
I noticed a lifeguard in his wooden hut talking on the phone. After
he finished, I went over and introduced myself, and thanked him
for watching out for our safety. I then asked him, "If you were talking on the phone and you noticed someone drowning, could you
in good conscience turn away and let him sink to his death so that
you could continue your phone conversation?" He said, "Of course
not!" Then I explained that, just as he would do anything in his
power to save the life of a drowning victim, I too needed to give

him something to think about. I asked him to please read the tract. With a puzzled look, he told me he would and said, "Thanks."

Since I've become passionate about reaching the lost, I realized that the gospel on paper is infinitely better than no gospel at all. Also, I've had many people come back after receiving a tract and tell me that they really appreciated it because it made them reconsider their spiritual beliefs. If you don't like any of the tracts you've seen in the past, try our unique tracts (we call them "Ice Breakers," and you can view them at www.wayofthemaster.com), or grab a napkin and write your own! What's important is that you do something to reach out to the lost. —KC

11 | WELL VERSED

As I was waiting to witness to a couple of young ladies, I couldn't help but overhear some of the filthy language one of them was using to describe a situation that displeased her. When I found a gap in the conversation, I handed them a couple of our tracts, along with two pennies embossed with the Ten Commandments, and swung the conversation to the Law. The young lady with the dirty mouth claimed she was a Christian, but when I said that I had heard her language and that something wasn't right, she admitted she was a backslider. She was very well versed in the knowledge of the way of salvation, but she was adamant that one should not come to Christ because of the fear of Judgment Day, hell, or the wrath of God. She said that we should come to Christ because of God's love, as expressed in the Cross.

It was obvious by her sinful lifestyle that she had mere head knowledge of God's love and that she didn't consider it a love worthy of her attention. When I told her, "Jesus said not to fear him who has power to kill your body, and afterward can do no more, but to fear Him who has power to kill the body and cast your soul into hell, she replied, "I think that you were sent to me today."

We can look at these verses (Luke 12:4-5) without realizing their implication. Think about it. Someone bursts into your home at night. He's holding a fourteen-inch, razor-sharp hunting knife. He walks toward you and says, "I am going to slit your throat." *He's about to kill your body ... and Jesus is saying not to be afraid?* Of course you are going to be afraid. You are going to be *terrified.* Who in his right mind wouldn't be? Self-preservation is a God-given instinct.

Jesus is using hyperbole—a statement of extremes. He is saying, "Is someone going to kill you? Is that a fearful situation to be in? It's *nothing* compared to the terror of being in your sins and standing before Almighty God on Judgment Day." Such talk is foreign to modern evangelism.

In *The Knowledge of the Holy,* A. W. Tozer writes:

> *God's justice stands forever against the sinner in utter severity. The vague and tenuous hope that God is too kind to punish the ungodly has become a deadly opiate for the consciences of millions. It hushes their fears and allows them to practice all pleasant forms of iniquity while death draws every day nearer and the command to repent goes unregarded. As responsible moral beings, we dare not so trifle with our eternal future.*

Author and evangelist Mike Smalley writes, "Many feel secure in their sins with no fear or worry of Judgment Day because 'God is a God of Love and will overlook my sins.' They forget the fact that love has no place in a courtroom. The purpose of a court is to present evidence and determine guilt or innocence. That will be the case on Judgment Day. All that will be evident then will be God's Holy burning love for absolute perfection. We should fear God above all others and all else in the world because He *is* a God of love. Why? The simple reason is this: you and I are not the only thing He loves. He loves righteousness. He loves holiness, and He loves justice."[1]

A close friend of mine told me that as a young, professing Christian he had lacked the fear of God. To him, God was just a good friend. One day he found out that his girlfriend's parents were out of town. He immediately dropped to his knees and earnestly prayed, "Lord, this could be of You. I want to lose my virginity today. I will know it's of You if she says to come on over." She invited him over, and he became a fornicator that day. Then he earnestly thanked God for what he saw as the Lord giving him his heart's desire. Some time later, he found a place of genuine repentance and is now soundly saved and fervently serving God.

A lack of the fear of God isn't confined to the pews. Almost 40 percent of *pastors* who were polled admitted that they'd had an extramarital affair since beginning their ministry.

Those who lack the fear of God will not stop at fornication. A wise man once said, "Most I fear God. Next to Him, I fear him that fears Him not." If someone has no fear of God, he will lie to you, steal from you, and even kill you . . . if he thinks he can get away with it.

How Many Lies?

A six-year-old boy once approached his father, who, as a pastor, understood the importance of a sinner having knowledge of sin. The child said that he wanted to "ask Jesus into his heart." The father, suspecting that the child lacked the knowledge of sin, told him that he could do so when he was older, then sent him off to bed.

A short time later, the boy got out of bed and asked his father if he could give his life to the Savior. The father still wasn't persuaded of the son's understanding, and not wanting the child's salvation to be spurious, he sent him back to his room. A third time the son returned. This time the father questioned him about whether he had broken any of the Ten Commandments. The young boy didn't think he had. When he was asked if he had lied, the child said that he hadn't. The father thought for a moment, then asked him how many lies he had to tell to be a liar. When it was established that one lie made a person a liar, the child realized he had lied and he broke down in uncontrollable tears. When the father then asked him if he wanted to ask Jesus into his heart, the child *cringed* and nodded his head. He was cringing because he now had a knowledge that he had sinned against God. That produced fear. At this point, he could do more than experimentally "ask Jesus into his heart." He could find a place of godly sorrow. Even at such a young age, the boy could exercise repentance because he now understood that he had offended God.

After speaking of the importance of the place of fear, L. E. Maxwell said: "Is the majesty of the Moral Ruler to meet with no respect? Is the authority of His Law of no consequence? Is there nothing in God to fear? An effete dilettantism would feign tell us so. Nevertheless all history and Scripture and experience cry out against such an emasculated and effeminate theology."

It is the fear of God that should stop Christians from diluting the message with which they've been entrusted and thereby trifling with the eternal well-being of sinners. Their devotion to the truth will be rewarded: "Those who rebuke the wicked will have delight, and a good blessing will come upon them" (Proverbs 24:25).

It seems that John Wesley knew preachers in his day who refused to preach the Law to bring the knowledge of sin. They justified their method by saying that they preached "Christ and Him crucified." So Wesley pointed to Paul's method of preaching "Christ crucified":

> *When Felix sent for Paul, on purpose that he might "hear him concerning the faith in Christ;" instead of preaching Christ in your sense (which would probably have caused the Governor either to mock or to contradict and blaspheme,) "he reasoned of righteousness, temperance, and judgment to come," till Felix (hardened as he was) "trembled" (Acts 24:24-25). Go thou and tread in his steps. Preach Christ to the careless sinner, by reasoning "of righteousness, temperance, and judgment to come!"*

The Bible gives us further insight into Paul's reasoning. In Acts 28:23 we read, "When they had appointed him a day, many came to him at his lodging, to whom he explained and solemnly testified of the kingdom of God, persuading them concerning Jesus from both the Law of Moses and the Prophets, from morning till evening."

Our aim in preaching is to persuade sinners "concerning Jesus." *He* is the way, the truth, and the life. Without Him they will perish. How did Paul preach? He used both prophecy *and* the Law of Moses. Prophecy appeals to a person's intellect and creates faith in the Word of God. As a person realizes that the Bible is no ordinary book—that it contains hundreds of indisputable prophecies that substantiate its supernatural origin—he begins to acknowledge Scripture's credibility. The Law of Moses, on the other hand, appeals to a person's *conscience* and brings the knowledge of sin. Paul used both, because prophecy alone doesn't bring an awareness of sin.

A New Gospel Presentation

A well-known charismatic couple whose aim is to reach millions with the gospel say that they have discovered a new method to get people saved. They maintain that an angel told the woman how to get instant decisions. Let's imagine that you are in a restaurant and you want a waitress to make a decision for Christ. This is what you would say:

"Do you know there are two kinds of beautiful waitresses?"

Her answer: "Really?"

Then you say, "Yes! Those who are saved and those who are about to be. Which one are you?"

If her answer is anything other than, "I am saved," say, "Repeat this after me: 'Father, forgive my sins. Jesus, come into my heart. Make me the kind of person You want me to be. Thank You for saving me.'"

Then ask the waitress: "Where is Jesus right now?"

If she answers, "In my heart," say, "Congratulations on being a child of God!"

If her answer is anything else, have her repeat the prayer after you again.

This couple also insists, "When you talk to someone, use the same words the angel said. It works! If you change the words, it does not work!"

This technique that the "angel" gave the woman isn't new. It is the age-old selling approach of manipulating "customers" so they will answer in the way you want them to. However, there is one important difference. Waitresses are trained to be congenial to customers—not only for the sake of their job, but because the size of their tip depends on it.

Why would an angel of God, after two thousand years of evangelism, suddenly announce a method that isn't in line with God's revealed Word? Did God suddenly figure out a new way to reach the lost and then send His angel to tell us? Did He change His mind about how to reach the world?

If an angel tells us of a gospel (or a method of gospel promotion) that isn't in line with Holy Scripture, we should reject it without a second thought. Why would we do such a thing, even if it *seemed* to work? Simply because we fear God in light of the apostle Paul's sober warning in Galatians 1:8: "But even if we, *or an angel from heaven,* preach any other gospel to you than what we have preached to you, let him be accursed" (emphasis added).

I cannot adequately express my anguish over this type of evangelism. My heart's cry is for people to be saved from hell, and yet modern methods work *against,* not *for* that end. Dare I say it, but they are doing the *devil's* work rather than the Lord's. In Matthew 13:25 we are told, "While men slept, his enemy came and sowed tares among the wheat and went his way." As Christians, we must be alert to the workings of the enemy, understand about true and false conversions, and fear God enough to follow in the steps of *biblical* evangelism. We should heed Paul's warning against "peddling God's Word [shortchanging and adulterating the divine message]" (2 Corinthians 2:17, AMP). John Wesley said that those who didn't bother to use the Law were either "babes in Christ, or strangers to regeneration."

> ➤ Feel free to check out the Way of the Master School of Biblical Evangelism, our comprehensive training on sharing your faith. Go to www.wayofthemaster.com and click on "School." —KC

A pastor of a large church in the South told me that almost everyone in the Bible Belt parrots the same phrase when they are personally challenged about their salvation. They say, "I have received Jesus Christ as Lord and Savior. I've dealt with that." Yet this pastor knows in his heart of hearts that there are no signs of regeneration. He said that it's as if the people have been inoculated against the truth. They *have* been.

I received the following letter from a very concerned mother:

> *It was at a youth camp that my oldest son "gave his heart to Jesus" and was baptized, but since then he has shown no real desire that I can see to live for the Lord. I don't want to seem critical, but I just don't see the desire in any way, shape, or form. I don't want to see the same thing happen with my other two kids.*

God only knows how many others have had the experience of seeing false professions of faith from loved ones. When these false converts fall away, they often become bitter, and their latter end becomes *worse* than the first. They are inoculated against the truth. What can this mother now say to her son?

I deal with so many who are more than false converts—they are venomous backsliders. They have enough ammunition to do great damage to the cause of the gospel. Yet, as they pour out their hatred and filthy blasphemy, my heart goes out to them because they are the sad product of manipulative, modern evangelistic methods.

The next time you meet someone who is into the occult or some weird cult, dig a little, and don't be surprised when you find that they once "gave their heart to Jesus." Scripture warns that many false converts will leave the church: "Now the Spirit expressly says that in latter times *some will depart from the faith,* giving heed to deceiving spirits and doctrines of demons" (1 Timothy 4:1, emphasis added).

The Driving Power

Charles Spurgeon reiterates the importance of emphasizing the coming Day of Judgment:

> *God hath appointed a day in which he will judge the world, and we sigh and cry until it shall end the reign of wickedness, and give rest to the oppressed. Brethren, we must preach the coming of the Lord, and preach it somewhat more than we have done; because it is the driving power of the gospel. Too many have kept back these truths, and thus the bone has been taken out of the arm of the gospel. Its point has been broken; its edge has been blunted. The doctrine of judgment to come is the power by which men are to be aroused. There is another life; the Lord will come a second time; judgment will arrive; the wrath of God will be revealed.* Where this is not preached, I am bold to say the gospel is not preached. *It is absolutely necessary to the preaching of the gospel of Christ that men be warned as to what will happen if they continue in their sins.*
>
> *Ho, ho sir surgeon, you are too delicate to tell the man that he is ill! You hope to heal the sick without their knowing it. You therefore flatter them; and what happens? They laugh at you; they dance upon their own graves. At last they die! Your delicacy is cruelty; your flatteries are poisons; you are a murderer. Shall we keep men in a fool's paradise? Shall we lull them into soft slumbers from which they will awake in hell? Are we to become helpers of their damnation by our smooth speeches? In the name of God we will not.[2] (emphasis added)*

In *Striking Incidents of Saving Grace,* Henry Breeden tells of a preacher in Colliery, England, who saw a number of conversions take place under his ministry. Then in 1861 a "stranger" passed through and conducted meetings in which "there were great numbers of persons" who professed faith in Jesus. The preacher then recounts the sad effects:

> *But many of them were, in a short time, gone back again into the world. Indeed, so complete was the failure that the Minister who succeeded me in that Circuit said, "There was not one single person, out of about ninety who professed to obtain Religion through that man's services, that continued to be a member of the Colliery Church."*
>
> *I had observed the same sort of thing before in regard to the efforts of suchlike persons in other places. And, therefore, I was very desirous to find out what was the cause of such failures. I was sure that the persons, said to be brought in under my own ministry, had nearly all of them held on their way, and were then members—either in the Church above, or in the Church below. So I set myself calmly to consider the whole affair. In doing this, I soon found that the preaching that does not address the sinner's conscience, and strive to break the unconverted spirit down by enforcing the Law of God, scarcely ever leads to the salvation of the soul. And these men scarcely ever preach the Law.*
>
> *Yes, that is it, and nothing else—"By the Law is the knowledge of sin." Let a minister get that important sentiment burnt into his very soul by the Light and flaming Love of God. And then let him go forth and preach the truth as it is in Jesus, and many, many precious souls will soon be saved. But let him omit preaching the Law, and whatever else he may do—for he can accomplish many great things—yet, under that man's ministry, conversions will be scarce.[3]*

I couldn't give a more hearty "Amen!" to his conclusion: "Yes, that is it, and nothing else—'By the Law is the knowledge of sin.'" This teaching is so foundational, and yet many have failed to see its simple truth.

> ➢ When I first grasped the concept of using the Law in witnessing, I was thrilled to have the feather duster of modern evangelism replaced with the concentrated firepower of the Ten Great Can-

nons. Yet as I understood the function of the Law to bring a person to the Cross in humility and brokenness, I wondered if the message of grace had somehow been lost in the process. Other Christian friends often reminded me of the truth that we are "saved by grace, not by the Law." Where was the love in telling people that they have violated God's Laws and would therefore go to hell? Does the Law save them? No! Will the fear of God's wrath save them? Never!

The beauty of the Law is that it breaks proud hearts and shows people their guilt before God. Once they've been broken and their sin exposed before God, they can see their need for mercy and forgiveness. They are no longer proud and arrogant, but rather humbled and thirsty for the kindness and mercy that God offers in the Cross. With an understanding that *death* is what they deserve, they can now appreciate that "God demonstrates His own love toward us, in that while we were still sinners, Christ died for us" (Romans 5:8). Now sinners can truly appreciate the precious blood of Christ that saves them.

The harsh demands of God's Law *magnify* His free gift of grace. Once the light of the Law shone on my heart, I was horrified, embarrassed, and ashamed—I had violated it terribly. But then, as clear as day, I could see the beauty of the Cross! The Law *magnified* my thirst for Jesus. I finally understood why Jesus is the only way to the Father (John 14:6). I am deeply grateful for what the Law did to drive me to and glue me to the Savior.

Without the Law, the message of Jesus on the cross will not make sense. Just as taking chemotherapy if you don't think you have cancer would be foolish, so would surrendering your life to Jesus when you don't think it's necessary. It would be like selling your house to pay for a crime you don't think you've committed. Without knowledge of the Law, the masses will perceive Jesus' death as the unfortunate fate of a good man, the just punishment of a religious lunatic, or simply an ancient legend. But with an understanding of God's Law, they can *clearly see* and *fully understand* that He is their only hope of ever going to heaven.

The Law enables grace to make sense. If I don't understand that I've broken the law, then someone telling me I'm going to jail seems unreasonable. If I don't think I deserve to go to jail, I won't appreciate the judge offering to post my bail. I may think it's a kind gesture but completely out of line, because I don't think I should have been arrested in the first place. I'd appeal the case, defend myself, and accuse the prosecution of harassment. In the same way, if a person doesn't think he's guilty of sin and deserves hell, he won't fall on his face and beg God for mercy and forgiveness. He won't appreciate Jesus' blood being shed for him because he doesn't think he needs it.

If there is no conviction of guilt, there's no confession and no repentance. But if the criminal clearly understands that he is guilty of breaking the law and knows he is deeply indebted to it, then he might humbly admit his guilt, confess his crimes, and ask the judge for mercy.

God gave us the Ten Commandments to show us that we have violated an eternal Law, offended the judge of the universe, and will be guilty when tried in the "court of no compromise." Only when sinners *actually perceive* that they deserve punishment in hell will they fall on their knees like the man in the temple and say, "God, be merciful to me a sinner!" (Luke 18:13). Only when sinners understand the filth in their own heart will they cling with all their might to the cleansing power of the Cross and never let go. Only when they see themselves naked before the eyes of an all-seeing God will they treasure the pure white robe of the righteousness of Christ.

The problem with omitting the Law when witnessing is that most men and women think that they're good people, believing that their own good deeds will be enough to earn them a place in heaven. But the Bible says that even though "there is none who does good, no, not one" (Romans 3:12), still each man will proclaim his own goodness. It's true! The majority of people (including most professing Christians) consider themselves to be "good."

Look at Luke 18:18-23 to see what Jesus said to a man who inquired about eternal life. Jesus used the Law to expose this man's sin of idolatry (his god was his money) and to bring an awareness of his need for forgiveness. Shouldn't we follow in the Master's footsteps? Jesus used the Law when He witnessed to a proud, self-righteous sinner. Only when He was talking with an already humbled, repentant person (like the thief on the cross and Nicodemus) did He simply share the good news of God's grace. Jesus wasn't eliminating grace from the way of salvation; He simply knew that the Law was designed for hard-hearted sinners—*to prepare the way* for the gospel of grace. —KC

In the next chapter, we will look at the importance of a sinner's motive in his response to the gospel.

12 | THE MOTIVE AND THE RESULT

Two men are seated in a plane. The first is given a parachute and told to put it on because it will improve his flight. He's a little skeptical at first; he can't see how wearing a parachute on board a plane could possibly improve his flight.

After some time, he decides to experiment and see if the claims are true. As he straps the apparatus to his back, he notices the weight of it on his shoulders and he finds he now has difficulty sitting upright. However, he consoles himself with the flight attendant's promise that the parachute will improve his flight, and he decides to give it a little time.

As the flight progresses, he notices that some of the other passengers are laughing at him because he's wearing a parachute inside the plane. He begins to feel somewhat humiliated. As they continue to laugh and point at him, he can stand it no longer. He sinks back in his seat, unstraps the parachute, and throws it to the floor. Disillusionment and bitterness fill his heart because as far as he's concerned, he was told an outright lie.

The second man is also given a parachute, *but listen to what he is told.* He's told to put it on because at any moment he'll have to jump out of the plane at 25,000 feet. He gratefully puts the parachute on. He doesn't notice the weight of it upon his shoulders, nor is he concerned that he can't sit upright. His mind is consumed with the thought of what would happen to him if he jumped without the parachute.

Let's now analyze the *motive* and the *result* of each passenger's experience. The first man's motive for putting on the parachute was solely to improve his flight. The result of his experience was that he was humiliated by the other passengers, disillusioned, and somewhat embittered against those who gave him the parachute. As far as he's concerned, it will be a long time before anyone gets one of those things on his back again.

The second man put on the parachute solely to survive the jump to come. And because of his knowledge of what would happen to him if he jumped without it, he has a deep-rooted joy and peace in his heart, knowing that he's been saved from certain death. This knowledge gives him the ability to withstand the mockery of the other passengers. His attitude toward those who gave him the parachute is one of heartfelt gratitude.

As we've seen, many modern evangelistic appeals say, "Put on the Lord Jesus Christ. He'll give you love, joy, peace, fulfillment, and lasting happiness." In other words, Jesus will improve your flight. The sinner responds, and in an experimental fashion puts on the Savior to see if the claims are true. And what does he get? Temptation, tribulation, and persecution. He finds it difficult to live an upright life. Not only that, but other people mock him for his faith. So what does he do? He takes off the Lord Jesus Christ; he's offended for the Word's sake; he's disillusioned and somewhat embittered—and quite rightly so. He was promised peace, joy, love, and fulfillment, and all he got were trials and humiliation. His bitterness is directed toward those who gave him the so-called Good News. His latter end becomes worse than the first—he's another inoculated and bitter backslider.

Instead of preaching that Jesus will "improve the flight," we should be warning sinners that one day they will have to jump out of the plane. "It is appointed for men to die once, but after this the judgment" (Hebrews 9:27). When a sinner understands the horrific consequences of breaking the Law of God, he will flee to the Savior solely to escape the wrath that is to come. If we are true and faithful witnesses, that's what we'll be preaching—that there is wrath to come, and that God "commands all men everywhere to repent, *because* He has appointed a day on which He will judge the world in righteousness" (Acts 17:30-31, emphasis added). The issue isn't one of *happiness* but one of *righteousness*.

It doesn't matter how happy a sinner is or how much he is enjoying the pleasures of sin for a season; without the righteousness of Christ, he will perish on the day of wrath. The Bible says, "Riches do not profit in the day of wrath, but righteousness delivers from death" (Proverbs 11:4). Peace and joy are legitimate *fruits* of salvation, but it's not legitimate to use these fruit as a drawing card *for* salvation. If we do, the sinner will respond with an impure motive, lacking repentance.

Can you remember why the *second* passenger had joy and peace in his heart? It was because he knew that the parachute was going to save him from certain death. In the same way, as believers we have joy and peace because we know that the righteousness of Christ is going to deliver us from the wrath to come.

With that thought in mind, let's take a look at another incident aboard the plane. We have a brand new flight attendant. It's her first day, and she's carrying a tray of boiling hot coffee. As she's walking down the aisle, she trips over someone's foot and slops the hot coffee all over the lap of our second passenger. What's his reaction as that boiling liquid hits his tender flesh? Does he say, "Man, that hurt!"? Yes, he does. But does he then rip the parachute from his shoulders, throw it to the floor, and say, "That stupid parachute!"? No; why should he? He didn't put the parachute on to protect himself from spilled coffee or to have a better flight. He put it on to save himself when the time comes to jump. If anything, the hot coffee incident causes him to cling tighter to the parachute and even look forward to the jump.

If we have put on the Lord Jesus Christ for the right motive—to flee from the wrath to come—when tribulation strikes, when the flight gets bumpy, when we get burned by circumstances, we won't get angry at God, and we won't lose our joy and peace. Why should we? We didn't come to Christ for a better lifestyle but to flee from the wrath to come.

Tribulation drives the true believer *closer* to the Savior. Sadly, multitudes of professing Christians lose their joy and peace when the flight gets bumpy. Why? Because they are products of a man-centered gospel. They came lacking repentance, without which they cannot be saved.

What Was Pharaoh's Problem?

Why did it take so long for Pharaoh to bow to the will of the God of the Israelites, who were his slaves in Egypt? One would think that one plague would have caused him to immediately let God's people go. The answer is given to us in Exodus 9:27-28. After a number of terrible plagues, Pharaoh called for Moses and Aaron and said, "I have sinned this time. The Lord is righteous, and my people and I are wicked. Entreat the Lord, that there may be no more mighty thundering and hail, for it is enough. I will let you go, and you shall stay no longer." Such talk would seem to show that finally he was repentant. However, Exodus 9:30 gives insight as to what was still lacking. Moses said, "But as for you and your servants, I know that you will not yet fear the Lord God." Pharaoh saw his sin as something he had done "this time," and in his heart he didn't yet fear God enough to obey Him.

There are many who profess faith in the Savior who are like Pharaoh. A lack of knowledge of the Law has left them with a shallow understanding of the exceedingly sinful nature of sin. They admit that they have sinned "this time." They think sin is something they have done rather than something that saturates their very nature. They lack the fear of God, and like Pharaoh, these "believers" entreat the Lord simply because they find themselves in the midst of thunderous trials. Then, like the king of Egypt, when the plagues of life stop, they sin once again and harden their hearts to the will of God (Exodus 9:34).

What is it, then, that will break the will of a stubborn, rebellious sinner who gives mere lip service to God but doesn't fear Him? Not only does he need to be terrified by the plagues of God's Law, but he must also see the death of the Firstborn. After the Law has done its terrifying work on the sinner, the gospel gives light regarding the cost of his redemption. His heart will tremble with fear when he realizes that his liberty from wrath came through the death of the firstborn Son of God.

However, the death of Jesus of Nazareth, which purchased our salvation, didn't come swiftly. Jesus Himself told us that He would suffer (Luke 9:22). When commenting on Psalm 22:14, Charles Spurgeon said:

> *The placing of the cross in its socket had shaken Him with great violence, had strained all the ligaments, pained every nerve, and more or less dislocated all His bones. Burdened with His own weight, the august sufferer felt the strain increasing every moment of those six long hours. His sense of faintness and general weakness were overpowering; while to His own*

*consciousness He became nothing but a mass of misery and swooning
sickness....To us, sensations such as our Lord endured would have been
insupportable, and kind unconsciousness would have come to our rescue; but in His case, He was wounded, and felt the sword; He drained the
cup and tasted every drop.*[1]

The risen Savior retained the scars of the cross for a reason. Calvary's grisly
wounds must remain before the eyes of Christians. They stand as a fearful
testimony, not only of God's unfathomable love for sinners, but of His
incredible love for justice.

> As I began to understand the use of the Law to bring repentance,
> the question arose in my mind, "But if we tell unbelievers about the
> Law, sin, righteousness, judgment, hell, and *then* the Cross, are we
> underemphasizing God's love and grace? After all, isn't love what
> the gospel is all about?" A few good friends have also asked me this
> question, and I am grateful for their bluntness because it gets to the
> heart of the matter.
>
> The Bible consistently defines the love of God toward sinners in
> two words: *the Cross.*
>
> - *"For God so loved the world that* He gave His only begotten Son"
>   *(John 3:16, emphasis added).*
> - *"But God demonstrates His own love toward us, in that while we
>   were still sinners,* Christ died for us" *(Romans 5:8, emphasis
>   added).*
> - *"And walk in love, as* Christ also has loved us and given Himself
>   for us, *an offering and a sacrifice to God for a sweet-smelling
>   aroma" (Ephesians 5:2, emphasis added).*
> - *"By this we know love, because* He laid down His life for us"
>   *(1 John 3:16, emphasis added).*
> - *"In this is love, not that we loved God, but that He loved us and
>   sent His Son to be the propitiation for our sins" (1 John 4:10,
>   emphasis added).*
>
> Always and without fail, God uses the Cross as the supreme
> example of His love toward sinners. Sure, God expresses His love
> toward *the saved believer* by offering daily comfort, joy, inner

peace, patience, self-control, and a safe harbor in times of trouble, but never does He offer these to the unbeliever. Check it out yourself. Look in your Bible to find any instance of Jesus, an apostle, or a prophet offering an unrepentant sinner any form of God's love other than Jesus' blood on the cross. Rather, God's wrath is on them! The Cross is love's masterpiece. The Cross is God motivated by love, running toward the sinner to rescue him from the flames of eternal punishment.

If I were to pinpoint a time in my life when my earthly father clearly demonstrated his love for me, it would be the time he saved my life. I was four years old, playing on a boat dock, when I fell into the water and was drowning. I likely would have died if my father had not been there to save me. He dived into the water and rescued me. I know that my father loves me *because he saved my life.* I couldn't want better proof that my father loves me than the fact that he risked his own life to save mine, and every other demonstration of love pales in comparison to that supreme moment of mercy.

So when it comes to telling sinners about the heavenly Father's love, if we have to point beyond the Cross, where Jesus rescued them from the waters of eternal death, we are missing the focal point of God's love. If you feel the simple message of the Cross is not enough to describe the love of God, will you say that to the Father who sacrificed His one and only Son, or to Jesus who loved you and gave His own life for you, or to the countless martyrs who died simply because Jesus loved them and died for them? To promise an unsaved sinner anything more than the full mercy and compassion of the Cross is to go beyond Scripture. As Paul said to the sinful Corinthians, "I determined not to know anything among you *except Jesus Christ and Him crucified"* (1 Corinthians 2:2, emphasis added).

Perhaps the problem isn't that sinners need more than "Christ crucified," but that they need to hear a better explanation of the One who loved us and gave Himself up for us. As messengers of life to a dying world, we must point people to Jesus and magnify the love of God in Him. We must expound the love that held Jesus to the cross and fill the mind of the unsaved with the knowledge of

God's solemn promise, written with His own blood, to forgive those who believe in Jesus. God help us to proclaim faithfully the full love of God in the Cross.

Believer, do you understand that love yourself? Do you understand what you were saved from? Have you ever looked for yourself into the mirror of God's Law and seen your own heart's exceedingly sinful reflection? Do you know how hot the flames burn in God's eternal prison? Have you ever wept tears of gratitude for the precious blood Jesus spilled to save you? If not, you will no doubt find it difficult to explain the Cross to others.

These are sobering thoughts for me as well as for anyone who has not yet fled to the Savior to escape the wrath to come. A fool will dismiss them as judgmental, but a wise person will examine himself to see if he is in the faith (2 Corinthians 13:5). —KC

In the next chapter, we will draw from the wisdom of men whose results the Church admires but of whose methods many are sadly ignorant.

13 | EXPERIENCE: THE TRUE TEST

Let's now draw on the experiential wisdom of eminent men of God from the past. Martin Luther, in his commentary on Galatians, writes: "Satan, the god of all dissension, stirreth up daily new sects, and last of all, which of all other I should never have foreseen or once suspected, he hath raised up a sect as such as teach . . . that men should not be terrified by the Law, but gently exhorted by the preaching of the grace of Christ."

Luther's words perfectly describe the methods of most of contemporary evangelists. Modern evangelists would never think of using the Law to terrify, but instead they prefer to gently exhort by preaching the grace of Christ. Luther further stated, "The true function of the Law is to accuse and to kill; but the function of the gospel is to make alive."

> ➢ Although the Law serves as a moral guide to genuine believers, its primary function is to kill and destroy self-righteousness. All hope in our good works must be put to death if we are ever to depend on Jesus, who alone can bring life. The Law brings that necessary death. —KC

In his book *Holiness,* J. C. Ryle writes of the sinner's motivation in coming to Christ:

People will never set their faces decidedly towards heaven, and live like pilgrims, until they really feel that they are in danger of hell. . . . Let us expound and beat out the Ten Commandments, and show the length, and breadth, and depth, and height of their requirements. This is the way of our Lord in the Sermon on the Mount. We cannot do better than follow His plan. We may depend on it, men will never come to Jesus, and stay with Jesus, and live for Jesus, unless they really know why they are to come, and what is their need. Those whom the Spirit draws to Jesus are those whom the Spirit has convinced of sin. Without thorough conviction of sin, men may seem to come to Jesus and follow Him for a season, but they will soon fall away and return to the world.[1]

Dr. Martyn Lloyd-Jones spoke of the function of God's Law in gospel proclamation:

The trouble with people who are not seeking for a Savior, and for salvation, is that they do not understand the nature of sin. It is the peculiar function of the Law to bring such an understanding to a man's mind and conscience. That is why great evangelical preachers 300 years ago in the time of the Puritans, and 200 years ago in the time of Whitefield and others, always engaged in what they called a preliminary "Law work."

John R. W. Stott, commenting on Galatians 3:23-29, writes, "We cannot come to Christ to be justified until we have first been to Moses, to be condemned. But once we have gone to Moses, and acknowledged our sin, guilt, and condemnation, we must not stay there. We must let Moses send us to Christ."

Addressing Some Concerns

Let me take a moment to address some questions that may have arisen in your mind.

Romans 2:4 tells us that "the goodness of God leads [us] to repentance." Some try to use this verse to justify a message devoid of sin, righteousness, and judgment, saying that we need merely to speak of God's goodness to see sinners saved. However, it should be pointed out that this verse is sandwiched between some of the harshest statements of God's judgment and wrath. If Paul were saying that we should speak only of God's goodness to sinners, he wasn't practicing what he preached. The great hymn writer Isaac Watts said, "I never knew but one person in the whole course of my ministry who acknowledged that the first motions of religion in his own heart arose from a sense of the goodness of God, 'What shall I render to the Lord, who has dealt so bountifully with me?' But I think all besides who have come within my notice have rather been first awakened to fly from the wrath to come by the passion of fear."

I hope that you don't get the impression that I'm suggesting that we preach only God's judgment and never give sinners the message of grace. The truth is that we must continually preach God's love as shown in the Cross. That is the focus. We are *determined* to preach Christ, and Him crucified. When we are witnessing and preaching, John 3:16 is where we should be heading, but we must make sure that we get to it via Biblical Avenue.[2]

I also hope you don't think that my asking someone if they are good or have lied or stolen, etc., is a method of my own devising. As much as I would like to take the credit for such a wonderfully effective way of awakening sinners, I can't. I learned it from the greatest Evangelist. It is the way of the Master to correct sinners regarding their understanding of the word *good*, and to ask if they have kept the commandments (see how Jesus does it in Luke 18:18-23).

> ➤ To see real-life witnessing using the Law, see The Way of the Master
> Foundation Course video series, available at www.wayofthe
> master.com. —KC

Modern evangelists who may be tempted to discard this teaching because they think it is simply a "method" should also consider their own ways. Can the rehearsed catchphrases used while preaching, the counselors coming forward to draw out decisions—heads bowed, eyes closed, music playing, etc.—be shown to be biblical, or are they man-made methods used to get decisions? We should determine our evangelistic methods solely in light of Holy Scripture.

The Conscience Bears Witness

A Nazi soldier was once questioned about why he mercilessly shot Jewish women and children during World War II. He told the interviewer that one of the motivations was "curiosity." He calmly said, "I just fired and they fell." When the interviewer asked if he felt bad about doing such things, he said, "I was given twenty years, and I served twenty years." In other words, he had paid his debt to society for his misdeeds; the scales were now balanced; justice had been served.

However, when the interviewer asked him about his conscience, he refused to speak any further, and immediately terminated the interview. Conscience speaks of more than guilt for transgressions of civil or criminal statutes. The conscience bears witness to the Moral Law. It reminds men that there is a God whose Law we have transgressed.

Paris Reidhead spoke these wonderfully wise words:

> *If I had my way, I would declare a moratorium on public preaching of "the plan of salvation" in America for one to two years. Then I would call on everyone who has use of the airwaves and the pulpits to preach the holiness of God, the righteousness of God and the Law of God, until sinners would cry out, "What must we do to be saved?" Then I would take them off in a corner and whisper the gospel to them. Such drastic action is needed because we have gospel-hardened a generation of sinners by telling them how to be saved before they have any understanding why they need to be saved.*
>
> *Don't use John 3:16. Why? Because you tell a sinner how to be saved before he has realized that he needs to be saved. What you have done is gospel-hardened him.*

What did he say? *Don't use John 3:16?* That sounds like heresy! Of course, we should use John 3:16; it should be the focal point of the gospel message—at the proper time. Reidhead is simply saying that we should not prescribe the cure before we have convinced the sinner of the disease. D. L. Moody said:

> *It is a great mistake to give a man who has not been convicted of sin certain passages that were never meant for him. The Law is what he needs. . . . Do not offer the consolation of the gospel until he sees and knows he is guilty before God. We must give enough of the Law to take away all self-righteousness. I pity the man who preaches only one side of the truth—always the gospel, and never the Law.*

The Light Didn't Awaken Him

Peter lay soundly asleep in Herod's prison (Acts 12:5-11). This is faith in action. Faith rests, even in a storm. Stephen had been stoned, James had just been killed with a sword—yet Peter slept like a parishioner in the back row of a dead church. He was bound with chains between two soldiers. More guards stood before the door of the prison. Suddenly an angel of the Lord appeared and stood by Peter, "and a light shone in the prison" (v. 7). There is a strong inference that the light didn't awaken Peter from his sleep, because the Scriptures then tell us that the angel struck him on the side. As Peter arose, his chains fell off, he girded himself, tied on his shoes, put on his garment, and followed the angel. After that, the iron gate leading to the city opened of its own accord, and Peter was free.

The sinner is in the prison of his sins. He has been taken captive by the devil. He is bound by the chains of sin, under the sentence of death. He is asleep in his sins. He lives in a dream world. However, it isn't the gospel light that will awaken him. How can "Good News" alarm a sinner? No, the Law must strike him. He needs to be struck with the lightning of Sinai and awakened by its thunderings. That will rouse him to his plight of being on the threshold of death. Then he will arise, and the gospel will remove the chains of sin and death. It will be "the power of God to salvation" (Romans 1:16). Then he will gird himself with truth, tie on his gospel shoes, put on his garment of righteousness, follow the Lord, and the iron gate of the Celestial City will open of its own accord.

Our nation is full of people—both inside and outside of the Church—who have come under the light of the gospel but who have never been struck by the Law. (In a later chapter, we will look at how many this may actually be.) They are still asleep in their sins, unaware of their terrible plight, because the Law has never awakened them. The power of the commandments must open their eyes before the light of the gospel can be of benefit. Look at this *sequence* in what Paul writes to the Ephesians: "Therefore He [the Lord] says: 'Awake, you who sleep, arise from the dead, and Christ will give you light'" (Ephesians 5:14). There must be an awakening before Jesus Christ gives us light. Dr. Timothy Dwight, former president of Yale University, concluded: "Few, very few, are ever awakened or convinced by the encouragements and promises of the gospel, but almost all by the denunciations of the Law."

I received the following story in a newsletter from someone in New York. It illustrates how the gospel makes little sense without the Law:

> We went to visit [our 96-year-old grandmother] every week and even though she has not received the gospel so freely these past few years, we kept sharing the truth of Jesus with her each time. Mike would play songs about Him. Wendy would talk to her. We would pray for her physical strength and add into the prayer how we wanted God to reveal His Son to Nana.
>
> Then last week, Wendy got the flu, and while she was in bed feeling miserable, she read Ray Comfort's book . . . which challenges us to share the whole gospel and not sugarcoat it. It talks about using the Law when talking to a sinner to make them see how they have personally broken God's Law and are doomed without a Savior who paid the price for them. It says in Psalm 19:7 that the "Law of the Lord is perfect, converting the soul." God spoke to Wendy's heart that she needed to share the Law with Nana before Nana could ever see the grace and mercy of God in the cross.
>
> So after committing the day and every detail to God, we went over to visit Nana. She was more alert and less distracted than usual. While Mike was praying, Wendy read her God's Commandments from Exodus 20:1-17 and then asked Nana pointblank, "Nana, have you ever lied? Or stolen anything, even a little thing?" She replied, "I guess so." Wendy shared about God's very real judgments, hell, and heaven, that one day Nana would be standing face-to-face before God and would have to give an account of her life. Then she read from Isaiah 53:5-6 and told Nana about Jesus and the horror of His cross. Nana looked shocked that someone would have those awful things happen to Him. Wendy shared some of her testimony and then asked Nana if she wanted to ask God to forgive her of her sins. She said yes! And she asked God to forgive her and wash her clean in the blood of Jesus.

This ninety-six-year-old woman didn't know that she was sinning against God until the Law, in the hand of the Spirit, did its work. Read this letter I received from a pastor in Tullahoma, Tennessee:

I have some great news to share with you. I found out this morning that my father was in the hospital. On the way there to see him, I prayed that God would give me wisdom with the words I was to speak. After being there a few minutes I asked if he had thought any more about our conversation several months ago about heaven and hell. He replied that he had and said he was ready if it was his time. I pressed him further and then began to use the Law first, going through the Ten Commandments. He began to cry some and admitted he was a Law breaker. I was then privileged to lead him in the prayer of salvation. He looked at me and began crying. I had to leave for a little while and when I came back I told him how glad I was that we had prayed together. He said he was glad too and began to cry again. I am so thankful that at 1:50 p.m. on this day, my dad became a child of God. Thank you, sir, for your obedience in teaching what you do. When my dad saw how utterly sinful he was and that he was without hope and God, he was willing to bow his head and accept Jesus with contrition. He was the first person I have witnessed to using the Law instead of grace first, and I praise God that my dad's salvation is the firstfruits. I used the Law again a few hours later at a store and the guy couldn't say a word. He saw himself as a sinner. Again, thank you.

Romans 7:9 says, "I was alive once without the law, but when the commandment came, sin revived." In his comments on this verse, Martin Luther writes:

So it is with the work-righteous and the proud unbelievers. Because they do not know the Law of God, which is directed against them, it is impossible for them to know their sin. Therefore also they are not amenable to instruction. If they would know the Law, they would also know their sin; and sin to which they are now dead would become alive in them.

Jonathan Edwards stated, "The only way we can know whether we are sinning is by knowing His moral law." George Whitefield said to his hearers, "First, then, before you can speak peace to your hearts, you must be made to see, made to feel, made to weep over, made to bewail, your actual transgressions against the Law of God." When we preach the whole counsel of God, we merely work with the Holy Spirit to convince people of sin. In *Today's Gospel: Authentic or Synthetic?* Walter Chantry writes:

> *The absence of God's holy Law from modern preaching is perhaps as responsible as any other factor for the evangelistic impotence of our churches and missions. Only by the light of the Law can the vermin of sin in the heart be exposed. Satan has effectively used a very clever device to silence the Law, which is needed as an instrument to bring perishing men to Christ.*
>
> *It is imperative that preachers of today learn how to declare the spiritual Law of God; for, until we learn how to wound consciences, we shall have no wounds to bind with gospel bandages.*

Pastor John MacArthur says essentially the same thing: "God's grace cannot be faithfully preached to unbelievers until the Law is preached and man's corrupt nature is exposed. It is impossible for a person to fully realize his need for God's grace until he sees how terribly he has failed the standards of God's Law."

According to John Newton, "Ignorance of the nature and design of the Law is at the bottom of most religious mistakes." Charles Spurgeon stated, "I do not believe that any man can preach the gospel who does not preach the Law." Then he warns:

> *Lower the Law and you dim the light by which man perceives his guilt; this is a very serious loss to the sinner rather than a gain; for it lessens the likelihood of his conviction and conversion. I say you have deprived the gospel of its ablest auxiliary [its most powerful weapon] when you have set aside the Law. You have taken away from it the schoolmaster that is to bring men to Christt. . . .* They will never accept grace till they tremble before a just and holy Law. *Therefore the Law serves a most necessary purpose, and it must not be removed from its place. (emphasis added)*

> ➢ Listen to the wisdom of great men of God from ages past:

- Charles Spurgeon: "The Law cuts into the core of the evil, it reveals the seat of the malady, and informs us that the leprosy lies deep within."

- John Bunyan: "The man who does not know the nature of the Law, cannot know the nature of sin."
- J. I. Packer: "Unless we see our shortcomings in the light of the Law and holiness of God, we do not see them as sin at all."
- Martin Luther: "The first duty of the Gospel preacher is to declare God's Law and show the nature of sin. . . . We would not see nor realize it (what a distressing and horrible fall in which we lie), if it were not for the Law, and we would have to remain forever lost, if we were not again helped out of it through Christ. Therefore the Law and the Gospel are given to the end that we may learn to know both how guilty we are and to what we should again return."
- John Wesley: "It remains only to show . . . the uses of the Law. And the first use of it, without question, is to convince the world of sin. . . . By this is the sinner discovered to himself. All his fig-leaves are torn away, and he sees that he is 'wretched and poor and miserable, blind and naked.' The Law flashes conviction on every side. He feels himself a mere sinner. He has nothing to pay. His 'mouth is stopped' and he stands 'guilty before God.' To slay the sinner is, then, the first use of the Law; to destroy the life and strength wherein he trusts, and convince him that he is dead while he liveth; not only under the sentence of death, but actually dead unto God, void of all spiritual life, 'dead in trespasses and sins.'. . . He cries out, 'O what love have I unto thy Law! all the day long is my study in it;' he sees daily, in that divine mirror, more and more of his own sinfulness. He sees more and more clearly, that he is still a sinner in all things—that neither his heart nor his ways are right before God; and that every moment sends him to Christ. . . . Therefore I cannot spare the Law one moment, no more than I can spare Christ; seeing I now want it as much to keep me to Christ, as I ever wanted it to bring me to Him. Otherwise this 'evil heart of unbelief' would immediately 'depart from the living God.' Indeed each is continually sending me to the other—the Law to Christ, and Christ to the Law."[3]
—KC

Look at how the Law did its part in bringing Robert Flockhart, one of Spurgeon's favorite preachers, to the Cross:

I consider the language of the apostle in Romans 7:9 not inapplicable to my situation at that time, "but when the commandment came, sin revived, and I died." Sin, that had been asleep before, came like a giant upon me. I saw myself in the mirror of God's Law. That Law was spiritual and extended to the thoughts and intents of my heart. Dreadful and blasphemous thoughts, like sparks out of a chimney, now came out of my heart. I was afraid to open my Bible or even to look up, for fear the Lord would send a thunderbolt out of heaven to crush me.

What a translation from darkness to light, from the kingdom of darkness to the kingdom of God's dear Son! My guilt removed and my pardon sealed, peace flowed like a river into my soul.[4]

Perhaps the modern evangelist's reticence to preach that which produces fear is simply due to concern about the reaction of sinners. Some may worry that the message may be aligned with what is commonly called hellfire preaching. Yet there is a vast difference between the use of the Law and hellfire preaching. Understandably, the thought of the existence of hell, without the use of the Law to justify its existence, is unreasonable to a sinner's mind. How could a God of love create a place of eternal torment? Imagine if the police suddenly burst into your home, angrily shouted, "You are going to be put away for a long time!" and thrust you into prison. Such conduct would undoubtedly leave you bewildered and angry because it would be *unreasonable.*

However, if the police burst into your home and told you specifically why you were in trouble ("We have discovered ten thousand marijuana plants growing in your backyard. You are going to be put away for a long time!") at least you would understand why you were in trouble. Knowledge of the law that you transgressed furnishes you with understanding. It makes judgment *reasonable.*

Hellfire preaching without use of the Law to show sinners *why* God is angry with them will more than likely leave them bewildered and angry—for what they consider unreasonable punishment. However, when we use the Law lawfully, it appeals to the reason of sinners. Paul *reasoned* with Felix about his sins and the judgment to come, to the point where the governor "was afraid" (Acts 24:25). Hell became reasonable. No doubt the "righteousness" Paul spoke of was the righteousness which is of the Law, and the result was that the fear of God fell upon Felix's heart.

Those who come to the Savior with such knowledge are not strangers to fear, even after they understand the significance of the Cross. They tremble at the cost of their redemption. They gaze with fear-filled hearts at the grisly sight of Calvary's cross. They work out their own salvation "with fear and trembling" (Philippians 2:12) because they were not redeemed with "silver or gold, ... but with the precious blood of Christ" (1 Peter 1:18-19).

In his wonderful book *Fresh Wind, Fresh Fire,* Jim Cymbala, rightly frustrated by the lukewarm contemporary Church, says of the disciples:

> *Once they were empowered on the Day of Pentecost, however, they became the church victorious, the church militant. With the gracious manifestation of God's Spirit in the Upper Room, the disciples encountered their first audience. Peter, the biggest failure of them all, became the preacher that day. It was no homiletical masterpiece, to be sure. But people were deeply convicted—"cut to the heart," according to Acts 2:37—by his anointed words. Three thousand were gathered into the church that day.[5]*

The inference is that the key was the empowerment of the Holy Spirit. This is true. However, we have the same Holy Spirit today, yet we rarely see such a harvest of souls. Why not? Simply because Peter properly prepared the ground upon which he was sowing. His audience was composed of "devout men" who were gathered at Pentecost to celebrate the giving of God's Law on Mount Sinai.

Even though these were godly Jews, Peter told them that they were "lawless"—that they had violated God's Law by murdering Jesus (Acts 2:23). He drove home that fact by saying, "Therefore let all the house of Israel know assuredly that God has made this Jesus, *whom you crucified,* both Lord and Christ" (Acts 2:36, emphasis added). It was then that they saw that their sin was personal. They were "cut to the heart" and cried out for help. Only after the Law convicted them of their sinfulness did Peter offer them grace (v. 38).

This was also the case with Nicodemus and Nathanael. Nicodemus was a leader of the Jews, whom Jesus called a "teacher of Israel" (John 3:10). He was therefore thoroughly versed in God's Law. He also had a humble heart.

Here was a leader of the Jews acknowledging the deity of the Son of God (John 3:2). The Law was a schoolmaster to bring this humble, godly Jew to Christ.

According to John 1:47, Jesus said that Nathanael was an Israelite (brought up under the Law) in whom there was "no deceit" (he didn't twist the Law as the Pharisees did; he no doubt read "the way of God in truth" [Luke 20:21]). The Law also served as a schoolmaster to bring this godly Jew to the Savior.

14 | THE BADGE OF AUTHORITY

America has chosen to live in moral darkness. We have become a lawless nation—a nation that has lost the fear of God. In 1999 alone, there were 89,110 reported rapes, 12,658 murders, and 409,670 robberies. That same year, there was an incredible total of 23,677,800 crimes.[1] The Constitution has replaced Holy Scripture as the point of moral reference. The writings of men have become sacred. Take, for instance, the issue of pornography. Why should our government tolerate such moral perversion? To them, the answer is clear from the writings of our forefathers—it is a "constitutional right" to produce unclean literature, even if it is morally offensive. However, ask a man who advocates pornographic literature if *child* pornography is legitimate, and he will usually draw his moral line. Ask him then at what age "immoral" child porn crosses the divide and becomes "morally acceptable." With a little digging, you will find that the dividing line is often the line of *personal pleasure.* He doesn't gain pleasure from looking at a thirteen-year-old child, but he does from a seventeen-year-old young woman. His love for sin clouds his moral judgment.

The Constitution of the United States is being used for something it was never intended. When a legal document is employed as a moral beacon, we end up with morally blind legislators leading a morally blind nation. Both fall into a dirty ditch. However, the argument for pornography is concluded with one statement from Holy Scripture: "Whoever looks at a woman to lust for her has already committed adultery with her in his heart" (Matthew 5:28). Case closed.

When we specifically point to the Scriptures as an ethical beacon, we must make it clear to those who will listen that our express reference is the Moral Law of God. There is great reason for this. In 1989, when I first came to the United States from New Zealand, I was preaching in the open air at Venice Beach, California. Unbeknownst to me at that time, the police there wore shorts and rode around on bicycles.

When I stood on a soapbox and began to speak on the edge of the wide sidewalk, a crowd of about eighty people gathered around to listen. Suddenly, a man in shorts stood right in front of me and told me to stop preaching. On my soapbox, I was elevated above him, and his badge was out of my sight, so I paid him no more heed than I would to an ordinary civilian who was telling me to stop. When I ignored him, he became very indignant and told me once again to stop. I asked, "Are you a police officer?" He then became angry and said through gritted teeth, "If you don't stop right now, I will arrest you!" It was then that I noticed a badge on his belt, which told me he *was* an officer of the law. Suddenly, his words carried a great deal of authority!

Those who are representatives of the living God yet don't point to the Law as the core of their authority will not gain due consideration from the world. Jesus stood before the multitudes as One who was a representative of the Law of God. The Bible says the Messiah would bring justice to the earth and that "the coastlands shall wait for His law" (Isaiah 42:4). He repeatedly referred to the Law as the point of His authority: "Do not think that I came to destroy the Law.... I did not come to destroy but to fulfill. For assuredly, I say to you, till heaven and earth pass away, one jot or one tittle will by no means pass from the law till all is fulfilled" (Matthew 5:17-18); "This is the Law and the Prophets" (Matthew 7:12); "Have you not read in the law ...?" (Matthew 12:5); "It is easier for heaven and earth to pass away than for one tittle of the law to fail" (Luke 16:17).

Abortion is wrong. Adultery is wrong. Pornography is wrong. We can shout our moral convictions from the highest housetops, but the world will not listen. People exalt themselves above the claims of Christian morality.

Without the conviction of sin that comes through the preaching of the Law, they have no incentive to open their hearts to what we have to say.

> ➤ While I was on an airplane recently, a flight attendant asked me if it was true that I was very religious. After I told her about my love for Jesus, she smugly replied, "Well, we all have our own opinions, right?" True, we each have our own opinion. That is why we must not assert just a personal opinion, but the true, authoritative Word of God. When a man hears from the Supreme Judge of his soul that what he is doing is wrong, he realizes the foolishness of his rebellion. —KC

Why did I suddenly take notice of the man who was telling me to stop my open-air preaching? *It was his badge that caused me to take notice.* His badge said that if I didn't heed his words there would be coming judgment. To tell the world that it's wrong to kill, to steal, or to commit adultery, without reference to future punishment, is to point an unloaded cannon.

Some may listen simply because morality has a positive influence. Theft can ravage a society. Adultery can ruin families. Lying can shatter friendships. In that context, morality makes sense. However, when we tell the world to repent because God has "appointed a day on which He will judge the world in righteousness" (Acts 17:31), they will have an inducement to obey the gospel. It will begin to dawn on them that their own eternal welfare is at stake.

For the Church to neglect to point to the Law of God is to hide the badge of our authority from the world. Understandably, sinners will disregard what we have to say. The gospel we preach is only there because God stands by the holiness of the Law. If God's eternal Law did not exist, then there would have been no need for a sacrifice. The Law demands retribution. It was the divine fire of God's Law that fell on the sacrifice of Calvary.

If the people of the world *knew* that there was an eternal Law they must face, and that the Law necessitates death and hell for transgression, then they would seriously consider the claims of the gospel. If they understood that the long arm of the Law will reach right down into the heart of humanity, they would repent. If they knew that Almighty God is "angry with the wicked every day" (Psalm 7:11), that His wrath abides on them, they would flee to the Savior.

Let me put it another way. Each of the Ten Commandments is of itself a *key*. However, these are not keys that *release*; rather, they are keys that lock the sinner in the holding cell of sin and death. Paul writes of being "kept under guard" by the Law. He was left without hope, condemned, waiting for capital punishment from the hand of the Law he had so blatantly violated.

When speaking of God's Law, Charles Spurgeon said, "Having thus removed the mask and shown the desperate case of the sinner, the relentless Law causes the offense to abound yet more by bringing home the sentence of condemnation. It mounts the judgment seat, puts on the black cap and pronounces the sentence of death. With a harsh unpitying voice it solemnly thunders forth the words 'condemned already!'"

It was in the darkness of the Law that Paul saw the light of the glorious gospel. The grace of God pointed him to another door—the door of the Savior. He could leave the cell because his fine had been paid in full by the shed blood of the spotless Lamb of God. It was the Law that showed Paul that he was unable to save himself. He knew that salvation was an act of mercy—that his deliverance from death was the result of God's grace, not something in his own character that drew mercy toward him.

> ➤ The Law didn't help me; it just left me helpless. It didn't make me a good person; it made me realize that I'm not. The Law is the mirror that shows you and me that we're in trouble with God and cannot help ourselves; we must rely completely upon Jesus to save us. I thank God for the Law. Without it, I'd still be living in a dream world, thinking I was going to heaven when, in reality, I was on my way to hell! —KC

This principle was clearly illustrated as I was open-air preaching on the Third Street Promenade of Santa Monica, California, where I had a permit to speak. I had been taking a team there each Friday night for more than two years, and only once before had I seen such antagonism toward the gospel. There was the usual bitter animosity from the products of modern evangelism. One man, betraying his "Christian" background, started preaching about his hamster dying for the sins of the world, and if only we would give our hearts to him, we would find peace and joy. When a professing atheist named James began to mock the things of God by yelling "Praise Jesus," among other things, my suspicions were confirmed when he admitted that he had once given his heart to Christ. A teenage girl, a Mormon, kept shouting that I was Satan, and tried to shock me by baring her breasts (I looked the other way). Others were spitting and using language that would make your hair curl tighter than a pig's tail. Among a number of others, three teenage girls came to the "heckler's microphone" and said that they were witches. A few years ago I would have doubted what they said, but I believed their testimony.

For many years I have used a mannequin called Lazarus, which lies under a sheet as a crowd-getter. Often people stop and ask, "What have you got *that* there for?" To which I reply, "It's to get people to stop and ask, 'What have you got *that* there for?' It works, doesn't it?"[2]

On this particular night, Lazarus was receiving his share of persecution. One young man began doing lewd acts on him, much to the delight of the crowd. While I was speaking, another youth burst through the crowd, rushed up to Lazarus and stomped on his head. It was such a violent act that Lazarus's plastic face actually burst. I jumped off my soapbox, grabbed the youth by his shirt, and said, "That dummy cost me a lot of money. Give me eighty dollars right now or you are in big trouble." I looked him in the eyes and said, "You are under citizen's arrest for willful damage of my property. I'm calling the police."

He looked scared and said, "You can have everything I have." He immediately handed me a fistful of dollars. I passed it to a friend, who counted it and said that there was only twenty-eight dollars. I told the youth that wasn't enough and I wanted the full eighty dollars. He protested that he didn't have any more cash.

By this time a large crowd had gathered. Still holding the youth by the shirt, I said, "Just as I am holding this man because he has transgressed the law, so God has placed you in a holding cell for transgression of *His* Law. The sentence for your crimes against God is death."

I then went through the Law and into grace, saying, "God is rich in mercy and sent His Son to pay the fine for you." I preached the Cross, faith, and repentance—still holding the young man tightly by his shirt. I told the crowd that because Jesus paid the fine in full for us on the cross, God can extend His mercy toward us. We are free to go.

Then I turned to the youth, stuffed the money in his hand, and said, "Here's your money back. Neither am I going to call the police. You are free to go."

It was such a clear illustration of God's mercy. The young man's guilt was evident—he had been caught in the act. He couldn't make atonement. He deserved nothing but judgment, but instead he received mercy. His mouth dropped open in disbelief.

I don't know what happened to that young man, but I'm sure he will never forget that moment. Neither will I forget the moment when God let go of my shirt and said, "You are free to go." Every time I think of the Cross, my mouth drops open in disbelief.

Sin's Pleasure

Someone once called me and asked for my advice about a publication he wanted to produce. It was to help men who were addicted to pornography. He was going to write his experience in tract form, relating how pornography had ruined him. The vice had produced guilt, ruined his marriage, and made him a slave to his passions. He thought that the negative fruit of the sin would steer men away from it.

His philosophy sounds good, but it rarely works. If it did, we wouldn't have so many people smoking cigarettes, abusing drugs, gambling, and drinking alcohol. The evidence that smoking results in a slow and painful death doesn't deter smokers. Drug abuse kills. Gambling destroys homes and lives. Alcoholism and drunk driving take countless lives each year. Cities with legalized gambling have been found to have higher rates of crime, suicide, bankruptcy, and other social ills—yet people gamble. People know the consequences of a sinful lifestyle, but the immediate pleasure far outweighs the fear of long-term negative consequences. Sinful people will not give up their darling lusts unless they have a good reason to. Hell is a good reason.

> ➤ In speaking with my father about reasons why we should obey God, he said that hell definitely grabs his attention, and that he didn't want to go there because he has a very low tolerance for pain. —KC

In the next chapter, we'll look at how the Ten Commandments can be used effectively in personal witnessing.

15

DON'T LEAVE ME LIKE THIS!

I was in Baltimore on a Sunday night and had finished all my meetings, so I decided to change my plane ticket to go home early. When I called, the reservation agent gave the name of the airline, told me her name was Fran, and asked how she could be of help to me. I explained my situation, made her laugh a little, and got to a point where I felt I had the liberty to ask about her spiritual life. I said, "Fran, are you a Christian?" She answered, "No. I don't accept the Virgin Birth." I explained to her that the Virgin Birth wasn't the issue with her at the moment, but that her big problem was the Ten Commandments. I asked, "Have you ever told a lie?" She said she had. She also admitted that she had stolen. When I explained that Jesus said that lust was the same as adultery in God's sight and asked her if she had lusted, she said, "Of course."

I said, "Fran, by your own admission, you are a lying, thieving adulterer at heart, *and we have looked at only three of the Ten Commandments.* You have to face God on Judgment Day." I then said, "I would like a window seat if possible."

She didn't appreciate the change of subject. She said, *"Don't leave me like this!"*

Gently, I said, "What's wrong, Fran, don't you like being left with your conscience?" I went on to reason with her about her salvation, about Judgment Day, and then about the Cross.

We shouldn't be afraid to make sinners tremble. Which is worse: a little trembling because of guilt, or eternity in the lake of fire? Men like Whitefield and others preached until the Law "stopped the mouth" of sinners and they hung their heads in shame. These great preachers weren't afraid to use the terrors of the Law to drive men to the Cross. A resurrected and accusing conscience is the first evidence of the beginnings of the work of the Holy Spirit. It is a great mistake to muffle its voice with talk of God's forgiveness before it has a chance to do its precious work.

Fran didn't get angry at me. I wasn't judging her. She was the one who admitted her sins. Besides, what could she say: "I thought lying, stealing, and lusting were all right"? She couldn't *begin* to justify her sins in light of her quickened conscience. It is because of the ally of the "work of the Law" that we can gently say "hard" things to sinners.

It is interesting to note that the conscience doesn't join in with the pleasures of sin. The unregenerate person loves sin with all his heart, mind, soul, and strength. However, the judge in the courtroom of the mind stands aloof and makes an impartial judgment. It is the "conscience also bearing witness, … their thoughts accusing or else excusing them" (Romans 2:15). The judge gives a *guilty* or *not guilty* verdict based on the evidence.

In parts of Africa during the drought season, antelope are drawn by thirst to pools of muddy water. Without a drink they will die of dehydration. Hidden in the foul waters lie hungry and vicious crocodiles. The only thing visible in the water, to the discerning eye, is the naked eye of the monster as it watches the antelope's every movement.

Desire so consumes the antelope that they slowly venture to the water's edge and completely let down their God-given guard as they drink in the life-giving liquid. Instinct warns them of the danger, but their unquenchable thirst drives them to the water. Suddenly, great jaws open and amid the splashing of water, an antelope is pulled to a terrifying death.

Likewise, sinners are drawn to the muddy pool of iniquity by their uncontrollable thirst for sin. The cries of their God-given conscience are muffled at the sight of what lies before them—their desire. Then in an instant, death seizes upon them and they are gone forever, swallowed by the jaws of everlasting hell.

The Law reveals the crocodile *before* it attacks. As sinners drink in the muddy waters of iniquity, they suddenly see sin's terrible form as it lies hidden in the pool. This is what Paul is speaking about in Romans 7:8-12. The Law showed him the appetite in the eye of the beast, causing him to draw back quickly from the pool of iniquity.

So Long, Pal!

Our ministry regularly receives calls on our 800 number from people who misdial the number they are trying to call. Very early one morning a deep-voiced gentleman phoned, thinking he was calling a company that sells farm supplies. I told him that he had transposed the last two digits, then said to make sure he read his Bible. He said he wouldn't, because he was an atheist. For the next few minutes I reasoned with him about the necessity of having a maker for everything that was made. It was a spirited fight, but it was merely swordplay. The moment would come when I would have to get my point across, to go for the kill. I took the Ten Commandments in hand and lunged toward the heart: "Do you think you have kept the Ten Commandments?" He said he thought he had. "Have you ever told a lie?" He had, but he would not hold still for a second and admit that he was a liar. He jumped back and forth, insisting that someone who told lies was "human," just told "fibs," or was "weak, like everyone else."

When I pressed the point, he suddenly spat out, "Okay, I'm a liar!" We touched on two other commandments (which he admitted to transgressing), the existence of his conscience, and the fact of Judgment Day. Suddenly, his references to evolution, other people's sins, and hypocrisy in the Church were no longer the issue. He was mortally wounded...cut to the heart. He protested, "I'm a good person!" I thrust back, "No, you're not. You're a lying thief!" The pain was too much for him. He said, *"So long, pal!"* and hung up in my ear.

I sat by the phone and wished that he had stayed in the fight for another minute. I would have told him that he was just adding self-righteousness to his sin. I would also have liked to tell him to study Matthew 24 and Luke 21, which would prove to him that the Bible is the Word of the Creator. Then I prayed that God's hand would be upon him.

About ten seconds later, the phone rang again. When I picked it up, I heard a deep-voiced and mystified man mumble, "What's going on? How did I get you again? I tried to call this number, and instead I get one that makes my blood hot!"

Hot blood means that life is present. He was no longer a cold-blooded atheist. *I was beside myself with joy.* I told him to read Matthew 24 and Luke 21. Then I gave him my name and said he could call our 800 number anytime. When he kept mumbling, "Why did I call you again?" I could think of only two answers. Either he was a dummy and had called the same wrong number twice, or God's hand was upon him. I told him that it was because God's hand was upon him. He didn't argue about that, and this time our parting was more congenial.

Right Number

One Friday afternoon, the phone rang, and when I answered it I heard, "Is this Direct Imports?" I said it wasn't and asked what number the man wanted. He gave our number, so I said, "Well, that is our number, but before you go, *make sure you read your Bible.*" He became quiet, then asked, "Why's that?" I said so that he could find how to secure his eternal destiny and added, "There's nothing more important than that, is there?" He said, "Yi, yi, yi...I'd better sit down for this!" I asked, "Are you Jewish?" When he said he was, I told him that I was also Jewish and remarked, "Remember, you've got to face the Ten Commandments on Judgment Day."

His reply was interesting: "I have done research, specifically on the adultery one, and I've come to the conclusion that you can fool around with a woman as long as she's not married." I said, "If you as much as look with lust, the Bible says that you commit adultery in your heart. Have you ever told a lie?" He had. I asked if he had stolen. He had. So I gently told him that he was, by his own admission, a lying, thieving adulterer, and that's why he needed the Savior, Jesus Christ, to save him from God's anger. I told him to read his Bible and seek God for the salvation of his soul. I also invited him to call my number anytime if he wanted to talk in the future. His voice sounded quite depressed as he said, "Thank you very much for talking to me." I think I ruined his weekend, but I was thankful to see the convicting power of the Holy Spirit at work.

In the next chapter we will look at how you can put this teaching into practice in your own life.

> When I first heard the the principles of bibical evangelism, I was wide-eyed, filled with energy and enthusiasm to share my faith, and I had a new appreciation for my own salvation. I immediately wanted to put these biblical principles into action and test them out on the unsaved. All of a sudden, fear gripped my heart. I understood the concept of how the Ten Commandments show sinners their need of God's forgiveness, but what would I say to my grandmother, my Buddhist friend, or my father? How could I make sure I wouldn't offend anyone in my newfound zeal to destroy their self-righteousness with the razor sharp ax of the Law? Ray and I discussed the subject for hours and hours. Eventually, we collaborated to form a new ministry called the Way of the Master; we produced a brand-new "reality" Christian television program and designed an eight-week study course to teach you how to share your faith simply, effectively, biblically—the way Jesus did. The next chapter contains portions of that study course and will take you by the hand, leading you through some of the basic "how to" principles. For the complete eight-week personal or group training course, order The Way of the Master Foundation Course from our Web site, www.wayofthemaster.com, or call (877) 496-8688. —KC

16 | HOW TO SHARE YOUR FAITH

Perhaps you haven't been sharing your faith as you know you should, and you are wondering how to get started. At the same time, you have a very real fear of approaching strangers and talking about the things of God. And if you do approach someone, you don't want to blow it. These thoughts combine into one big, cold, ever-increasing snowball.

Strangers are hard enough to approach. What do you say to someone you don't know? How about your neighbors? They are *even harder* to approach (if that's possible). If you make a mess of witnessing to your neighbors, you don't want to start a lifetime feud. Then there's your mother-in-law. *Upsetting her could cause really big problems.*

These are fears that all of us have, and they are very real. However, there are certain principles that can help us to at least bring our fears into perspective. Think of what you fear, then think of the terrible fate of those who die in their sins. Which is worse? Remember, when it comes to evangelism, you have a similar responsibility to that of a firefighter. Think of his moral obligation as he looks at the mother screaming for help from a six-story building. You must deal with your fears in light of the sinner's terrible fate.

Here are some simple suggestions for getting started: Be friendly. Talk with people. Practice at the park, at the gas station, or at the grocery store.

Perhaps you already have an outgoing and friendly personality, but if you tend to be shy and introverted, try to open up a little and start talking with people. A simple "Hi, how are you?" isn't hard. "Nice day isn't it? My name is so-and-so ..." With a bit of practice, anyone can learn to be friendly. Most people respond warmly to warmth. Once we see that this is true, it will help to calm our fear-filled imaginations.

Someone e-mailed our ministry and told us about how he and a friend went to the park on a Saturday afternoon just to practice being friendly to strangers. They had so much fun that they couldn't wait to get out the next weekend to take the next step.

After you have gained a measure of confidence in simply being friendly and talking to people, you are ready to learn the next step—how to swing the conversation to the subject of spiritual things.

Don't Open with Grace

It may be a relief to know that you shouldn't walk up to someone and begin a conversation by talking about Jesus. They'll most likely think you're strange. Bright light in the eyes is always offensive. Instead, start in the natural realm (talking about everyday things) and then swing the conversation toward the spiritual realm (talking about spiritual things). That's what Jesus does in John 4:7-26. When He meets the woman at the well, he begins by talking about natural things (a drink of water). He then swings the conversation to spiritual things ("living water"). You may start off talking about football or the weather, and then perhaps use something in the news to swing into the subject of spiritual things. Or you might simply ask if the person knows of a good church in the area. Perhaps you can use a gospel tract. Just say, "Hi. Where are you from? I'm from such-and-such, etc." Then you muster up the courage to say, "Did you get one of these? It's a gospel tract.... Have you had a Christian background?" It doesn't matter *how* you do it, only *that* you do it. Start in the natural realm so they don't think you're a religious nut and then make the transition any way you want. That will lead you directly into a conversation about God. Remember, most people are not offended when the subject of God comes up, despite what our overripe, fear-filled imaginations tell us.

WDJD: The Four Stepping-Stones

If you can remember four stepping-stones, you can confidently lead *any* witnessing encounter, and you will be in control of *every* conversation you have about your faith. Imagine, you will know exactly where you are and you will know exactly where the conversation is going. You don't have to study Greek, you don't have to understand archaeology, just remember four points and you can begin to say good-bye to most of your fears about evangelism. There is no doubt that the most difficult thing to do is to bring up the things of God. The next hurdle isn't quite so high. It naturally issues out of asking someone about spiritual things.

The stepping-stones are represented by four letters: WDJD, which stand for "What Did Jesus Do?" Remember the question and the acronym to help you to remember the four stepping-stones.

W: Would you consider yourself to be a good person?

You will be surprised to find that people are not offended by your asking if they consider themselves to be a good person. If they say no (which is highly unlikely), ask them what they mean. Remember, you are asking them about their favorite subject—themselves. Most likely you'll find that they are kidding or that they've done something in their life that they feel bad about. Otherwise, expect them to say, "I'm a pretty good person" or "I'm a *really* good person." This reveals their proud self-righteousness. Now you are ready to use the Law (as expressed in the Ten Commandments) to humble them ... the same way Jesus did (see Mark 10:17-22).[1]

D: Do you think you have kept the Ten Commandments?

Some will say yes, others will say that they haven't. Either way, you simply continue by saying, "Let's take a look at a few and see." You may want to start with the ninth commandment ("You shall not bear false witness against your neighbor"), because most people will readily admit to having lied—at least once. Next, you may want to ask about stealing, then adultery (lust), then taking the Lord's name in vain.[*] Here is how to go through each one (in the order that we typically use):

---

[*] I normally deal first with lying, stealing, and lust, because people can more easily acknowledge them as evident sins. It seems that this is what Jesus does in Luke 18:20.

The ninth commandment ("You shall not bear false witness against your neighbor"):

After you've said, "Let's take a look at a few of the commandments and see," simply ask, "Have you ever told a lie?" Some will admit to lying; others will say they have told only "white lies"; and a few will claim they have never told even one lie. If so, gently press the issue: "Do you mean to say that you have never told anyone a lie? Even once?" Usually they will say something like, "Maybe when I was a kid." Ask, "What does that make you?" They will hesitate to say it, but get them to admit it: "A liar."

It may surprise you to know that people don't get angry at this approach; instead, they become sober. They may try to sidetrack you by saying, "I don't believe in the Bible." Simply continue on your course. If they argue about the Bible, say, "I know you don't believe in it. I am simply sharing with you what the Bible says. Okay? Let's keep going."

The eighth commandment ("You shall not steal"):

"Have you ever stolen anything?" Many will claim that they haven't. "Have you ever taken anything that did not belong to you, regardless of its value ... anything? Even when you were younger? Be honest before God." Some will try to trivialize theft by saying that they stole when they were a child. Ask, "What does that make you?" and press them to say, "A thief."

The seventh commandment ("You shall not commit adultery"):

"Have you ever committed adultery?" Again, most will say no. Add, "Jesus said whoever looks upon a woman to lust after her has committed adultery with her already in his heart. Have you ever looked at someone with lust?"

The third commandment ("You shall not take the name of the Lord your God in vain"):

"Have you ever taken the Lord's name in vain?" Some will try to wiggle out of this, but just push a little: "You mean you have never used God's name to express anger?" Most will admit to this one. Then gently explain, "So instead of using a four-letter filth word to express disgust, you have taken the name of the One who gave you life and everything that is precious to you, and used it to express disgust. That is called 'blasphemy,' and God promises that He will not hold anyone blameless who takes His name in vain."

At this point, you should be noticing something: The individual will either grow quiet (shut up under the Law, Romans 3:19) or will be getting agitated. If the person seems to recognize his guilt, you may want to say at this point, "By your own admission, you're a lying thief, a blasphemer, and an adulterer at heart, and we've only looked at four of the Ten Commandments."

If he is still trying to defend himself ("I'm not a bad person"), go through a few more commandments.

The sixth commandment ("You shall not murder"):

"Have you ever murdered anyone?" Obviously, most will say that they haven't. Simply point out that "Jesus said that if you merely call your brother a fool, you are in danger of judgment, and the Bible says if you've ever hated anyone, you are a murderer in God's eyes. God does not simply judge actions. He knows the intentions of the heart."

The first commandment ("You shall have no other gods before Me"):

"Have you always put God first in your life?" Most will admit that they haven't. "God says that He is supposed to be the primary love of our lives. In fact, Jesus said that our love for God should be so great that our love for our parents, kids, friends, even our own lives should seem like hatred by comparison."

The second commandment ("You shall not make for yourself an idol"):

"Have you ever made an idol, a god to suit yourself?" People will usually say that they haven't. "Have you pursued money more than God? Then you have made money an idol. Have you given work more attention than God? Then work is an idol. If you think, 'God is loving and wouldn't send me to hell,' you are correct; your god wouldn't send anyone to hell, because your god doesn't exist. He is a figment of your imagination. You created a god in your own mind that you're more comfortable with, and that is called 'idolatry.' It's the oldest sin in the book and God warns us that idolaters will not inherit the kingdom of God."

The fourth commandment ("Remember the Sabbath day, to keep it holy"):

"Have you kept the Sabbath holy? God requires one day out of seven for you to rest and acknowledge Him, and you have failed to give Him what He has commanded. How many times have you neglected to bow your head before your meal and thank Him for the food He has provided? How many thousands of times do you think you've just greedily dug in without thanking your Provider?"

The fifth commandment (*"Honor your father and your mother"*):
"Have you always honored your parents, treating them in a way that is pleasing to God?"

The tenth commandment (*"You shall not covet ... anything that belongs to your neighbor"*):
"Have you ever coveted, or jealously desired something that did not belong to you? Covetousness reveals a lack of gratitude for what God has already given you."

J: On the Day of Judgment, if God judges you by the Ten Commandments, will you be *innocent* or *guilty?*
If the individual has not yet begun to show signs of conviction, he will more than likely start now. Most people will sense where you are going with the conversation and will say, "Innocent." But they must understand and confess their guilt if they are ever to come to Jesus. Here is how to help them do that:

Them: "I'm a pretty good person."

You: "You just told me that you broke God's commandments. By your own admission, you're a lying thief, an adulterer at heart, a murderer, and a blasphemer. Think about it. Will you be innocent or guilty?"

Them: "But I haven't done those things for a long time."

You: "Imagine saying that in a court of law. 'Judge, I know I am guilty but it has been years.' He won't ignore your crime. He will see that justice is served and will punish you no matter how much time has elapsed. The courts punish war criminals from decades ago, and God doesn't forget sin, no matter how long ago a person did it. Do you think you will be innocent or guilty?"

Them: "But I have done more good than bad."

You: "Again, think of a court of law. If you have broken the law, you are guilty. It doesn't matter how many good deeds you've done when you are being tried for your crime. You have broken God's Law. Will you be innocent or guilty?"

Them: "But that's man's law. God is different."

You: "You're right. God can never be bribed. And His standards are much higher than a human judge's. He loves justice and has promised that He will punish not only murderers and rapists, but also liars, thieves, adulterers, and blasphemers. You are in big trouble, aren't you?"

Often, people become awakened—*aware* of their sin—but not alarmed. In other words, they understand they have broken God's Law, but it seems that they just don't care. Your goal is to see them alarmed, because they should be—they are in great danger. The following line of reasoning can help:

"Let's imagine that a computer chip had been placed behind your ear, and it records everything that runs through your mind for a whole week: every secret thought, every deed, and every word that comes out of your mouth. Then all of your friends and family are called together and all of your thoughts are displayed on a big screen for them to see. How would that make you feel? Embarrassed? Ashamed? That is just what will happen on the day when God requires you to give an account for everything you've said and done for your whole life. All of your secret thoughts will be laid before Him. You are in big trouble."

It is wonderful to get a confession of guilt, but if the person simply won't be honest and admit his guilt, at some point you may have to help him. Say, "If you would just be honest, you know you will be guilty before God. Besides, that is what the Bible says and if you claim to be innocent, you are calling God a liar."

D: Destiny—will you go to heaven or hell?

Gently ask, "Do you think you will go to heaven or hell?" People won't be offended, because you are simply asking a question rather than telling them where they're going. Some will say, "Hell," but most will say, "Heaven." If they think they are going to heaven, use this analogy:

Consider this. You are standing in a court of law, guilty of a serious crime. There is a fifty thousand dollar fine. The judge says, "You are guilty. Anything to say before I pass sentence?" You answer, "Yes, judge. I'm sorry for what I have done. Please forgive me." Can a good judge let you go simply because you say that you are sorry or that you won't do it again? Of course not. There is a fifty thousand dollar fine that must be paid. However, if someone pays the fine for you, can the judge then let you go? Yes. Once the fine has been paid, your debt to the law has been satisfied and the judge can set you free.

In the same way, each of us is guilty before God, and He will not let us go simply because we say that we are sorry or that we won't do it again. Of course, we should be sorry, and we shouldn't do it again. However, the fine for our crime must still be paid. Two thousand years ago, someone paid our fine for us. Jesus Christ, God's only begotten Son, suffered and died on the cross on our behalf. If we turn from our sins and trust in Him, God will dismiss our case—not just because we are sorry, but because Jesus paid our fine.[2]

If the person responds by saying that this is *man's* justice, and that God's ways are different, agree with him. Say that God's justice is far stricter than man's justice, and that His standards are infinitely higher.

Do not be afraid to tell people that if they die in their sins, the Bible makes it clear that they will go to hell. Ask, "Does that concern you?"

If they say that it doesn't concern them, or if you sense they are not humbled and don't recognize their need of God's forgiveness, it's very helpful to describe what hell is like until they show signs of concern. According to the Bible, hell is a place of eternal, conscious torment, where "their worm does not die, and the fire is not quenched" (Mark 9:44), there is "weeping and gnashing of teeth" (Luke 13:28), "everlasting punishment" (Matthew 25:46), "shame and everlasting contempt" (Daniel 12:2), and "eternal fire. . . . the blackness of darkness forever" (Jude 1:7, 13). Tell them that you don't want them to go to hell and God doesn't want them to go to hell. Plead with them. If they do not seem concerned, it may be that they are just hiding it.

Don't feel pressured to share the Good News with a proud, self-righteous sinner (rebellious, cussing, arrogant) who is not willing to admit his guilt before God. Remember, Jesus didn't present the gospel to the rich young man because he needed the Law to humble him first. You will have to watch and listen carefully, because humility is not always obvious.

If the person admits that the possibility of going to hell does concern him, only at that point should you present the gospel. If you are able to detect humility (the person is no longer justifying and defending himself), or his responses indicate that he has been humbled, you now have the glorious pleasure of sharing the Good News.

Sharing the Gospel

Begin your presentation of the gospel this way: "Do you know what God did for you so that you wouldn't have to go to hell? He provided a way for you to be forgiven. The question is, how do you obtain this forgiveness?" Take the time to explain the plan of salvation thoroughly: "God loves you so much that He sent His only Son to suffer and die in your place, taking your punishment for you so that you could live. Then Jesus rose from the dead and defeated death. It is this simple: you broke the Law and Jesus paid your fine. If you will repent—turn away from sin—and place your trust in Jesus Christ as your Savior, God will forgive you and grant you everlasting life. He will change you from the inside out and make you a new person in Christ."

This is the time to *magnify the love of God* to the sinner. Now you have the green light—go for it! Don't hold back: Show the amazing length, width, depth, and height of God's love for the person as a sinner. This is the moment to pull out John 3:16. God offers complete forgiveness of sin and the gift of everlasting life *freely* to those who will surrender everything to Him through faith in Jesus Christ.

Ask the individual if he understands what you have told him. If he is willing to confess and turn from his sins and trust the Savior for his eternal salvation, have him pray and ask God to forgive him.

The Prayer of Confession

Should we pray the traditional sinner's prayer with someone who we think is willing to turn from sin and receive Christ? Perhaps an analogy will shed some light on the subject: If someone you know committed adultery, would you lead him back to his wife and say, "Repeat after me: 'I am really sorry. I should not have slept with that woman.'" More than likely, you wouldn't. If someone says he wants to pray right then and there, encourage him to do so. You might like to say, "You can pray right now. Confess your sins and turn from them, and then tell God you are placing your trust in Jesus as the Lord and Savior of your life. Surrender your heart to Him. After you've prayed, I'll pray for you."

Make sure the person has a Bible (get him one if necessary), and encourage him to read it daily and obey what he reads. Also, encourage him to get into a Bible-believing, Christ-centered church.

If the person doesn't invite you to pray with him, let him go on his way, but encourage him to think deeply about your conversation and to get his heart right with the Lord as soon as possible. You can then leave him in the hands of a faithful God, who will continue to speak to him through His Holy Spirit and bring him to genuine repentance in His time.

Inoculated "Almost Christians"

If you are dealing with an inoculated churchgoer who knows a few Bible verses (such as John 3:16), you probably have the toughest encounter of all. The person may answer all the questions correctly, but you know he doesn't live like a Christian should. Here are some questions that might reveal his level of understanding:

1. "Are you born again?" If he says he isn't, remind him that Jesus said a man must be born again to enter the kingdom of God (John 3:5).
2. "When was the last time you read your Bible?" If he says it has been a long time, express your concern by asking, "What would you think if you sent love letters to your wife and she never took the time to read them? You would start to suspect that maybe she isn't very interested in you. God sent you sixty-six letters and you rarely read them. What should He conclude about your love for Him?"

Encourage the person to examine himself to see if he is in the faith (2 Corinthians 13:5). If there are no signs that he has been born again, if there is no fruit in his life to indicate that he is a child of God, ask, "Do you consider yourself to be a good person?" If he says yes, something is radically wrong, and you should take him through a presentation of the Law.

What about Grandma?

Someone who had just heard the teaching expounded in this book said, "I see what you are saying, and I agree with you. Let's say I'm on my way to witness to my elderly grandmother, who's not a Christian but thinks she is. Does this mean I'm going to have to say, 'Grandma, have you ever looked at someone with lust?'"

Good question. The answer is a definite yes and no. Here's how you can say what you want to say without seeming disrespectful. First, gently swing into the subject by asking about her Christian background—when she started going to church, and so on. Then say, "You know what convinced me that I was a sinner? It was the Ten Commandments. I didn't realize that Jesus said, 'Whoever looks upon a woman with lust has committed adultery already with her in his heart.' I didn't know that God sees our thought life. Do you think that you have kept the Ten Commandments, Grandma? Would you consider yourself to be a good person?"

When she tells you that she's a good person, say, "Well, let's look at some more commandments to see if we have kept them." Always bear in mind that you are not alone in your witness. You not only have the Holy Spirit to help, but you have Grandma's conscience working with you.

The Issue of Suffering

What if someone asks, "What about the issue of suffering? Little kids are born deformed, people die of terrible diseases, and there are earthquakes and tornadoes that cause havoc. This proves that there is no God. We are on our own." How do you answer that? I'll often tell the following story:

Three philosophers are seated in a plane on an overnight flight. The first man said, "I heard that during the night, while many of us were sleeping, hijackers took over the cockpit and are now flying the plane." As he spoke, the plane lunged to the left and thrust a number of passengers against the wall, seriously injuring some of them.

After the second man regained his composure, he said, "Because of what just happened, *I don't believe that this plane was designed or manufactured.*" Even though his statement didn't make sense, he continued to maintain that the entire plane, with its seats, windows, lighting, air conditioning, engines, etc., happened by accident.

As the third philosopher began to respond, the plane again lunged to one side. This time it was so violent that many passengers were seriously injured and two elderly people were killed. The man was obviously shaken, but he was able to share his thoughts about what had happened. He said that despite what was happening on the plane, he believed that all was well in the cockpit.

Just then, someone passed a handwritten note to the first man. It read: *Hijackers! All to be thrust out of the plane. Parachute under seat. Put it on now. Going to cut the lighting. Be ready to jump!* As he read these words, his eyes widened. The note confirmed that something was radically wrong. He quickly reached under his seat, put on the parachute, and then passed the note on to the second philosopher.

The second man read the words on the note. He smiled and said, "This note hasn't used correct grammar. '*Parachute under seat*' isn't even a complete sentence ..." With that, he crumpled the note and dropped it to the floor.

The third man, still shaken by the recent events, picked up the note and read it. He said, "It sure looks authentic. It's written on the airline's letterhead. What's happening on the plane does add up to there being something radically wrong.... Yes, I think I now believe there is something wrong." He sat back in his seat, but he didn't bother to put on his parachute, nor did he pass the note on to others.

Here we have three common reactions to the message of the gospel. The first passenger is a genuine convert. He understands that the issue of suffering—disease, pain and death—shows that something is radically wrong between God and man. The knowledge that he must jump through the door of death causes him to trust in the Savior (to "put on the parachute," the only means of salvation).

The second man is an atheist. He uses the issue of suffering to somehow make an illogical leap into the philosophy that there is no God. Despite all evidence, he clings to the belief that the whole of creation, with its flowers, its birds, the sun, the moon, the animal kingdom, the beauty of the seasons, the incredible variety of succulent fruit trees, etc., all happened by accident. The notion that such reasoning borders on insanity doesn't enter his unthinking and sin-loving mind. He doesn't bother to humbly study the warning of Scripture. Instead, he exalts himself above the mind of his Creator, and he condescendingly becomes a critic of the Word of God. He maintains that it is full of errors and therefore can't be trusted.

The third man is an average person. He believes in God. He even believes the Bible. He is easily convinced that something may be wrong between man and God ... but he doesn't see his urgent need to put on the Lord Jesus Christ.

How do we awaken these two men?

For the answer, let's go back to the airplane. The first man should ask the other two philosophers to look out the window for a moment and to think about taking a twenty-five-thousand-foot fall. Their knowledge of the unbending law of gravity should kick in, and from there common sense should do the rest. The reality of their predicament should cause both men to look under their seat for the parachute.

The issue of suffering is not something that Christians should avoid. It is glaring evidence that man has rejected God—*all is not well on board the flight*. The reality of suffering works *for* our cause, not against it. All these things—pain, disease, droughts, tornadoes, earthquakes, etc.—should cause the thinking person to investigate the claims of the "note"—God's Word— and heed its advice.

The ultimate convincing agent, of course, is the unbending Law of God. The knowledge of the Law and the terrifying consequences of transgressing its precepts should cause fear to kick in—and common sense should then cause sinners to seek after the Savior who died and rose again so that they might be saved.

The Place of Apologetics

Although apologetics (the systematic defense of the faith) plays an impor- tant part in evangelism, it's vital to realize that they have a limited function in reaching the lost. If we confine our evangelism to arguing about the exis- tence of God, the inspiration of Scripture, the age of the earth, etc., we are like a man who goes fishing with bait but no hook. Although he may attract the fish, they will end up fat and happy—and they will get away. The function of bait is to attract the fish and disguise the hook. When the fish come around, the fisherman pulls the hook into the jaw and catches his fish. Apologetics are the bait, and the hook is God's Law. It is the Law that appeals to a man's conscience and brings the knowledge of sin.

Tone of Voice

It is imperative that we ask God for the right spirit, tone, and attitude in our witnessing encounters. We don't want to come across like a know-it-all or as arrogant. Our attitude should be humble compassion mixed with a deep concern. Be resolute but gentle. Don't be smug or condescending with your arguments. We're called to speak with gentleness and respect, like compassionate doctors with a cure. We should never become angry or even raise our voice. We have the freedom to speak very boldly if the hearer senses that we are coming from a place of love and concern.

Gestures

Be careful of your body language. Don't point your finger at someone in a judgmental way. Don't stand above people if you can help it; sit down beside them. Don't have a smug grin on your face as if you are winning an argument or fold your arms as if you are scolding a child. Remember, above all, that you are only a fellow sinner saved by God's grace, pleading with others to come to the Savior.

Practice

As you've read these principles, you may have thought that you could never remember all the information. You don't have to. Just remember the WDJD stepping-stones and practice them. Find a friend and role-play. You've had to practice almost everything else in life—walking, writing, reading, riding a bike, and driving a car. Evangelism is no different. Once you have the four stepping-stones memorized and begin putting them into practice, you will start an incredible evangelistic adventure. You will be amazed that the responses of those you speak to will be very predictable. In no time at all, sharing your faith will become second nature to you. What's more, God will be with you every step of the way.

Being a witness of Jesus Christ is a mind-set. Here's a role-playing scenario to help you put your mind in the proper frame: Imagine you're in the garden of Gethsemane. You drop to your knees in prayer and sweat great drops of blood at the thought of sharing your faith. Now say, "Not my will but Yours be done." This exercise will give you the mind-set to deny yourself and daily pick up the cross. You only have to bear the reproach of the cross for a short time. The day will come when you will exchange it for a crown. So if you have dealt with your fears in the garden, every time fear knocks at the door, you can send faith to answer it. When your cowardly, cringing heart says, "You can't do this," you simply ignore its whispering and say, "I dealt with you in the garden. Now I can do all things through Christ who strengthens me."

The next time a telemarketer calls your home, you may be tempted to get rid of him by saying, "I'm busy at the moment, so give me your home phone number and I will call you back later tonight." Instead, resist temptation and think of God's will, not yours. No doubt these poor folks get abused and hung up on, on a regular basis. So, let your little light shine through the phone. When he says, "My name is Greg. I have a real deal for you. It won't cost you a thing. All I need is your name and address." Say, "Hi Greg. It's good to hear from you. Have you been having a good day?" Listen to his reaction. Your genuine warmth will probably shock him. Then say, "May I ask you a few questions? (He's been trained to be congenial and will no doubt react positively.) Do you consider yourself to be a good person?" If you mess up, say, "Gotta go. Thanks for calling," then hang up.

Don't stay in the tomb of dead silence. Ask God to send His angels to roll the stone of fear away. Then come out of the tomb. Please. You are needed. This chapter may seem complex, but it's not. Let me share with you a typical witnessing encounter.

Sue and I were recently in an appliance store. The assistant was very helpful. While he was serving us, I gave him a few tracts, for which he was genuinely grateful. One was "101 of the World's Funniest One-liners." He laughed as he read the cover. He also loved my business card. It is a tract that looks like a business card but it says, "Department of Annoyance ... Director." The back is printed in reverse, so that you have to go to a mirror to read it. When he looked at the back and turned it upside down to try and read it, I said, "Annoying, huh?" He laughed again.

As we walked across the store, I thought, *If I care about this man, I will witness to him.* In came the excuses: *"You can't do this. You don't have time. You shouldn't do this in the store. He will be offended. ... blah, blah, blah, ad infinitum."* I ignored the whisperings and said, "Those things I gave you were gospel tracts." He said, "Huh?" So I said, "They were *Christian* tracts. Have you had a Christian background?"

He said, "Catholic."

"Do you consider yourself to be a good person?"

"Yes."

"Can I ask you a few questions to see if that's true?"

"Sure."

"Have you ever told a lie?"

"Yes."

"What does that make you?"

"A liar."

"Have you ever stolen something?"

"Yes."

"What does that make you?"

"A thief."

"Jesus said that whoever looks at a woman to lust after her has committed adultery with her already in his heart. Have you ever done that?"

"Yes."

"Will you be innocent or guilty on the Day of Judgment?"

"Guilty."

"Will you go to heaven or hell?"

"Somewhere in between."

"There's no such place."

"Hell, then."

His eyes were wide and his face was sober, so I said, "Do you know what God did so that you would not have to go to hell?" He said that he didn't, so I took him through the gospel. When he heard about God's forgiveness and His gift of everlasting life, his facial expression changed, and he said, "Wow!" There was no offense. None of my fears were realized.

I asked him if he had a Bible, and then I left him with some more literature. All this happened in about two minutes.

Find Another Horse

It is very important to realize that you are going to have what may *seem* like failures. I have given out hundreds of thousands of gospel tracts. I have seen many people react very positively. They say things like, "This has made my day! Thank you." However, if I get a thousand positive results and one negative result, for some reason it is the negative experience that remains in my mind. If someone coldly says, "No thank you," it cuts right into my heart. I never get used to rejection.

When rejection bucks you off your evangelistic horse, don't stay in the dirt. Get up. Say, "I've got to find another horse!" Then keep reaching out to the lost until the feeling of rejection is lost in the dust of your gospel trail.

Failure is often a part of learning. In August 2003, Kirk Cameron, my associate Mark Spence, and I were in Ottawa, Canada, at the invitation of our Canadian agent, Pastor Chris Curry, conducting a Way of the Master seminar. After Kirk left to keep another commitment, Mark, Chris, and I went out into the city to look for prospective interviews for our upcoming television program.

Most Christians are a little apprehensive about approaching strangers, so I was going to demonstrate how easy it is. The key was to create a relaxed atmosphere. I would simply walk up to strangers (wearing a hidden microphone), befriend them (using our unique tracts), and then explain what we were doing. Afterward we would ask for permission to use the film.

As I stood in front of the camera, I tried to look relaxed as I said, "I'm going to show you how easy it is to befriend strangers, using tracts."

An hour earlier, I had made the same pronouncement, but just as I finished speaking, a young man spotted our "hidden" camera and angrily ran toward us with his middle finger pointed skyward. He was really mad. Afterward, he told us that he thought we were police officers, and he suggested that Mark take off his sunglasses next time because they made him look like a cop.

On this try, at a public park, Mark wasn't wearing his sunglasses, and the camera couldn't be spotted. Four youths were sitting on a seat with their backs to us, so we carefully positioned ourselves behind them, and I did my introduction. It was simply a matter of approaching them, and after I had shown how easy it was to befriend strangers, I would call Mark over, have the young men sign a form granting us permission to use the videotape, and then interview them about the things of God.

As I casually approached the youths, their dog walked menacingly toward me. The animal had a similar look in his eye as the youth with the skyward finger. That didn't help to make the atmosphere as relaxed as I would have liked it to be. Thankfully, its owner called it back and apologized for the dog's territorial attitude.

As I greeted the four guys, suddenly an argument broke out behind me between one of them and someone else that had joined the group. That didn't help keep a relaxed atmosphere either, especially in light of the fact that it was obviously an argument about a drug deal of some sort.

Within seconds, two older men joined our little party. These two looked like dealers. One had a decidedly nervous expression. The other had a long, platted red beard. Mr. Nervous asked who I was and what I was doing. There was impatience in his tone. Then he spotted the camera. Oh, dear. That didn't help his nerves (or mine). Mark realized that he had been spotted and sensed that there was tension in the air, so he positioned Chris in front of him with a microphone, to give the impression that he wasn't filming me.

The air was electric. I was now looking directly at the two pushers who were demanding who I was and why we were filming them. Chris's standing in front of the camera didn't seem to fool them. I suddenly became aware of the fact that two inches of microphone wire were very visible. I knew that it could be seen as it ran across my belt, but it hadn't seemed to matter a few minutes earlier.

Also, a week earlier some kind Christian had given me a plastic card with the letters *F-B-I* boldly emblazoned on it. In fine print across the bottom, it said, "Firm Believer in Christ." I loved it, and put it in the window on my wallet. I had even pressed it down in the window so that "Firm Believer in Christ" couldn't be clearly seen. It gave me a buzz to think that someone might actually think that I was an FBI agent. My predicament wasn't good.

I glanced across at Mark for some sort of consolation that I wasn't alone in such a tense situation. All I could see was Chris being interviewed. It seemed to me that Mark thought that what I was doing was boring, and that Chris would make a better interview.

As I began to try to explain what I was doing, one of the pushers angrily said, "You are a fake!" He had no doubt seen the microphone wire. If they grabbed me and found my "FBI badge," they weren't going to bother with the fine print. I thought, "Great, I'm not going to be killed for my faith, but for being an undercover cop . . . and it's not even going to be filmed."

Suddenly, the spokesman said, "I'm getting out of here!" His red-bearded friend looked at me, then speedily followed him. The argument behind me had come to a conclusion, so I turned to the three young men who were still checking out the tracts and began to share my faith with them. They were so out of it that they probably didn't have any idea what I was talking about.

Thankfully, the entire incident was captured on film, showing just how easy it is to approach strangers and befriend them, using tracts.

The moral of the story is this: If at first your efforts don't succeed, keep trying until you get it right. Not every time will be a rousing success, but even planting a seed can later yield good fruit. If you will follow the four stepping-stones and allow the Law to do its intended work of breaking up the soil of hardened hearts, you will begin to see people respond with repentance. Remember, you can do all things through Christ who strengthens you.

In the next chapter we will look at what it is that puts a burning passion for the lost in the hearts of believers.

17 | FORGET ABOUT JONAH

Most of us who know the Lord are aware that one doesn't have to commit intellectual suicide to become a Christian. Although it may console us to point out to the world that the Scriptures are scientifically and archaeologically accurate, there is something important we must understand when we choose to take the "intellectual road." It should only be used as an *on-ramp* to the "freeway of conscience." If we don't learn to accelerate when we're on the on-ramp and quickly merge into the lane that will get us to our destination (the conversion of the sinner), we will cause all sorts of congestion. Appeals to the intellect should simply be a means to an end. Here's why.

Let's talk for a moment to Mr. Albert Proudheart. He's a professing intellectual who maintains that there are mistakes in the Bible. For example, 1 Kings 4:26 informs us that "Solomon had forty thousand stalls of horses for his chariots, and twelve thousand horsemen." But 2 Chronicles 9:25 disagrees with this count. It tells us that "Solomon had four thousand stalls for horses and chariots, and twelve thousand horsemen." Albert cynically asks, "Was it four thousand stalls or forty thousand? Surely one of these verses is wrong."

You explain that you believe that this isn't one account. It is two different narratives from two different times in the life of Solomon. Albert doesn't buy that. He smiles cynically, shakes his head in a condescending way, and moves on to another "mistake." And he has many.

Albert even believes that the day will come when science is going to discover the bones of a thirty-three-year-old Jewish male who was crucified outside the gates of Jerusalem. He says that the bones will be proven to be two thousand years old. He laughs and says, "What are you going to do then? I'm sure that despite the evidence, you will carry on in your blind faith. No doubt."

You feel embarrassed. He has just stripped you of your intellectual dignity. You want to say, "Please, don't classify me as a no-brainer, fundamentalist 'born-again.' I'm really *not* stupid." You want to convince him that Christianity *is* intellectual, but you will never do it—for one simple reason. Let's say you adequately answer all of Albert's cynical questions. You stump him with powerful arguments, using archaeological and scientific evidence. You have intellectually dwarfed him. Now all you have to do is convince him that Noah actually built an ark and brought in the animals two by two, that Jonah was swallowed by a whale, that Samson killed a thousand men with the jawbone of an ass, that Daniel was really in the lions' den, that Moses really did divide the Red Sea, and that Adam and Eve ran around naked... and ate from the tree of the knowledge of good and evil. Can you *prove* all of that to him?

Look at what the apostle Paul said about how he persuaded men about God: "And I, brethren, when I came to you, did not come with excellence of speech or of wisdom declaring to you the testimony of God" (1 Corinthians 2:1).

Why didn't Paul dazzle his hearers with eloquent speeches and intellectual wisdom? Bible scholars who have studied his letters tell us that he was extremely capable intellectually. First Corinthians 2:5 tells us why he deliberately stayed away from worldly wisdom: "that your faith should not be in the wisdom of men but in the power of God." If sinners are converted by the intellect (the wisdom of men), they will fall away by the intellect. If they are merely *argued* into the faith, they will just as easily be argued *out* of it whenever a respected scholar reports that "the bones of Jesus" have been found.

However, if sinners are converted by "the power of God," they will be kept by the power of God. No intellectual argument will cause them to waver because they will know the life-changing reality of their conversion, and their faith will be secure in the eternally solid and secure Rock of Ages.

If we want to reach the lost, we must stop believing that we have to be intellectual know-it-alls, stop wasting time arguing over every alleged mistake in the Bible, and rather think of something infinitely more important—the sinner's eternal salvation. Think about it: God could settle every intellectual argument in an instant—He could answer every possible question—but He chooses not to. He allows unprovable things to exist, which the proud use as an excuse to reject Him but the humble accept by faith as they surrender their lives to Him.

We need to make ourselves "of no reputation." God did (Philippians 2:7). He humbled Himself to become flesh. He rode as the King of kings on the back of a donkey. That's about as lowly as you can get. If He could humble Himself for our redemption, can we not do the same for the sake of the salvation of the world? We can ride this one out.

This is the donkey that God, in His great wisdom, has sat the Church upon: "God has chosen the foolish things of the world to put to shame the wise, and God has chosen the weak things of the world to put to shame the things which are mighty; and the base things of the world and the things which are despised God has chosen, and the things which are not, to bring to nothing the things that are, that no flesh should glory in His presence" (1 Corinthians 1:27-29).

God has chosen a unique way to grant eternal life to humanity. Unlike everything we achieve in this world, in the kingdom of God no one can boast that they have merited salvation (Ephesians 2:8-9).

Many years ago, I ran a children's club. One day I told one hundred kids to line up for some candy. There was an immediate rush, and the line sorted itself into what I saw as being a line of greed. The bigger, selfish kids were at the front, and the small and timid ones were at the back. I then did something that gave me great satisfaction. I told them to turn about-face. Everyone did. I said to stay where they were, and I took great delight in going to the other end of the line and giving the candy to the smaller, timid kids first.

In a world where the rich get richer, the poor get stomped on, and those that can achieve do achieve, we are informed that God has gone to the other end of the line with the message of everlasting life. How has He done that? Simply by choosing that which is weak, base, and despised. You can see evidence of this by asking a proud skeptic, "Do you believe that the following biblical accounts actually happened: Adam and Eve, Noah's ark, Jonah and the whale, Joshua and the walls of Jericho, Samson and his long hair, Daniel and the lions' den, Moses and the Red Sea?" Of course he doesn't. To say that he believed such fantastic stories would mean that he would have to surrender his intellectual dignity. Who in their right mind would ever do that? I'll tell you who: *Those who understand that God has chosen foolish, base, weak, and despised things of the world to confound those who think they are wise.* And by the way, none of those biblical accounts has yet been, nor ever will be, disproved.

Humbling though it may be not to have every answer to every question, learn to relax as you sit on this lowly donkey. Trust God. His Word is sure and true. This humble beast of burden is actually making a triumphal entry. This is the way of eternal salvation. So, in your heart, say, "Blessed be the name of the Lord," because you know that this is the path that leads lost sinners to Calvary. They cannot be saved through their intellect. They must be reached through their conscience—driven to the Savior, stripped of their self-righteousness, thirsting for the righteousness of God that comes by faith. Each of us must humble ourselves, be condemned, and then be crucified with Christ, so that we can be resurrected in His likeness. There's no other way.

I'll say it again: Sinners cannot keep their dignity if they want to enter the door of the kingdom of heaven. It's too lowly for the dignified. They must humble themselves and become as little children (Mark 10:15). This does not mean believing things that are false, but rather believing God's Word even when we are not yet able to intellectually prove it. The reason that Christians can wholeheartedly trust God's Word (even in the face of supposed evidence to disprove it) is not because they have chosen to ignore their intellect, but because they *know* the transforming truth of God's Word through conversion. Intellectual dignity and a proud heart are bedfellows. If you don't believe that, take the time to share your faith with a typical secular university student. The Bible tells us that "knowledge puffs up" (1 Corinthians 8:1), and it's in our colleges that you will find many who are swollen with pride at what they think they know. God resists those who are proud of heart; they are an "abomination" to Him (Proverbs 16:5, kjv). Let's therefore stop trying to accommodate sinners by satisfying their proud and unreasonable intellect. If we want to see them saved, the Law must humble them. Charles Spurgeon said, "There must be true and deep conviction of sin. This the preacher must labor to produce, for where this is not felt, the new birth has not taken place." So, accelerate up the on-ramp and quickly get to the conscience. Simply ask people, "Do you consider yourself to be a good person?" Shut them up under the Law. Show them that they have sinned against heaven (whether they believe in heaven or not, their conscience will affirm the truth of it), and that eternal justice calls for their sinful blood. God's Law is like an unleashed, razor-sharp guillotine, swiftly falling toward the sinners' stiff and sinful necks. They have no time to argue.

Meet Dr. Knowright

Dr. Knowright has a stubborn-hearted patient in an isolation room. The man has a rare disease that will kill him if he doesn't breathe pure oxygen. But the obstinate patient doesn't see his peril. He refuses to believe the diagnosis of the good doctor and breathe from the oxygen tank. Instead, he is consumed by something he finds to be far more interesting—he's feeding his mind on a dirty television program.

Dr. Knowright doesn't panic. He doesn't try to argue. He simply leaves the room, closes the airtight door, and turns on the air-removal switch.

He waits at the viewing window. It's a very predictable scenario. His patient begins to become fidgety. He then wipes sweat from his brow. He is distracted from the television program as his breathing becomes labored. He eyes the oxygen hose. He then begins to heave as he tries to catch his breath. Suddenly he lunges for dear life at the oxygen hose, adjusts the mask over his nose and mouth, and begins to breathe freely. Dr. Knowright whispers. "It never fails.... The will to live is paramount."

It's important to realize that some people do have genuine intellectual hindrances to faith, and these should be addressed.[1] However, Albert Proudheart's dilemma is a little deeper than he would have you know. The Bible warns us that in these last days men will scoff and say that there is no such thing as the flood of Noah (despite the mountain of evidence). We are even told that their motivation for being "willingly ... ignorant" is their love of lust (2 Peter 3:1-7, KJV). No, Albert Proudheart doesn't really have an *intellectual* problem with Christianity. He has a problem with his own heart. He *loves* sin. He drinks it in like water. Because of this, he has no concern for his eternal salvation. His mind is overtaken by something *far more interesting.* He's feeding on sin's succulent pleasures. Don't panic. Don't argue with him. Instead, flick the switch that will suck the air from him. Learn to do what Jesus did. Use the Law (Mark 10:17-22).

Andrew Murray writes, "To convince the world of the truth of Christianity, it must first be convinced of sin. It is only sin that renders Christ intelligible."[2] Show sinners the nature of sin by taking them through the Ten Commandments. Their reaction will be very predictable. Watch them become fidgety as their conscience does its work. Watch sweat come to their brow. Look for the fear in their eyes as they begin to see their peril. The Holy Spirit is faithful to do His wonderful work. He convinces sinners that God's wrath is above them...and there is a yawning hell beneath them (John 16:8). Unless they humble themselves, repent, and trust in Jesus Christ, *they will perish.* The razor-sharp blade of eternal justice "abides on him" (John 3:36). Forget about Jonah and the whale. Who cares how many horse stalls Solomon had? If you can't answer those questions, don't worry about it. Jesus purposely didn't answer every question He was asked by the skeptics (Matthew 21:27). Instead, He accelerated past the intellect and addressed the real issues separating people from God—He moved directly into the area of the conscience. We should do the same.

It is the knowledge of danger that makes a sin-loving sinner gasp for dear life and cling to the life-giving Savior. After you have seen this happen a number of times, you too will whisper, "It never fails.... The will to live is paramount."

18 | TAKE TWO TABLETS AND CALL ME WHEN YOU'RE MOURNING

Why are there so few front-line soldiers within the body of Christ? There are many who say that they love God, read the Word, pray, and praise God with a passion, but there are so few who have what Spurgeon referred to as a deep "tenderness." These are the ones who carry an anguish of soul for the fate of the ungodly. They break out of their complacency and seek by any means to save the lost. "The love of Christ compels [them]" (2 Corinthians 5:14). The Greek word translated "compel" denotes that God's love arrests them, preoccupies and presses them to reach out to the lost. They take off their jackets of condescension, put on the armor of light, and go to battle for the souls of men. These harvest workers are the ones of whom Jesus said there was a great and tragic lack (Matthew 9:37-38). He commanded us to pray that God would send more.

For years I couldn't discover what it was that forged these rare and hardy souls. Were they merely diamonds that sparkled more than others because of a God-given temperament? Were these people born fearless by nature and their bold and zealous witness came naturally to them, out-sparkling others who lacked such a virtue? No, some of the most zealous and bold witnesses for Christ I have known have been of a quiet or even a shy disposition.

One night in late 1994, I found the answer. A friend, Pastor Mike Smalley, and I were at the home of Winkie and Faye Pratney deep in the heart of Texas. Winkie is a fellow New Zealander, so it was something special for us to get together for dinner—it called for steak.

Winkie went outside to put the steaks on the barbecue, but a few minutes later reluctantly brought them back inside when the barbie ran out of propane gas. As he cooked them inside, he said something about them not being as tender as they would have been if he had cooked them on the intense heat of the barbecue.

After a few minutes, the entire house filled with smoke from his cooking; but it was well worth it—the steaks melted in the mouth. Besides, the fans in the house soon cleared the air.

When I remarked about the tenderness of my steak, Winkie shared his secret. He explained that the way to keep a steak tender is to sear it on both sides for forty seconds on a very hot hotplate. That seals the juices in the steak; then you cook it slowly until it is done.

About three o'clock the following morning, it dawned on me what produces the much-desired tenderhearted Christian. When a sinner comes under the intense heat of the Law of God, it has the effect of sealing within him a tender heart. This is how it happens: As the spirituality of the Law bears down on him, it shows him the exceeding sinfulness of his heart. It reveals to him that the very core of his nature is vile, that his lust is adultery, his hatred is murder, and he is a liar, a thief, and a rebel—a selfish and ungrateful sinner for whom hell is the only appropriate destination.

He begins to see that he has loved what is abhorrent to his Creator. The Law shows him that even his so-called good works are tainted by a self-centered motive. This knowledge, coupled with the fact that he has *greatly* angered God by transgressing His Law, is the heat that seals in the tenderness of soul.

When grace is revealed, it is embraced as a man dying of thirst embraces a jug of water. The experience of the searing heat of the Law bringing him to the point of death, yet being freely given the waters of life, forever secures the virtue of unspeakable gratitude. And that makes him a laborer for life. The Law gives him understanding that in the gospel he is forgiven much, so he loves much—vertically, and therefore horizontally.

Such tenderness is difficult to cultivate in someone who already possesses knowledge of God's grace in Christ. His realization of God's goodness deprives him of the fear of wrath. Only those who can sing "and grace my fears relieved" see grace as being truly amazing. This is why I believe it is a mistake to tell a guilty, unregenerate sinner "God loves you." Such knowledge doesn't allow fear to enter his heart. Instead, it deprives him of a depth of gratitude he would otherwise have had if fear had been allowed to do its work.

This is why enlightened evangelists are not afraid to gently put on the heat when speaking with sinners. They know that when the smoke of the wrath of the Law condemns the prisoner before them, it is actually preparing his heart for a pardon that will be welcomed *because of the fear gripping his heart.* They know that the tears that fear produces will be wiped away by the gentle hand of God's grace. They know that the gentle hand will not be fully appreciated if the Law is not allowed to do its most necessary work. It is the Law of God that exposes sin, and when sin is viewed under the penetrating light of the Law, as we have seen, it makes grace abound. The Greek word used to explain this in Romans 5:20 is *hyperperisseuo,* which means to "superabound."

If I were a physician and I knew you had a terrible disease, I would be unwise to give you a cure without first carefully explaining to you that you had the disease. However, I wouldn't merely tell you that you had the disease; I would actually let fear work for your good. I would use it to cause you to *want* to take the cure. As I showed you X-rays, I would watch beads of sweat drip from your brow and I would say to myself, "Good, he's beginning to see the seriousness of his disease." The fear will not only cause you to embrace the cure, it will (when the cure is received) give you tremendous appreciation for me as your doctor for providing the cure.

> ➤ One day I determined to witness to a very dear friend of my family who had stopped by for a visit. Her name is Kristy, and at the time she was thirteen years old. We began talking about spiritual things in a casual conversation. I told her I wanted to read her something, and I read her a portion of Revelation 20 about Judgment Day. I reasoned with her about God's love for justice and told her that God must punish sin wherever it is found. We read other passages about false believers and where they would spend eternity. She was frightened for them, and we talked about the mirror of the Law to see if we ourselves are safe on Judgment Day. When we went

through the Ten Commandments, she felt guilty and began to confess secret sins of theft, lying, hatred, etc. I had her read from the Scriptures about the destiny of liars, thieves, blasphemers, slanderers, and idolaters, all of which she admittedly was. She concluded that she'd be guilty on the Day of Judgment and would therefore go to hell for eternity. She was visibly upset and concerned. I could see tears begin to form as she held her head low. To see her realize her hell-bound destiny broke my heart but thrilled it as well, because I knew that this girl was about to hear the best news of her life. Fear and guilt, produced by her conscience, had thoroughly gripped her heart; the soil was now ready for the seed of the gospel.

I asked Kristy if she knew what God had done so she wouldn't have to go to hell. She didn't know, although she mumbled the word, "Forgiveness?"

I told her about Jesus' suffering death as payment for her sins. She broke the Law, and Jesus paid her fine. I read her Isaiah 53:5-6 and showed her the way of salvation through repentance and faith in Jesus. I asked her if she'd ever been born again. She said she hadn't, but she wanted to receive the new heart that is promised in the Scriptures, because she feared that even if God forgave her of her sins, she might sin again. What a wonderful attitude! To cower at the thought of offending God even one more time—oh, beautiful Spirit of God, please sustain that holy fear in me! "The fear of the Lord is the beginning of wisdom." Because of her fear of the Lord, I had the privilege of detailing the wonders of God's faithfulness to create in her a new heart with new desires, and His promise to forgive and cleanse her of all unrighteousness (1 John 1:9).

Kristy silently prayed for forgiveness and a new heart of obedience. Then I prayed for her protection, blessing, and her new life in Christ. When I asked her how she felt, her face broke into a huge smile as she said, "Much better." She gave me a hug and thanked me for talking with her. I bought her a teen Bible and encouraged her to read it every day. She was very excited.

Later my wife, Chelsea, said that Kristy was so grateful to finally understand why Jesus died on the cross for her. Kristy said that it had never made sense to her before—not even when she went forward to "accept Jesus" in church. The day she responded at the altar, she simply raised her hand at the invitation to "accept Jesus into your heart and have your sins forgiven so you'll go to heaven." Who wouldn't accept that? The problem was that she had no real knowledge of her sin, so she couldn't repent or understand the Cross. But when the Law revealed her exceedingly sinful heart, she ran into the arms of Jesus for forgiveness and a new heart. And to think that I once thought the Law was outdated and useless! Praise God for continuing to teach me! —KC

A great preacher once asked a well-known actor how it is that when performers present a story, they often bring the audience to tears. Yet rarely does a minister move a congregation to such a degree. The actor responded that the performers portray fiction as if it is reality, whereas ministers of the gospel too often portray reality as if it is fiction.

If we really believed that unregenerate souls were going to hell, we would preach with overwhelming passion. Our hearts would groan in constant prayer. We would run to sinners with solemn words of warning, take hold of them, and beseech them to turn from sin. Instead, we lack any real sense of urgency. We are afraid to speak frankly with sinners about their personal sins. We think that searing them under the heat of the Law will do harm rather than good. But consider how Jesus spoke with the woman at the well in John 4. He applied the heat of the Law (v. 18) and spoke of her *personal* transgressions—and what was the result? She became an immediate laborer (vv. 28-29).*

I received the following letter about one of my books. It shows the power of the Law to bring a thirst for righteousness:

> *This friend of mine has always told me for the last eight years, whenever the opportunity popped up, that the Law was finished with and that the*

---

* The woman at the well is often cited as evidence that we come to Jesus for happiness. However, to say that the "thirst" spoken of in John 4:13-15 is a thirst for happiness is mere conjecture. The biblical reason that we come to the Savior is for righteousness, not happiness. The only way for this woman to drink of the living waters of eternal life was to pass through the door of righteousness. Jesus said that those who hunger and thirst for righteousness are blessed (Matthew 5:6). He said that unless our righteousness exceeds that of the scribes and Pharisees, we won't enter the kingdom of heaven. He told us to seek first the kingdom of God and His righteousness. The woman at the well had transgressed the seventh commandment, and without the righteousness of Christ, she would perish. The Law makes us thirst after a righteousness that we would otherwise have no desire for.

Ten Commandments were basically useless. Of course, I tried to gently suggest that the knowledge of sin could not come by any other way than the Law, but this was always smothered in a sugary reference to love and grace . . . so I kept quiet.

But I stuck my neck out last week and gave the book to this friend, and the next day he handed it back to me. He was crying and shaking with emotion. He could hardly speak. He said, "I've just been born again!" What really happened, I think, was the full impact of the power of God's Law had struck him and wounded him, showing him clearly how bad his sin really was. He was in quite a state for several days after that, and kept breaking out into praise to God.

It was the two tablets of the Law that caused the mourning in his heart.

Seven Scared Sinners

Late in 1994, I arrived in Baton Rouge to do a series of meetings. A young man named Jeff picked me up and told me of the plan he had for me to speak open-air at a fake funeral.

After a short nap in my hotel, I met with the others, briefed the pallbearers, the corpse, and the crowd as to the dos and don'ts of an open-air setting, and we drove to the site of the preaching.

When we pulled into the parking lot of a Wal-Mart, I thought we were going to buy something, but it was actually the location Jeff had chosen for us. After I had preached for about five minutes, one of the security guards approached me and said I could speak for another five minutes, then I had to stop. I was thankful for the extra time and afterwards mentioned this to the local pastor who had come with us. He smiled and said, "When you started, I told the security guard, 'See all those people around the preacher? They go to my church, and we all shop at Wal-Mart.'"

After that, we drove to an area near the local university campus and set up the funeral once again. This time Jeff had decided he would give my voice a break by preaching himself. Just as we were organizing the pallbearers, a siren shrieked behind me. I turned to see a traffic officer on a motorcycle angrily waving over a van full of teenagers. As the van pulled to the side of the road, the police officer jumped off his bike, ran to the van, opened the door, and cursed the driver. He then grabbed him, violently pulled him out of his seat, and thrust him against the vehicle. The officer then gave him a body search, once again using obscenities as he did so. The scared youth didn't resist as he was frisked and yelled at.

From what I could gather, the officer had waved the van over and they had failed to stop. Some of the passengers in the van had thought the incident funny, which had caused the officer to boil over. Here was a wrath-filled, slightly out-of-control officer of the law, "God's minister, an avenger to execute wrath on him who practices evil" (Romans 13:4).

We decided that it wouldn't be wise to preach there with the law so upset, so we moved to the entrance of a bar about thirty yards away, across the parking lot. While Jeff preached, semidrunken teenagers came out of the bar and mocked him. It was a replay in the spiritual realm of what I had just seen in the natural realm. These teens were refusing to listen to the Law, and they were storing up wrath that would be revealed on the Day of Wrath. The day would come when an angry Law would pull them from the seat of the scornful, and from that there would be no escape.

After about five minutes, the manager came out and stopped Jeff from preaching. (The local church members didn't patronize his bar.) As we wandered back to the van, we passed the youths the officer had stopped. I went over to the group and asked what had happened. The driver was obviously still upset and told me that he had driven through a stop sign, had his lights out, and had failed to stop when the officer first waved him over. His six friends who were with him were also shaken by what had taken place. I couldn't help but sympathize a little with the driver and shared how I thought the officer had clearly lost control of himself. He agreed.

I wanted to witness to them, but felt I lacked the right approach. It would be like putting salt on the wound of a distressed child. I was sure that if I mentioned sin, righteousness, and judgment at that point I would be told in no uncertain and colorful terms to depart from the area. Reluctantly, I simply said I would see them later and walked back to our group.

As I stood there, someone asked if I had witnessed to them. I said I hadn't. I said I didn't know how to approach the subject and that I needed a little time to get some thoughts together.

A moment later, I walked back to them determined to say something about their eternal salvation, even if I did get abused. Suddenly, I remembered that I had put about ten one-dollar bills in my wallet to give away at the open-air presentation, something I often do to illustrate a number of points. When I asked how much the fine would be, the driver looked up and said, "About $200." I took my wallet out, pulled out the handful of bills and said, "This isn't much, but I would like to give this toward the fine." As I referred to the money, I looked down at it in amazement. Clearly visible was a ten-dollar bill, making the wad of bills look like far more than it was. *It looked like a fortune!*

Different teens in the group said, "Wow ... you can't do that ... that's really nice of you ... you don't even know us." The driver graciously declined the money, but the offer struck a chord in their hearts. They could see that I really cared about them and the suggestion had given me license to speak to them about their salvation. I said, "I'm a preacher. Here is a gift for each of you." I then handed each of them a penny with the Ten Commandments pressed onto it and asked if they had kept the Law. When I asked if they had lied, stolen, lusted, etc., every one of them admitted that they had broken the commandments.

Then I turned to the driver and asked him if he was scared when the law enforcement officer pulled him from his vehicle. He said he was terrified. I then said, "Tonight you transgressed civil law, but now you know that you have also transgressed the Divine Law. If civil law scared you, wait until you face God on Judgment Day—it is a fearful thing to fall into the hands of the living God." I explained the gospel, asked if they had Bibles, and told them to dust them off and read the Gospel of John. I then shook their hands, thanked them for listening, and left them in the hands of a faithful Creator.

While I had been speaking, the driver was peeling masking tape from around his ankles. He had strapped sealed plastic bags of whiskey under his socks—something the officer hadn't found when he frisked him. God only knows what may have happened that night if the driver had downed the whiskey and driven home with six drunken friends in his van.

The officer of the law missed that hidden offense, but God's Law won't miss a thing.

Both the civil and the Divine Law did a deep work in some young hearts that night. It is my prayer that seven "steaks" were seared to a crisp and that some day seven tenderhearted and faithful laborers will enter the harvest fields and gladly toil for their Master.

> ➤ The information in the next chapter is what really lit a fire in my heart to abandon my comfort zone and reach out to the lost—*now!*
> —KC

AN ANGRY GOD

If our theology ignores the centrality of the Law and thus overlooks the necessity of the Holy Spirit's conviction of sin, we will see nothing wrong with leaving a sinner with false peace. In Jeremiah 8:11, God says of the prophets and priests of Israel: "They have healed the hurt of the daughter of My people slightly, saying, 'Peace, peace!' when there is no peace."

This is how to give false peace to a sinner. Simply ask, "Do you have assurance that you will go to heaven when you die?" Who in his right mind doesn't want to go to heaven? So a good number will say something like, "I *hope* I'm going to heaven when I die." Now say, "God wants you to have that assurance. All of us have sinned and come short of the glory of God, but God sent His Son to die on the cross for us so that we could have peace with God. When we repent and trust in Him, God will give us everlasting life. He writes our name in the Book of Life. Would you like to accept Jesus into your heart right now and have your name written in heaven? I could lead you in what's called 'the sinner's prayer' right now. Would you like to pray?" Many do.

You may be asking, "What's wrong with that?" Let me see if I can answer that question with an anecdote.

A blind man is unwittingly heading for the edge of a thousand-foot cliff. A modern evangelist draws alongside him and says, "Blind man, I am going to give you a wonderful gift that will give you peace." He then hands him a CD player and adjusts some earphones over his ears. The sightless man hears "Amazing Grace" being sung by a choir of ten thousand voices. His unseeing eyes widen with delight. He smiles and says, "What you said is true. This is truly wonderful. Thank you very much." He shakes the man's hand, turns up the volume on his new gift, and continues walking toward the thousand-foot cliff.

What has the modern evangelist done? He has failed to awaken the blind sinner to his true plight. Instead, he has given him *false* peace. Now not only is the blind man still heading toward a horrible death, *but he is deaf toward any further verbal warning.* The message of peace has done an unspeakable disservice to the blind sinner.

Millions of people have been given "assurance of salvation," yet they are strangers to biblical repentance. The Law has never awakened them. They have never been warned to turn from the cliffs of eternal destruction. Now, because of the techniques of contemporary evangelism, their ears are deaf to the true message of salvation.

A religious studies professor named Wade Clark Roof, in his book *Spiritual Marketplace: Baby Boomers and the Remaking of American Religion,* says that one-third of America's 77 million baby boomers identify themselves as born-again Christians. According to Roof, that means they've had a "highly personal spiritual experience that has changed their lives." Roof observes that only about half of those who call themselves born-again attend a conservative Protestant church. Twenty percent don't belong to *any* church at all, and one-third believe in astrology and reincarnation.

There is another hidden tragedy that has resulted from the effects of modern evangelism. After years of hearing the modern gospel message, most Americans have a concept of God as a benevolent father figure. The thought that a God of love would judge our nation with catastrophes is unthinkable to many. Therefore, the terrible tragedies of "natural" disasters and deadly diseases are considered the mere rumblings of "Mother Nature"— El Niño, La Niña, global warming, global cooling, environmental toxins—*anything but* the dealings of a holy God with a sinful nation. Still, it doesn't take a rocket scientist to see that this nation has lost God's blessing. The American Cancer Society estimates that in just one year there are almost 1.4 million new cancer cases. On top of that, recent years have brought an onslaught of hurricanes, devastating floods, earthquakes, droughts, and tornadoes.

The tragic dilemma facing the Church is how to go from preaching "God loves you" to "God is angry at the wicked every day." For many, it is too great a leap to take. Consequently, few preachers have the courage to say that America is under God's judgment, and those who do are considered a little fanatical. We're in this position because just over one hundred years ago modern evangelism forsook the scriptural stepping-stone of the Law of God. Without it, the world cannot conceive that God would be angry at humanity. Remember, without the use of the Law, judgment is totally *unreasonable*. C. S. Lewis said, "When we merely say that we are bad, the 'wrath' of God seems a barbarous doctrine; as soon as we perceive our badness, it appears inevitable, a mere corollary from God's goodness." The Law helps us perceive our badness.

God Is Nice

A sincere young lady once heckled me as I expounded the Ten Commandments to a crowd of mainly unsaved people. She boldly called out, "Don't listen to this man! *God loves you.*" I stopped speaking and asked her if she cared about the salvation of the people to whom I was speaking. She said she did, so I gently coaxed her up onto the soapbox and asked her to give her testimony. After she had (bravely) spoken for a few moments, I asked her where her hearers would go if they died without the Savior. She hesitatingly said, "Hell ... " Then she began to weep and added, *"But God is nice."*

God is many things—holy, perfect, righteous, loving, good—but there is no biblical foundation for saying that He is "nice." The young lady was nice. She was charming. But to tell sinners that their Creator is "nice" will give the impression that He is "pleasant, sweet, delicate, and agreeable." If that was this young lady's image of God, no wonder she was offended by the biblical revelation of His nature. Sometime after that incident, another young lady publicly reproved me for preaching about future punishment. She called out "God loves you ... just ask Jesus into your heart right now!" When I asked her where the crowd would go if they died without Jesus Christ, she said, "They won't go to heaven." I asked where they would go. She said, "They won't go to be with God." Again I pressed her as to the specific location, and she said, "To a *not very nice* place." Her dilemma was that the mention of hell, without the Law to make it reasonable, made her God look like a tyrant and brought with it the scorn of the world.

Professor Douglas Groothuis of the evangelical Denver Seminary said, "Even some evangelicals, who generally take a more literal approach to biblical teachings, view hell as 'a blemish to be covered up by the cosmetic of divine love.'"[1] They deliberately cover over any mention of the cliff toward which the blind man is headed. They don't want to alarm him.

No wonder the world has a misguided understanding of the nature of God. An article in the *Washington Post* put it this way:

> *Over the years, Ed and Joanne Liverani have found many reasons to summon God. But now, at middle age, they've boiled it down to one essential: "Not to get clobbered by life."*
>
> *So sometime in the past ten years the Liveranis began to build their own church, salvaging bits of their old religion that they liked and chucking the rest. The first to go were an angry, vengeful God and hell— "That's just something they say to scare you," Ed said. They kept Jesus, "because Jesus is big on love."[2]*

➢ At Camp Firefly, a yearly camp that my wife and I host for terminally ill children and their families, I went golfing with four of the fathers. On the first couple of holes, I made a few jokes and then used some "IQ Test" tracts to break the ice for witnessing (see these unique tracts at www.wayofthemaster.com). All the dads failed the IQ tests, allowing me to remind them that sometimes our eyes can play tricks on us, keeping us from seeing the truth even when it is plainly in front of us. Then I asked who would like to take another intelligence test. "This time," I said, "it's about God." Two men came closer. Dan was one of them.

Dan had a very strong and friendly personality. He lived in the inner-city with his wife and four children, and he had had a very hard life. The first question on the test was, "Is there a God?" Dan said, "Yes." Second question: "Does God care about right and wrong?" Dan said, "No." The other men and I looked at Dan with a sense of wonder at how he could say such a ridiculous thing. I had never heard of anyone who believed that God didn't care about right and wrong, good and bad. When I asked the next question,

"Is there a hell?" Dan didn't believe there was, because in his mind, if God didn't care about wrong then He certainly wouldn't create a place of punishment for wrongdoers.

It was obvious who I would be witnessing to on this golf outing. Before we teed off, I asked Dan how he would feel if someone took his wife into the field behind the golf course, abused her, slit her throat so she would bleed to death, and then stabbed her in the heart thirty times just to make sure she was dead. I asked him if he would care that someone did that to his wife. Of course, he did. He said, "I'd track him down and kill him myself." I then reasoned with him that if he, a mere man, cared about murder, how much more did God care about such a horrible act of violence. He didn't know how to answer other than to say, "God doesn't care about earthly things, only heavenly things." I felt that he was hiding something big, with an odd comment like that, but I didn't know what.

Then, following Jesus' example, and with the help of Dan's conscience and the Holy Spirit, I began to bring about the conviction of his personal sins. I did this by asking him if he considered himself to be a good person. He said, "Yes, I do." I asked him if he had kept the Ten Commandments. He said he didn't think so, but that it didn't matter, because he had plenty of relatives who went to church, and their kids had turned out far worse than his. His conclusion was that his way was better. "Have you ever told a lie?" I asked him. He said he had. When I asked him what that made him, he said, without hesitation, "A liar." I asked him if he'd ever stolen anything. He said, "Yes." I asked him what that made him. He said, "A thief." Then I told him that Jesus said, "Whoever looks at a woman to lust for her has already committed adultery with her in his heart." He easily admitted that he was guilty of looking at women with lust. Then I gently said, "Dan, by your own admission, you are a liar, a thief, and an adulterer at heart, and you have to face God on Judgment Day. And we've looked at only three of the Ten Commandments."

We went through some more of the commandments, and by the next tee station, Dan had admitted that he was also an idolater and a blasphemer. I asked him, "If God judges you by the Ten

Commandments on Judgment Day, will you be innocent or guilty?" He paused for a moment and said, "Guilty." I asked, "Do you think you'll go to heaven or hell?" He said, "I'll go to heaven, because God is forgiving and He doesn't care about earthly things. All you need is a tiny bit of faith and He will forgive you of all that stuff." I said, "Dan, if you were a criminal, guilty of serious crimes, standing before a judge and you said, 'Judge, I know I'm guilty, but I have faith that you're a forgiving man and that you'll just forget about what I did and let me go,' should that judge let you go?" He said no. We agreed that if a judge is a good judge, he cannot just overlook crime, but must see to it that justice is served and that criminals are punished. So I asked, "Dan, do you think God is good?" He answered yes. I said, "If God is good, then by nature, He will not overlook your sins, but will do everything in His power to see that justice is served and that you are punished."

Dan said angrily, "Don't tell me that!" We picked up our golf balls, got into our cart, and drove to the next hole.

We had finished only five holes, and we weren't playing anymore golf because we were so deep in conversation. The rest of the guys continued to play without us. Dan told me that his mother had always told him that he couldn't run away from God, that God would chase him down and would one day get him. Dan hated that. He was desperately trying to justify himself as a good person in his own eyes, believing that God didn't care about the sins of his past. I resumed the use of the Law. I told him that if he was honest, he knew that when God called him to give an account of his life on Judgment Day, he would be found guilty and receive the punishment he deserves. I shared with him what the Bible said about his fate: that all liars will have their part in the lake of fire, and that no fornicator, idolater, adulterer, thief, or blasphemer will inherit the kingdom of God. I explained that every time he sinned, he was storing up wrath for himself that will be revealed on the day of wrath, that he is an enemy of God because of his wicked works, and that "the wrath of God abides on him." I pointed out that if God gives him justice, he won't be going to heaven but will spend eternity in hell.

At this point, he had me locked in his stare, and I began to feel a great sense of pressure to stop the conversation. However, I knew that I had to press on in our talk, or the progress we had made would be lost and Dan would be in a worse place spiritually than when we began. I had to continue reasoning with him until he stopped justifying himself and coming up with excuses for his guilt. It wasn't easy, but eventually his expression of anger toward me changed to a look of fear and panic. He was guilty, and he knew it. Dan wasn't defending himself anymore—just staring at me, looking like a man who had been found out and didn't know where to turn for escape. He eventually turned away from me and looked at the golf cart floor, as if he were coming to terms with the fact that he was guilty before God and would one day be held accountable for his sins.

As he looked like his heart was sinking, I gently asked him if he could see his need for God's forgiveness. He said yes. Outside I was calm, but inside I was leaping with joy! Now that he knew his need for forgiveness, he could see his need for a Savior. Now was the time to tell him about Jesus. I said, "Although God is a God of justice, He is also a God of love and mercy, and He has made a way for you to be forgiven, Dan." He lifted his eyes and looked at me with curiosity. I said, "Dan, imagine that you're a criminal, guilty of serious crimes that have earned you a fine of five million dollars or a sentence of fifty years in prison. Without a dime to pay the court, you are being sent to prison for the rest of your life. Then suddenly, someone you don't even know steps forward and pays your fine for you. The judge examines the stranger's money and says, 'Dan, this man has paid your fine in full. You are free to go.' And then the stranger comes over to you and says, 'I know you don't know me, but I sold my house and all my possessions and emptied all my bank accounts to pay this fine for you. I did this because I love you.'" Dan was listening intently. Then I said, "Dan, that's what God did for you—He paid your fine. God became a man, Jesus Christ, and suffered and died on the cross to pay the price for your sin. You broke the Law, and Jesus paid your fine. It's as simple as that. And you're free to go, on the grounds that someone has paid your fine. That's how much God loves you, Dan!"

I explained that he'd never be able to earn his way into heaven. He had lied, stolen, committed adultery, was guilty of idolatry and blasphemy, and had no excuse. But God would give him forgiveness as a gift if he would repent of his sins and place his faith in Jesus Christ alone to save him. We talked about what repentance meant. I told him the story of the Prodigal Son returning to seek the forgiveness of his father. The father, seeing him far off in the distance, actually *ran* to his son, picked him up and rejoiced, because his son was lost, but now is found, he was blind but now he sees! I told Dan that his mother was correct in saying that God had been chasing him all his life, but what he didn't understand was that He was chasing him in love, so that if Dan ever came to his senses and turned away from his sin to humbly seek God's forgiveness, he would find that He was very nearby. Dan sat still and quiet as I magnified the love, grace, and mercy of God in Jesus Christ.

I spoke to him about the urgency of his need to turn from sin and put his faith in Christ. I asked him if he thought it was possible that he could die that night. Dan's daughter had cancer—that was the reason he had come to Camp Firefly. He knew that tomorrows were never guaranteed, and he understood that each day could be his last. I told him that because God's Word says, "Man is destined to die once, and after that to face judgment," nothing was more important than getting his heart right with God before he went to sleep that night. Dan nodded in agreement and said, "That's true."

We had reached the end of the golf course, each finishing with a score of thirty! (We didn't mention to the guys at the clubhouse that we had played only the first five holes.) As the other guys in our group turned in their clubs, Dan and I were still talking in the parking lot. He sat down on the front of the golf cart and began to cry. He said, "I've been running from God all my life, trying to get away from Him. But I don't want to run anymore." He began to sob as he held his face in his hands. I put my arm around this big man and said, "Dan, do you need God to forgive you?" He said with a heavy voice, "Yes." I asked, "Do you want to turn away from all

THE WAY OF THE **MASTER**

your sins and give your whole life to Jesus right now?" He said, "Yes, I do." In that moment, I was so overwhelmed with the Spirit's presence that I felt as if I were witnessing a miracle.

I told Dan to confess his sins to God—all of them. I told him that he needed to come totally clean before God and confess that he was a liar, a thief, and an adulterer. He must no longer hide his sins from God but must forsake them all, and ask God to help him to turn to Him and to love and obey Jesus with all his heart. He began to pray, quietly confessing his sins to God. Then I prayed for him. I thanked God for chasing Dan and catching him that day on the golf course. I thanked Him for Dan's broken heart and willingness to repent of all his sins and trust in God's mercy. I asked the Lord to bless him, to protect him and his family, and to change him into a godly man. While I prayed, I could hear him quietly saying, "Yes, Father . . . in Jesus' name . . . in Jesus' name." We were two gathered in the name of Jesus, and I was sure that God had just soundly saved a man in the middle of a parking lot.

I asked Dan if he had a Bible; he did, and he was going to start reading it. We had become good friends and he had become a new creation. Later that day, I saw Dan sharing his story with another person from camp. He was tearing up again, sharing the story of the God who had chased him down and caught him on the golf course that day. I was later told that when Dan was asked how his golf game went, he said, "It was the best day of my life, and golf had nothing to do with it." —KC

20 | A BURDEN FOR THE LOST

While David was on the run from King Saul and hiding in the blackness of Adullam's cave, he longed for a drink of the cool water of Bethlehem's well. However, Israel's sworn enemy, the Philistines, had a garrison in Bethlehem, making it a dangerous place to be seen. Still, his thirst would not subside. He remembered the hot days of his childhood, when his thirst drove him to draw fresh water from the deep well. The more he thought about it, the more his desire grew, until he whispered, "Oh, that someone would give me a drink of the water from the well of Bethlehem, which is by the gate!" (2 Samuel 23:15). The Scriptures then tell us:

> So the three mighty men broke through the camp of the Philistines, drew water from the well of Bethlehem that was by the gate, and took it and brought it to David. Nevertheless he would not drink it, but poured it out to the Lord. And he said, "Far be it from me, O Lord, that I should do this! Is this not the blood of the men who went in jeopardy of their lives?" Therefore he would not drink it. These things were done by the three mighty men. (2 Samuel 23:16-17)

The three mighty warriors had a love for David that was more than lip service, as evidenced by the fact that they risked their lives merely to get a drink of water for their beloved leader. Yet, David's reaction to their display of love was to pour the water out on the ground as a drink offering to the Lord.

Some might be tempted to say, "Surely, if those men went to such effort to get the water, at least David could have drunk it!" But we have here something far deeper than mere human gratitude. *David's conscience would not allow him to indulge in self-gratification.* He said, "Is this not the blood of the men who went in jeopardy of their lives?" *How could he drink it?* It was more than just a cup of water. It was an evident token, a symbol, proof of their love and devotion to him. The cost was too great. His only course of action was to give it to God, to pour that precious water out as a drink offering to the Lord.

One Big Gap

One morning, my wife, Sue, was awakened at four o'clock to the sound of the television set blaring. She immediately thought that one of our children couldn't sleep and was watching TV. However, it was so loud, she decided she would go downstairs and turn it down.

When she arrived in the den, she found that one of the family dogs had accidentally stood on the remote control and was watching the sports channel.

It fascinates us to see an animal imitate us—it seems to wink or smile, or it seems to watch the sports channel. However, despite the efforts of evolutionists to link us to the animals, there is one big gap. As humans, we know that we are "beings." We are aware of our destiny with death. We are aware of the existence of a Supreme Being. God has placed eternity in our hearts (Ecclesiastes 3:11).

A non-Christian friend of mine found out that he had six months to live. His friends told him to spend the last six months doing a "brothel crawl." He wasn't interested. He found that he had something within his heart considerably stronger than his sex drive—it was the will to live. Deep within, his heart cried, "Oh, I don't want to die!" Eternity was in his heart. Its deep whisper was, "Oh, that one would give me a drink of water from the wells of salvation."

Before the beginning of time, God saw not only the cry of his heart, but the cry within every human heart. The Mighty Three, the Triune God, broke through the hosts of hell to draw water from the well of Bethlehem. God was in Christ, reconciling the world to Himself. Now the offer to sinful humanity is this: "Whoever drinks of the water that I shall give him will never thirst. But the water that I shall give him will become in him a fountain of water springing up into everlasting life" (John 4:14).

True converts hold the cup of salvation in their trembling hands. They have seen the cost of their redemption. They see that they were not redeemed with silver or gold, but with the precious blood of Christ. Like David, they cannot drink of that cup in a spirit of self-indulgence. Rather than drink in the pleasures and the comforts of the Christian life, their reasonable service is to present themselves as living sacrifices, holy and acceptable, and pour his life out as a drink offering to the Lord.

A Delightful Heart

I was killing time in a department store when an elderly man struck up a conversation with me. It wasn't long before the conversation swung around to the things of God. When I asked this man if he had a Christian background, his answer was interesting. He said, "Oh, I am a churchgoer. I believe in God the Father—and the Son, *He's around too . . . somewhere.*" His reply was both humorous and tragic. This man went to church, obviously had faith in God, believed in the deity and the resurrection of Jesus Christ, *yet he was not saved.*

If you love God, your heart will go out to the millions who are in such a state. They are in "the valley of decision" (Joel 3:14). Valleys are often without direct light, and direct light is what sinners need. They don't understand the issues. They are so close to salvation; it is as near as their heart and mouth. Yet without repentance, they will perish. Such thoughts are grievous. If you are born of God's Spirit, you will find that something compels you to run to the lost, to reach out to the unsaved, because God gave you a new heart that delights to do His will.

Well-known author and pastor Oswald Chambers said, "So long as there is a human being who does not know Jesus Christ, I am his debtor to serve him until he does." Bible teacher C. F. W. Walther said, "A believer is ready to serve everybody wherever he can. He cannot but profess the gospel before men, even though he foresees that he can reap nothing but ridicule and scorn for it; yes, he is ready also to give his life for the gospel."

One cannot help but see the apostle Peter's passion for the lost, which is so evidently portrayed for us in the book of Acts. He put behind him the three times he had denied his Lord and stood before a multitude on the Day of Pentecost. When a crowd gathered around the lame man who had been healed, Peter boldly preached the gospel to them. He testified before the very ones who had murdered the Savior, and he convicted them of that very sin. He had a passion for his God and a passion for sinners.

Likewise, the apostle Paul's greatest longing, aspiration, and yearning was simply for the salvation of the lost. His greatest passion was for evangelism, as evidenced by his own words. In the introduction of his letter to the Romans, Paul writes that he was in debt to the world. His evangelistic zeal was so great that he said he would give up his relationship with Jesus Christ if it would mean that his brethren would be saved. Look at these sobering words: "I tell the truth in Christ, I am not lying, my conscience also bearing me witness in the Holy Spirit, that I have great sorrow and continual grief in my heart. For I could wish that I myself were accursed from Christ for my brethren, my countrymen according to the flesh" (Romans 9:1-3).

I have looked at a number of Bible commentaries to see what they make of these verses. Some contend that Paul could not be speaking of his own salvation; rather, the reference is to his willingness to be cut off from Israel. It's my understanding, however, that Paul was *already* cut off from Israel because of his faith in Jesus Christ. If it were merely a reference to being cut off from his people, why did he say that he had *already* "suffered the loss of all things" (Philippians 3:8)? If he counts all things as rubbish to him, why then does he have to back up his statement with (what seems like) oaths to make his point?

It is as if Paul is writing to hearers who would not be able to understand such love. How could evangelistic intensity weigh so heavy on a man that he was prepared to be cut off from any association with the Lord Jesus to see that desire fulfilled? Such a statement could not penetrate selfish minds without a thoughtful preparation. They would not believe him. So Paul testifies about that in what he was about to say:

- He is telling the truth in Christ. The very One who was truth itself was Paul's witness that what he was about to say was true.
- His Holy Spirit–regenerated conscience bore witness that he spoke

the truth. He had cultivated a conscience that was tender before God and man, and the "work of the Law" did not accuse him of lying. His words could not be dismissed as mere exaggeration or hyperbole.

Deep within the soul of this man of God lay a burden—a great sorrow, a continual grief. Horror of horrors—he was saved, but his brethren were not.

Perhaps you think Paul was lying when he said that his concern for the lost meant more to him than his relationship with Jesus. Moses said a similar thing when he asked that God would cut him out of the book of life rather than judge Israel.

In light of these thoughts, I don't know how anyone can call himself a Christian and not have concern for the lost. Charles Spurgeon, in a sermon at New Park Street Chapel in 1859, said: "The saving of souls, if a man has once gained love to perishing sinners, and love to his blessed Master, will be an all-absorbing passion to him. It will so carry him away, that he will almost forget himself in the saving of others. He will be like the stout, brave fireman, who careth not for the scorch or for the heat, so that he may rescue the poor creature on whom true humanity hath set his heart."

In a sermon at Exeter Hall in 1860, Spurgeon said: "If sinners will be damned, at least let them leap to hell over our bodies. And if they will perish, let them perish with our arms about their knees, imploring them to stay. If hell must be filled, at least let it be filled in the teeth of our exertions, and let not one go there unwarned and unprayed for."

When an emergency vehicle drives through a city, the law demands that every other vehicle must pull over and stop. Why? *Because someone's life may be in jeopardy.* It is to be given great priority. That's how we should be when it comes to the eternal salvation of men and women. There is an extreme emergency. *Everything else* must come to a standstill or we are in danger of transgressing the Moral Law, which demands, "You shall love your neighbor as yourself."

> ➤ I had no real concern for the salvation of others until I attained the knowledge of the Law. When I understood God's holiness, and therefore His anger against sin, I began to see why Paul said, "Knowing, therefore, the terror of the Lord, we persuade men" (2 Corinthians 5:11). —KC

Hell should be so real to us that its flames burn away apathy and motivate us to warn the lost. Do we see the unsaved as hell's future fuel? Do we understand that sinful humanity is the anvil of the justice of God? Have we ever been horrified or wept because we fear for their fate? The depth of our evangelistic zeal will be in direct proportion to the love we have. If you are not concerned about your neighbor's salvation, then I am concerned for yours.

The evangelistic zeal described on the previous pages should characterize a normal, biblical Christian. However, according to a 1994 article in the *Dallas Morning News,* 68 percent of professing Christians outside of the Bible Belt don't see evangelism as being the number one priority of the Church.[1] Also in 1994, the Barna Research Group found that among American adults who said that they were born again, 75 percent couldn't even define the Great Commission. A survey by *Christianity Today,* a major evangelical magazine, found that only one percent of its readers said they had witnessed to someone "recently." That means that 99 percent of its readers were lukewarm or cold when it came to concern for the fate of the ungodly. According to *Zondervan Church Source,* 97 percent of the Church has no involvement in any sort of evangelism.

In Luke 15, Jesus gives three parables in a row to illustrate God's profound concern for lost souls. How is it that so many in the Church can profess to love God yet neglect or even *despise* evangelism? The answer is frightening.

THE RICH MAN

Some years ago, I read the story Jesus told of Lazarus and the rich man and interpreted it in a radically different slant than most. In fact, I have searched many commentaries and haven't found even one with the same interpretation. I submitted it to seven godly men. Six passed it as being biblically sound. The seventh wasn't sure. Here is the story from Scripture:

> *There was a certain rich man who was clothed in purple and fine linen and fared sumptuously every day. But there was a certain beggar named Lazarus, full of sores, who was laid at his gate, desiring to be fed with the crumbs which fell from the rich man's table. Moreover the dogs came and licked his sores.*
>
> *So it was that the beggar died, and was carried by the angels to Abraham's bosom. The rich man also died and was buried.*
>
> *And being in torments in [hell], he lifted up his eyes and saw Abraham afar off, and Lazarus in his bosom. Then he cried and said, "Father Abraham, have mercy on me, and send Lazarus that he may dip the tip of his finger in water and cool my tongue; for I am tormented in this flame."*
>
> *But Abraham said, "Son, remember that in your lifetime you received your good things, and likewise Lazarus evil things; but now he is*

comforted and you are tormented. And besides all this, between us and you there is a great gulf fixed, so that those who want to pass from here to you cannot, nor can those from there pass to us."

Then he said, "I beg you therefore, father, that you would send him to my father's house, for I have five brothers, that he may testify to them, lest they also come to this place of torment."

Abraham said to him, "They have Moses and the prophets; let them hear them." And he said, "No, father Abraham; but if one goes to them from the dead, they will repent." But he said to him, "If they do not hear Moses and the prophets, neither will they be persuaded though one rise from the dead." (Luke 16:19-31)

Now I ask you, is this a picture of the way of salvation? If so, it's totally inconsistent with every other biblical reference to deliverance from death. Those who seek to justify good works as a means of entrance into heaven could find adequate evidence here. Let's look at the passage in light of this thought.

First, what was the rich man's sin? Obviously, it was failure to feed Lazarus. If that is the case, then he could have *earned* salvation. If a non-Christian wanted to earn his way into heaven, should he then give food to the homeless? How much food would merit eternal life? No, since salvation is "by grace [divine influence]... through faith,... not of works" (Ephesians 2:8-9), the rich man's sin could not have been a mere failure to give Lazarus free food.

Perhaps his sin was the fact that he was rich. Then Abraham should have been damned, for he too was rich. Was gluttony the rich man's sin? Not necessarily. According to *Vine's Expository Dictionary of New Testament Words*, the word *sumptuously* means "goodly."

Why the reference to his clothing? Was his apparel or the color of it abhorrent to God?

On the other hand, what did Lazarus do to merit salvation? Did his suffering in this life appease the wrath of God and gain him entrance into the next? If so, then let us seek suffering instead of the Savior. Let us inflict our bodies as did the prophets of Baal, or crawl up the steps of some cold cathedral until blood pours from festered wounds, then call for the dogs to lick them. If this is a picture of the way of salvation, then eternal justice can be perverted, God can be bribed, and the sacrifice of the wicked is not an abomination to the Lord.

The story, therefore, *must* have another meaning.

Who Is the Rich Man?

Let us establish several principles of biblical interpretation that will help us unlock the meaning of the story of Lazarus and the rich man.

- Purple is the biblical color of royalty—Esther 8:15.
- Fine linen represents the righteousness of the saints—Revelation 19:8.
- The Church is referred to as the "royal priesthood"—1 Peter 2:9.
- The tabernacle (a *type,* or symbol, of the Church) was made of fine linen and purple—Exodus 26:1.

The rich man is a type of the *professing* Church, and the leper (which is what most Bible commentators agree Lazarus was) is a type of the sinner.

Let's look first at Lazarus. The foul sores of sin permeate his very being. He is an unclean thing. His righteousness is like filthy, leprous rags. Those who touch him are commanded to "[hate] even the garment defiled by the flesh" (Jude 1:23). Unclean spirits, like hungry dogs, feed off the wounds of his sin, waiting to consume him at death. He is laid at the gate of the Church—that rich, fat Laodicean Church, the "royal priesthood" of believers, clothed in fine linen and purple, faring sumptuously on the teachings of prayer, prophecy, providence, justification, sanctification, and purification. This Church enjoys an "abundant life" of men's camps, youth camps, marriage seminars, ladies' meetings, worship, prayer, and praise; young people's meetings, Bible studies, audiotapes, videotapes, and CDs; it heaps to itself teachers, having "itching ears"—ears so scratched by feasting, so dulled by overconsumption, *that the muffled cries of Lazarus at the gate go unheeded!*

We have become like Israel when God spoke to them in their prosperity, but they said, "I will not hear" (Jeremiah 22:21). The sin of the Church isn't that it's rich *but that it hasn't the compassion to throw even a few evangelistic crumbs to starving sinners at the gate.*

The rich man's thoughts are only for himself. He is filled with his own ways. We have built for ourselves big beautiful buildings with cool clear acoustics and colorful carpets, where as cozy Christians we sit on padded pews, living in luxury while sinners sink into hell. We say that we are rich, but we are poor, blind, wretched, miserable, and naked. I thank God for comfortable pews and quality sound systems, *but not at the cost of neglecting the lost.* We have lavish luxury on the lifeboat, while people drown en masse around us.

I have watched vast multitudes crowd around ministries of "power," "healing," and "faith," and prayed that what I suspect is untrue. I have listened to the message that these men and women bring, and I have hoped that I was mistaken in my thought that there was something radically wrong. I'm not bothered by what they say, *but by what is left unsaid.* There *is* healing in the atonement (who doesn't pray that God would heal a sick loved one?); we *need* to have faith in God's promises; and historically God does bless His people and lift them out of poverty, hunger, and suffering. *But why don't these ministers preach Christ crucified for the sins of the world?* They consistently leave the Cross out of their message, other than to mention it as the means of purchasing healing and prosperity for God's people. Why is there no preaching against sin and exalting of God's righteousness?

I look at the vast seas of people surrounding these preachers and I think that there must be many who don't know God's mercy in Christ, yet they are not warned to flee from the wrath to come. Judgment Day isn't mentioned; neither is hell; nor is there a call to repentance. I try to feel gracious toward these preachers and excuse them by thinking that perhaps these are "teachers" within the body of Christ, whose particular gifting is to exhort and encourage rather than to seek to save what is lost. However, the most gifted of teachers cannot be excused for not caring about the fate of the ungodly. The apostle Paul was the greatest of teachers, yet he pleaded for prayer that he would share the gospel with boldness as he "ought to speak" (Colossians 4:4). He said, "Woe is me if I do not preach the gospel!" (1 Corinthians 9:16). What are the ethical implications of a fire captain who is preoccupied with making sure that his firemen are well dressed, while the people he should be saving burn to death?

I pray that the following letter I received doesn't represent the throngs who are followers of these preachers of power, peace, and prosperity:

I don't think I've thanked you lately for waking me out of my false con- version. Please don't let discouragement ever hinder you from continu- ing to preach "Hell's Best Kept Secret." I believe it's the perfect message to wake up anyone, regardless of their denomination. . . . I never, ever thought the day would come that I would call myself an ex–"Word of Faith"er. If Paul was a Hebrew of Hebrews, I was a faith guy of faith guys. A card-carrying, tape-listening-to, TV-preacher-watching, book- reading, seminar-attending, positive-confessing faith guy was I. And it was all a waste of time. I write this to show you that if one who was as extreme as I was can be snatched from such a slumber, I believe anyone with an ounce of self-honesty is a candidate for this wake-up call. Not that I am any more opposed to the errors of Word of Faith doctrine than those of others in contemporary Christendom, but it's what I'm most familiar with. Like any of them, its greatest error is that it's a broad way and a wide gate.

If the Prodigal Son had returned to his father *before* he realized that his desires were base, he may have come to him with a different attitude. Instead of seeing that his desires were for pig food and saying, "Father I have sinned. . . . Make me like one of your hired servants" (Luke 15:18-19), he might have said, "Father, I have run out of money." Rather than saying, "*Make* me," he would say, "*Give* me." Instead of wanting to serve his father, his father would have become his servant. That is the category of many who sit in the midst of the body of Christ. The Law has not been used to show them that their sinful desires are *exceedingly* sinful. God is merely a means to further their own ends.

Admirers of the Admiral

Few see how great a sin it is to neglect evangelism because so few have any concern for the lost. Many within the Church think we are here simply to worship the Lord, and evangelism is for the few who have that gift. For them, their call to worship is a higher calling.

There was once a respectable captain of a ship whose crew spoke highly of him. They esteemed him to a point where everyone knew of the crew's professed love for him.

One day, however, the captain saw, to his horror, that an ocean liner had struck an iceberg and people were drowning in the freezing water ahead of his ship. He quickly directed his vessel to the area, stood on the bridge, and made an impassioned plea to his crew to throw out the life preservers. But instead of obeying his charge, the crew lifted their hands and said, "Praise the captain... praise you... we love you! You are worthy of our praise."

Can you see that their adoration *should have been displayed by their obedience to his command?* Their "admiration" was nothing but empty words.

If we worship in spirit, we will also worship in truth. To lift our hands in adoration *to* God yet refuse to reach out our hands in evangelism *for* God is nothing but empty hypocrisy. "You shall worship the Lord your God, *and Him only you shall serve"* (Matthew 4:10, emphasis added) is more than a mere satanic rebuke. If the average church made as much noise *about* God on Monday as it does *to* God on Sunday, we would have revival.

Evangelist Bill Fay has spoken at more than fifteen hundred conferences and churches. At each meeting, he asks how many have shared their faith in the previous year. Never once has he found a church where more than 10 percent raised their hands. In December 1999, at a church of nearly four thousand in southern California, he found that only twelve had shared their faith in the previous year. Early in 2000, *The Gatekeeper,* a publication of a major denomination, revealed that 97 percent of its membership will go to their graves without sharing their faith. Evangelism should be the life's breath of the body of Christ. If the breath is not in the body, neither is the life.

This lack of concern for the lost may be because Christians haven't been taught the biblical priority of evangelism—even though it is so evident in Scripture. However, if we are aware of our debt to both Jew and Gentile and yet refuse to hold out the Bread of Life, we prove to be the rich man of whom Jesus spoke.

> ➤ The problem is that we as Christians think that every person we
> speak to about the things of God is going to be contentious. We
> create our own monster. But that proves to be false . . . usually. You
> will find that most people appreciate that you have taken the time
> to care about them. Every now and then someone may be upset
> when you mention the things of God. If that happens, quickly

assure them that you didn't mean to offend them, look around for another horse, and get back in the saddle. Remember, eternal souls are at stake. —KC

I have always maintained that the very reason the Church exists on earth is to evangelize the world—to be a light in the darkness, to preach the gospel to every creature. If we worship God yet ignore His command to take the gospel to every creature, then our worship is in vain. We might draw near to Him with our lips, but our hearts are far from Him. I have often said that if you want to find the "evangelism" section in your local Christian bookstore, you had better take your magnifying glass. This is not the fault of the store; it is an indication of where the modern Church's priorities lie.

With this concern in mind, I wrote a book calling Christians back to evangelism, and I sent the manuscript to an organization to review it. If they thought the book had potential, they would forward it to a publisher. This is what the reviewer said:

> *I like the content of this manuscript very much. It contains a much-needed message for Christians about the Great Commission. Nevertheless, I see a serious problem when it comes to marketing this material. In order for a book to be marketed successfully in the bookstores, its identity must be clear. Where does this book go in the store? Is it a devotional book? or a Bible study manual? or is it an inspirational, "Christian living" book?*

On that basis, they rejected it. Despite its being a "much-needed message," they think the "serious problem" lies not in the Church itself but in the marketability of the message.

The Evangelical Enterprise

One of America's more popular preachers made a statement that clearly revealed his priorities. He said, "I don't think anything has been done in the name of Christ and under the banner of Christianity that has proven more destructive to human personality and hence counterproductive to the evangelism enterprise than the often crude, uncouth, and unchristian strategy of attempting to make people aware of their lost and sinful condition."

What does he consider to be the "evangelism enterprise" if it's not to warn sinners to flee from the wrath to come? It is clear what the problem is. Modern Christianity has degenerated into merely a means of self-improvement, self-esteem, and self-indulgence. It is self-centered rather than centered on and in the will of God. This same preacher reveals the cause of his error by saying, "The Ten Commandments were designed to put pride and dignity in your life."

That's not what the Bible teaches. The Ten Commandments were given to do the exact opposite: to humble us. They show us that sin is "exceedingly sinful" and that we are in desperate need of God's mercy. The Bible tells us that "the law brings about wrath" (Romans 4:15). It shows us the reality of God's wrath abiding on us. It is God's purpose for us to use the commandments lawfully—to make people aware of their lost and sinful condition, crude and uncouth though it may seem to some.

In Luke 16:19-31, the rich man's problem was that he was idolatrous. His understanding of God was wrong. He lacked the knowledge of God and therefore didn't fear God, and because he didn't fear God, he didn't obey Him. He didn't love his neighbor as himself. Lazarus was starving at the gate, and the rich man didn't care.

The irony of the story is that the rich man waited until he was in hell before he became concerned for others.

> ➤ I have members of my own family who may never see the need to escape hell until they're already there. Then they will be concerned. However, if I am not concerned about their eternal destiny *now*, there's reason for you to be concerned about mine. —KC

22 | WHOSE COOKIES?

If you witness regularly, you will know that many in contemporary America think they are good people. This is the fruit of a nation that has forsaken God's Law. The Law is "good," but when there is no knowledge of the Law, "good" becomes subjective. This was the case with the rich young man's question: "Good Teacher, what good thing shall I do that I may have eternal life?" (Matthew 19:16). Jesus reproved his misuse of the word *good*. The young man was one who used the word without knowledge of its true meaning.

Sinners often say similar things. An athlete may say that "the good Man upstairs" helped him win a race. Or someone may seek to justify his sin by saying, "You're a good person; tell me why the Bible says . . . " This is why I find it frustrating when I do a good deed for someone who doesn't know that I am a Christian. If I help push a car, for example, I don't want them to think, *"I knew there were still good people. That restores my faith in human nature."* Often, the more "good" people sinners can find, the more they will try to justify their own goodness and reject God's mercy. Like the rich young man, they need to be enlightened as to what *good* is. The way to do this is to follow the way of the Master and obliterate their self-righteous pretensions of goodness by using the Ten Cannons of God's Law. When the rich young man claimed that he had kept the six commandments that

Jesus enumerated (see Matthew 19:18-19), Jesus blew a cannonball-size hole in the young man's facade by telling him to go sell everything he had—thereby exposing that the young man had in fact broken the first and second commandments. His wealth was the god that he served.

A famous Rodgers and Hammerstein musical contains a song with the words, "Somewhere in my childhood, I must have done something good." The young lady who sings the song has fallen in love and is brimming with happiness. It was her way of saying that God was rewarding her with the blessing of true love because she deserved it. Although God does reward good and evil, the young lady's words exemplify the world's erroneous philosophy. Any good that comes our way doesn't come to us solely because *we* have done something good but because *God* is good. Until we understand that "there is none who does good, no, not one" (Romans 3:12), we will expect blessings because we think we are good and therefore deserve them. When life brings us suffering, we become angry at God because we think God owes us happiness.

The Law not only gives us understanding of the grace of the Cross but of the grace of life itself—that God has not dealt with us according to our iniquities. The only thing God "owes" us is wrath.

A man in a London airport decided to purchase some English butter cookies. After finding a seat, he opened the small tin, took out a cookie, and set the tin aside. When he had waited for his flight for some time, a middle-aged woman came and sat next to him. A moment later, without a word of permission, she reached down, opened the tin of butter cookies on the seat between them, and helped herself to a cookie. The man was astonished by what this complete stranger had just done! Suspecting that it might be a local custom, he smiled at her and took one himself. A few minutes later, she took another one. He smiled—awkwardly now—and took another cookie himself. The woman then took a third. *Who does this woman think she is?* Finally, she took the very last cookie, looked at the man, then broke it in half and offered it to him. *The audacity of the woman!* Other words, such as *brazen, rude, impudent,* and *presumptuous,* flashed through his mind.

As he was about to express his thoughts, he leaned forward and saw that his identical tin of cookies was still at his feet where he had set it. In an instant, he realized that *he* had been the brazen, rude, impudent, and presumptuous one. *He had been eating the cookies of a complete stranger!* He also realized how her response to his actions had in truth been very gracious.

An unregenerate world judges God as being the guilty party for the sufferings of humanity. As far as they are concerned, He is unjust. But the Law of God gives sudden light to their misconception. It reveals who is eating whose cookies. *We* are the ones who are in transgression. It dawns on us that we are *more* than brazenly impudent in our accusations. We are guilty criminals standing before an unspeakably holy and gracious Judge, accusing Him of transgression. In light of God's holiness, it is hard to understand why He continues to let a sinful race such as ours even draw another breath.

Facial Injuries

In March 1993, Sue and I were involved in a head-on collision. Fortunately, we sustained only minor head injuries. I was on my way back from the bathroom in the early hours of the morning when Sue got out of my side of the bed. For some reason she looked down for a second and we collided head-on, leaving us both with a fat lip. She presumed that I would see her in the dark, but I was coming from a bright light into a blackened room. I couldn't see a thing.

To presume that the unregenerate man already has the necessary light to be saved is to have a head-on collision with the many Scriptures asserting that there is *none* who understands (Psalm 53:1-3; Romans 3:11-12; 8:7). If we *adulterate* the Word of God by making the Law invalid in its lawful use of bringing light to sinners, we will have *adulterous* converts. Their hearts will love the world and the things in the world. But as we teach all nations and, like the disciples, do not cease "teaching and preaching Jesus as the Christ" (Acts 5:42), we will see sinners come to "know His will, and approve the things that are excellent, *being instructed out of the law*" (Romans 2:18, emphasis added). "Instructed out of the law" suggests more than a casual reference to the Ten Commandments. It means to rightly divide the word of truth, as a father at the head of a table would break up bread for his children.

Charles Spurgeon, in lecturing his students on evangelism, said, "Explain the Ten Commandments and obey the Divine injunction; 'Show my people their transgressions, and the house of Jacob their sins.' Open up the spirituality of the Law as our Lord did."

Pastor Jack Hayford wrote an article in which he spoke of many people coming to the Savior after he taught a series on the Ten Commandments. He said, "As a pastor I've had to come to terms with a devastating fact: Through my teaching on God's grace, an alarming number of my flock have perceived that there is nothing to learn from the Commandments now that the Law, as a schoolmaster, has gotten them to Christ. Too many view their conversion as a graduation from accountability to the Law...which violates Jesus' own objectives."

He saw the consequences of an imbalance of Law and grace as being a "devastating fact." I would go further and say that what has occurred throughout the Church as a result of the modern gospel is utterly disastrous. An "alarming number" of people think they have graduated from accountability to the Law and they therefore live their lives accordingly—in lawlessness. They have a mere "form of godliness" (2 Timothy 3:5). They are hearers and not doers; they listen to the sayings of Jesus but don't do them.

Sinning Converts

The direct result of the Church being confronted with biblical teaching on God's immutable Law would be that "sinning converts" would no longer be consoled in their sins. Instead of dealing with the symptoms of sinners' nonaccountability lifestyles—their fornication, pornography, lack of discipline, lack of holiness, theft, wife beating, adultery, drunkenness, lying, hatred, rebellion, greed, etc.—pastors would deal with the *cause*. They would say, as Scripture does, "A good tree *cannot* bear bad fruit" (Matthew 7:18, emphasis added), and "No spring yields both salt water and fresh" (James 3:12). They would gently inform their hearers, "It sounds as if you have had a spurious conversion and you need to repent of your lawless deeds and make Jesus Christ your Lord." Then, using the Law of God, pastors should show the "exceeding sinfulness" of sin and the unspeakable gift of the Cross. This should awaken the false converts, put most Christian psychologists out of business, and cut counseling to a minimum.

A clear understanding of the reality of true and false conversion would give light to church leaders who are horrified at the state of what they see as "the Church." One respected leader said: "In survey after survey, researchers find that the lifestyles of born-again Christians are virtually indistinguishable from those of nonbelievers. The divorce rate among Christians is identical to that of nonbelievers. Christian teens are almost as sexually active as non-Christian teens. Pornography, materialism, gluttony, lust, covetousness, and even disbelief are commonplace in many of our churches."

Such teaching would also stop the insanity of modern evangelism's zeal without knowledge by showing that the category of lukewarm "converts" doesn't exist. There is no division in the kingdom of God for those who are tepid. We should be either hot and stimulating or cold and refreshing. Lukewarm "converts" are not part of the body of Christ; they merely weigh heavy within the stomach of His body until He vomits them out of His mouth on the Day of Judgment (Revelation 3:16). Because they didn't pass through the jagged-edged teeth of the Law of God, they remain hard and impenitent; they were never broken by the Law that they might be absorbed into the bloodstream of the body of Christ, to become His hands, His feet, and His mouth. They never felt the heartbeat of God, so their hands didn't reach out in compassion to the lost, their feet were not shod with the preparation of the gospel of peace, and their mouths didn't preach the gospel to every creature. This mass of converts is like the "backslider in heart" who is "filled with his own ways" rather than the ways of God (Proverbs 14:14). Their "Here I am Lord, send *him*," doesn't come from a fear of man but from rebellion to the revealed will of the God they call Lord and Master.

> ➤ I was guilty of being *lukewarm*. My desire for the lost was sincere,
> but I resigned myself to tasks other than evangelism because I
> didn't feel comfortable or effective in sharing my faith. God has
> since turned up the heat, bringing me to an understanding of the
> Law, and now I'm on fire. —KC

In 2 Kings 4:38-41, Elisha tells his servants to make some stew. However, "one went out into the field to gather herbs, and found a wild vine, and gathered from it a lapful of wild gourds, and came and sliced them into the pot of stew, though they did not know what they were." When the stew was being eaten, the guests cried out, "Man of God, there is death in the pot!" Elisha then put flour into the mixture, and "there was nothing harmful in the pot."

The servants of the Lord have gone into the field of the world and brought back the wild vine of the modern gospel, which they've added to the Church. Now there is death in the pot. What should give life-sustaining nourishment instead leads to death. As sinners are fed a gospel poisoned by modern evangelism, they are consuming a deadly mixture and becoming false converts.

The answer is to add the flour of brokenness. Just as flour is created by a process of brokenness—grinding wheat into powder—so too the weight of the Law causes the hard shell of human pride to be broken. Sinners are humbled under the grinding millstone of God's Law.

The Wide Gate

Jesus said, "Enter by the narrow gate; for wide is the gate and broad is the way that leads to destruction, and there are many who go in by it. Because narrow is the gate and difficult is the way which leads to life, and there are few who find it" (Matthew 7:13-14). He warned that the way that leads to destruction is broad. But more than that, He said it had a gate, and that many would go in that way. If the way of destruction is the way of the world, which is the usual interpretation, why did Jesus call it a gate that many would enter? Surely if that were the case, He would have said that the ungodly are *born* into the way of destruction. This thought is supported by the conjunction Jesus used to join verses 13 and 14. He said that the way of destruction is broad and many will enter into it *because* the way that leads to life is narrow. There are only two gates: if they don't go through the narrow they will end up going through the broad. Jesus said the wide gate is entered *because* the other gate is narrow.

It seems that Jesus, in His usual consistency, is speaking of true and false conversions, as He did in the parables of the sower, the wise and foolish virgins, the wheat and tares, the good and bad fish, the goats and sheep, and the wise and foolish house builders. He again uses the word *many* here in describing the false converts, as He did when speaking of those "who practice lawlessness" whom He never knew (Matthew 7:22-23).

Remember what Jesus likened to the kingdom of God? He said, "It is like a man going to a far country, who left his house and gave authority to his servants, and to each his work, and commanded the doorkeeper to watch"

(Mark 13:34). The doorkeeper should keep the door. He should watch, to allow in only those who should enter. Instead, we have forsaken our watch.

Acceptable Fodder

Again, the false convert is like the Prodigal Son *before* he understood that his appetites were base, that he had "sinned against heaven" and in his father's sight. Because modern evangelism fails to show him heaven's holy standard, he doesn't see that his sin is against God. He thinks it is quite acceptable to desire pig food. He returns to his father, but his heart is still with the harlots. He chooses to be with the people of God, but he secretly enjoys the pleasures of sin for a season. He also finds it easier to lie (white lies) than to speak the truth, easier to steal (white-collar crime) than to pay for something, easier to lust than to be holy, easier to live for himself than for others, easier to feed his mind on the things of the world rather than the things of God.

The professing convert's mind is on the things of the flesh *because he is still "bound by iniquity,"* as was Simon the sorcerer (Acts 8:23). Like Simon, he may believe, associate with the apostles, and see the miracles of God. He may pass through the waters of baptism and impress many with his subtle trickery, but those who understand the parable of the sower and its broad implications are not swayed. They see beyond his sleight-of-hand illusion into reality. They can see, to their horror, that by preaching a Lawless gospel, the Church is ushering multitudes through hell's broad gate... a gate that is oiled smooth by modern evangelism.

Nehemiah chose two men to be in charge of gathering citizens for Jerusalem. Their names were Hanani, which means "gracious," and Hananiah, which means "Jah [Jehovah] has favored." Scripture tells us that Hananiah was faithful and that he feared God. This was what Nehemiah charged them: "Do not let the gates of Jerusalem be opened until the sun is hot" (Nehemiah 7:2-3). God has favored humanity with the gospel of grace. Those faithful servants who fear God will seek citizens for the New Jerusalem, and they will not open the gates until the sun is hot. They will let the heat of the Law do its most necessary work.

23 | RAIDERS OF THE CONTENTS OF THE LOST ARK

As I sat in my car, I expected to receive a punch in the face. I had screened a series of television ads warning of rock music that advocated violence and murder. One group that stirred me up was called the Dead Kennedys. Their songs include lyrics such as these: "I kill children. I love to watch them die. I kill children, make their mommas cry. Crush them under my car, I love to hear them scream. Feed them poison candy, spoil their Halloween." Now I wondered if I would get my face rearranged by someone who didn't like what I had done—a gentleman in his forties, with a clenched fist and a determined look on his face, who was making his way toward my car.

As he approached the open window of my vehicle, he looked me in the eye and asked, "Are you Ray Comfort?" I meekly said yes. Without saying a word, he lifted his large fist, thrust it through the window . . . *and dropped twenty dollars in my lap.* Then he walked off without a word.

It would seem that God delights in bringing victory out of what appear to be disastrous situations. Israel stood at the Red Sea, trapped, with no possible way of escape. Then God did the impossible. He brought victory out of what seemed to be a sure fist in the face. Daniel found himself in a pit of ferocious lions. Again, God brought victory in the face of what appeared to be a devastating defeat. Jesus of Nazareth had been crucified. The disciples had been scattered. It seemed that the body had been stolen. *How much darker could life become?* Then God revealed the brilliant light of the Resurrection. He brought the ultimate victory out of the ultimate disaster.

Criminal Moral Code

The story is told of a mother who rushed her ten-month-old baby, who had an acute case of diarrhea, to a hospital near her village outside Bogotá, Colombia. When she came to get her baby the next day, his eyes were bandaged and he was covered with splotches of blood. Horrified, she asked what was wrong with the boy, but she was coldly dismissed by a doctor who told her that the child was dying.

In a panic, she raced her baby to another doctor, who examined his wounds and said, "They've stolen his eyes!"

Her baby was the victim of "organ-napping," where eyes are removed and the corneas sold on the black market. In one sense, the baby was fortunate—most victims are murdered.

In 1980, when the Ten Commandments were removed from the schools of the United States, the eyes of an entire generation were removed. "The commandment is a lamp, and the law a light" (Proverbs 6:23). Removal of the Law left a generation in the dark as to moral absolutes. We now live at a time when a breed of human beings can kill, steal, hate, dishonor their parents, and revile God without qualms of conscience.

In June 1993, six teenage gang members in northwest Houston raped and killed two girls, aged fourteen and sixteen. The leader of the gang, nineteen-year-old Peter Cantu, boasted how he and other members abducted the two young girls and raped and sodomized them before strangling them. According to his testimony, "It took a while for them to die." They kicked one girl in the mouth with a steel boot, knocking out three of her teeth, then strangled her with a belt until it broke. They strangled the other girl with a shoelace. Then they took turns stomping on their necks to make sure they died. Heinous crimes like this one are all too common in our lawless society.

Today's generation doesn't just lack the moral values of its grandparents; it doesn't have any moral values. In previous years, there was a "moral" code even among criminals, an "honor among thieves"—that when they stole from someone, they didn't blast him with their guns as they left. This is no longer true. What one generation permits, the next embraces as normal. Years ago, a woman would hesitate to walk in front of a group of men because they might whistle at her and undress her with their eyes. Nowadays, her fear is that she will be viciously raped, sodomized, and murdered.

In light of the statistics we looked at in the beginning of this book, it would seem that the enemy has removed from the body of Christ its ability to be salt and light in a dark and decaying world. Jesus warned that if the salt lost its flavor, it would be good for nothing except to be trampled underfoot by men. This is why so many hold the Church in contempt. The world has trampled us underfoot and is reaping terrible consequences.

We are living in times of gross darkness, but this is not a God-forsaken world—it is a world that has forsaken God. He can, in His great sovereignty, open Satan's clenched fist and drop the riches of revival in the lap of the Church. Eric W. Hayden, in his book *Spurgeon on Revival*, writes, "Almost every book dealing with spiritual awakening or a revival of history begins by describing the pre-revival situation in approximately the same words. For instance, you will read such words as these: 'The darkness before the dawn'; 'The sleep of midnight and gross darkness'; or 'dissolution and decay.' W. T. Stead, who was a child of the Welsh Revival of 1859, when writing of the later revival in the twentieth century, said of it: 'Note how invariably the revival is preceded by a period of corruption.' "

There is great hope for the masses of false converts who sit within the Church. It is a rich field of evangelistic endeavor. The fact that they are still there is a testimony to the fact that they remain open to the things of God. History shows us that virtually every major revival of the past has been birthed out of a great awakening of those who thought they were saved but were not. I have seen this teaching awaken many false converts to their true state. As a result, God has soundly saved them, and from there they have begun to be the witnesses they are commanded to be.

Enemy Attack

Let me share with you some insightful words from Martin Luther. When speaking of using the Law as a schoolmaster to bring sinners to Christ, he said, "This now is the Christian teaching and preaching, which God be praised, we know and possess, and it is not necessary at present to develop it further, but only to offer the admonition that it be maintained in Christendom with all diligence. *For Satan has attacked it hard and strong from the beginning until present, and gladly would he completely extinguish it and tread it underfoot"* (emphasis added).

The enemy has duped the Church into believing that it is advancing by getting decisions for Christ. Instead, Satan has invaded our ranks and stripped the gospel of its power. The ark has been raided.

John Wesley said to those who forsook the Law in its capacity to prepare the heart for grace: "O take knowledge what Satan hath gained over thee; and, for the time to come, never think or speak lightly of, much less dress up as a scarecrow, this blessed instrument of the grace of God. Yea, love and value it for the sake of Him from whom it came, and of Him to whom it leads. Let it be thy glory and joy, next to the cross of Christ. Declare its praise, and make it honorable before all men."

I know that his words are true. The enemy hates this teaching. I have many examples of the enemy's resistance, but one stands out in my mind. For years as I spoke on this subject, we tried to get a master audiotape of this teaching so we could share it with others. Each time we listened to the tape, we would find a mysterious buzz running through it, or a fifteen-second silence in the middle of an important illustration. However, in the late nineties, I spoke at a large church in Chicago that had a sophisticated sound system. They gave me a one-hour audio master with no flaws on the entire tape. That is, except for an eight-word sentence that had to be removed because it was cut in half when the sound man turned over the tape. That eight-word sentence that had to be deleted from a one-hour teaching was: "Satan doesn't want you to hear this teaching."

The devil is quite happy if the Church sings of the power of the presence of God. What terrifies him is when the Church begins to use that power of God's presence to reach the lost. Remember that in the Old Testament, the ark of the covenant signified God's presence. But it wasn't the ark that God prized—it was what the ark *contained.* Have you ever wondered why God manifested Himself in such a glorious way that the priests in the house of the Lord could not minister (1 Kings 8:10-11)? It happened when the priests brought in the ark of the covenant. Scripture tells what was in the ark:

"Nothing was in the ark except the two tablets of stone which Moses put there at Horeb" (v. 9).

It seems God so esteems His Law that He could not withhold His glorious presence from the temple. The psalmist didn't say, "Oh, how I love Your *ark!*" Paul didn't say, "I delight in the *ark* of God." It was God's holy Law that they loved and revered. That Law was written with the finger of God. It was an expression of His character. We (as individuals and as the Church) are the "temple of the Lord," and when we give the Moral Law its rightful place, perhaps we will truly see that power of His presence—something that causes demons to tremble.

Satan hates this teaching for a number of other reasons:

o It awakens false converts to their true state.
o It puts the fear of God in the hearts of Christians and therefore enables them to walk in holiness.
o It gives Christians a reason to reach out to the lost. The issue isn't the happiness of sinners in this life, but their eternal welfare in light of a wrath-filled Creator.

The following letter is typical of how the Law does its wonderful work:

> *I am fifty-three years old. Have committed all sins. I was baptized and saved by God's grace . . . or so I thought. Have long sensed something wrong. Last week my wife picked up a free cassette tape ("Hell's Best Kept Secret") placed at the cash register of a local sandwich shop. I played the tape as soon as my wife gave it to me. Bingo! I immediately understood what was wrong. I had not been brought to salvation by the Law. At the same time I realized that evangelizing is what I am to do . . . I play "Hell's Best Kept Secret" daily and have lost count of how many times I have listened to it. God has my heart. I have absolute faith, a Bible, a box and lots of open air. Anxious for your reply.*

The enemy has attacked the use of the Law in evangelism "hard and strong from the beginning until present." However, our great consolation is that this is God's teaching, and I believe it is also His timing to bring it back to light.

At the risk of sounding melodramatic, I would ask you to consider read-

ing this book again, simply because experience has taught me that its truths
will soon be snatched from your mind... unless you make a concerted effort
to let them sink deep into the soil of your heart.

> ➤ I have read and reread this book many times. I have examined all
> the associated Scripture verses and determined that these princi-
> ples are biblically rock-solid. Nothing in all of our Christian life is
> more important than learning how to effectively bring lost souls to
> Christ. The Lord's passion is to reach sinners, saving them from the
> fire, and bring them into a loving relationship with the Father—
> that's what He lived and died for. If we are following in the foot-
> steps of Jesus, in the way of the Master, then it should also be our
> greatest desire to seek and save the lost. —KC

A. W. Pink writes, "It is true that [many] are praying for worldwide revival.
But it would be more timely, and more scriptural, for prayer to be made to
the Lord of the Harvest, that He would raise up and thrust forth laborers
who would fearlessly and faithfully preach those truths which are calculated to bring about a revival." The use of the Law in evangelism is the
golden key to revival. It is heaven's answer to the prayers of those who yearn
for the salvation of a hell-bound world. If we want to see revival, we must
take a firm hold of that key with unwavering conviction.

Do you remember King David's experience with the ark (2 Samuel 6:3-8)?
Instead of having the sons of Kohath carry it on poles as the Scriptures commanded, he put it on an oxcart. As the ark was brought into Israel, the oxen
stumbled and the ark began to rock. When Uzzah reached out his hand to
steady it, God killed him. R. C. Sproul rightly said that Uzzah presumed his
hand was cleaner than the dirt.

We have put the ark of the gospel on the oxcart of modern evangelism.
Sincere though we may have been, we dare not presume that we can reach
out our sinful hand and steady the things of God, and then carry on the way
we have been going.

If we fear our Creator, we must discard our own ways and then do all
things according to the pattern given to us in Holy Scripture.

THE FINGER OF GOD

In John 8:1-11, the story is told of a woman caught in the act of breaking the Law. She had violated the seventh commandment, and according to God's Law (and the woman's accusers) she deserved death. Ignoring their accusations, Jesus bent down and wrote something in the sand that caused His hearers to come under conviction and leave. Have you ever wondered what it was that He wrote in the sand? Some think He wrote the sins of those standing around Him. If that were so, no doubt He would have needed a good-sized area of sand to write on.

There is, however, another way to convince people that they have sinned against God, and it doesn't require much writing. I suspect that when Jesus stooped down, He wrote the Ten Commandments. After all, what else does God write with His finger (Exodus 31:18)? The work of the Law was written on the hearts of His hearers, and they left one by one as their conscience did its accusatory duty, boldly verifying the truth of each commandment. The Law strips us of our holier-than-thou self-righteousness. We dare not point a finger at another when the ten condemning fingers of a holy Creator are pointed at us.

It was the Law that brought the sinful woman to the feet of Jesus. It left her with no other option than to run from its wrath to the Savior. That's its function. The Law sends us to Jesus for mercy. But more than that, it is the wrath of the Law that makes us *appreciate* mercy.

We are also told in the story that Jesus began to write as if He didn't hear the voices of the accusers. There is no reasoning with the Law. There is no insanity plea. It is written in stone. It grimly says, "The soul who sins shall die" (Ezekiel 18:4, NIV). The Law demands nothing but death. It doesn't hear a cry for mercy; it is cold and unmerciful. The ten great rocks of wrath call for justice and justice alone.

The first time God wrote His Law, it was engraved on hard stone. If it was the Law that Jesus wrote in the sand, it was symbolic that it can be erased only with a movement of God's mighty hand. That was what He did at the Cross.

The Bible also tells us that the accusers came to "trap" Him. Arrogant and sinful man stands as the accuser of a sinless God. Do you know of a skeptic who mocks God and His Word? Does he accuse God of crimes against humanity? Does he think that God is responsible for famines and wars that are fought in His name? Then don't be afraid to shut the accuser up under the Law; stop his mouth (Romans 3:19). Turn the wrath of the Law on him. Show him that he, not God, is guilty of heinous crimes.

I have repeated myself a number of times in this book because I want these principles to become second nature to you. People sometimes ask what sort of results we achieve with this approach to evangelism. The criteria for judging success should not be how many "decisions" we get, but whether or not we are following the way of the Master. As we've seen in earlier chapters, both Jesus and the apostles used the Law in evangelism to bring the knowledge of sin to their hearers.

The testimonies throughout this book, as well as in the appendix, attest to the effectiveness of this method. However, using these principles does not, of course, *guarantee* the salvation of those to whom you witness. Let me share something very personal. To date, only one of my immediate family members has become a Christian. My father made a number of professions of faith over the years, but there was never any fruit to confirm that he was genuinely saved. In July 2002, he had a heart attack, fell, and broke his hip. He was rushed to the hospital and it was found that his heart was working at only 15 percent of its capacity. Because this happened seven thousand miles away in New Zealand, I asked a Christian friend there to visit him. He spent twenty minutes talking with my father, then prayed with him for several minutes. I called the hospital and asked Dad if he was happy about that. He whispered, "Very happy." During this time, my brother, sister, and mother (none of whom are Christians) kept saying that there was a tremendous peace about him. Four pastors then visited him, and each assured me that it was evident that my father was genuinely saved. He died two weeks later, after some horrible suffering. There were many tears shed, but I thank God that He is faithful to His promises, and I'm looking forward to seeing my father again.

It has been thirty years since my conversion, and I have diligently prayed for the salvation of my siblings and parents every day. They listen to me preach. They gladly take my books and tapes. They are not anti-Christian; they are just apathetic when it comes to their eternal salvation. *Yet I teach Christians how to share their faith effectively.* People draw on my "expertise" almost daily—and to my grief, *most of my own beloved family members are not saved.* This keeps me genuinely humbled and shows me that what I share is not a "sure-fire method" to get people into God's kingdom. If it were, my entire family would be saved. It is instead *biblical* evangelism, and that means that no one can come to the Son unless the Father draws him. It shows me that we can faithfully preach the Law, but it is a dead, dry, and dusty letter if not accompanied by the life of the Spirit.

The Measuring Rod

I'm sure you are equally concerned about the eternal salvation of *your* loved ones. In light of that, here's a thought-provoking question: How deep is your love? Here's the way to measure it. You are concerned about your immediate family's salvation, but what about your other relatives? How about your closest neighbors? What about strangers? Are you concerned for the salvation of people you don't know? How about your enemies? Are you deeply worried about the salvation of people who have crossed you? Do you love your enemies enough to be troubled by the fact that they will go to hell forever if they die in their sins?

Here's one way to demonstrate the depth of your love for others. Do you say hello to strangers? It may not come naturally to you, but for the sake of the gospel, I would like you to try this experiment. The next time you are leaving a restaurant, or anywhere where someone is standing—maybe at a counter waiting to pay for something—study the person's facial expression for a moment. It will probably look a little grumpy. We don't like to admit it, but each of us does look a little grumpy while we are waiting for something; the burdens of the day tend to find expression on our face. Here now is the experiment: Forget about your fears, and with a warm and enthusiastic tone in your voice, say, "Hello." Then watch the person's expression change from grumpy to happy. They will almost certainly smile.

If by chance the person doesn't respond, you have lost nothing (you will just feel slightly silly). However, if there is a smile, there's your opportunity for the gospel. Reach into your pocket, and say (as if you had just thought of it), "Oh … did you get one of these?" (I do this with our tract "101 of the World's Funniest One-Liners."[1] With this tract, instead of being seen as a religious nut who is trying to ram religion down the throat of a complete stranger, I am seen as someone who is trying to brighten up the person's day.)

Here is something else that I have found to be very effective. One way you can gain instant credibility with young people, particularly teenagers, is to approach a group of two or three and ask, "Did you guys see this?" Then show them our pink and blue "Curved Illusion" tracts. That will get their attention. For credibility, have about ten one-dollar bills in your pocket, and ask (while holding the bills in your hand), "What's the capital of England?" When someone responds, "London," give him or her a dollar bill. If they don't know, ask for the capital of France, or the capital of your state. After two simple questions (and after giving another dollar bill) say, "Which of you folks think that you are a good person?" Usually someone will say, "I'm a good person!" Then ask, "Do you want to go for twenty dollars? I will ask you three questions. If you prove to be a good person, I will give you twenty dollars. Do you want to give it a try?" If one is interested in trying, ask the person's name (let's say it's John) and say, "Okay, John. I'm going to give you three questions to see if you are a good person. Here goes. Have you ever told a lie?"

Most people will say that they have. If John says that he hasn't, press him with, "Have you never told a fib, a white lie, or a half truth?" When he says that he has, ask what that makes him. Most will say, "A liar," while others may say, "Not a good person." If John doesn't want to call himself a liar, ask him what you would be called if you lied. That usually gets the person to admit that someone who has lied is called a liar. Once he has admitted that he is a liar, ask him if he has ever stolen something. If he says he hasn't, smile as you tell him that you don't believe him because he has just admitted that he is a liar. Then say, "Come on, be honest. Have you ever stolen anything… in your whole life . . . *even if it's small?*" When he says yes, ask what that makes him. He will more than likely say, "A thief."

Third question: "Jesus said, 'Whoever looks upon a woman to lust after her has already committed adultery with her in his heart.' Have you ever looked at a woman with lust?" Males usually laugh when they say that they have, so soberly say, "John, by your own admission, you are a lying, thieving, adulterer at heart, and you have to face God on Judgment Day. If God judges you by the Ten Commandments on the Day of Judgment, do you think you would be innocent or guilty?" If he says, "Guilty," ask him if he would go to heaven or hell. If he responds, "Hell," ask if that concerns him. If he says, "Heaven," ask why. Then follow it with this verse (paraphrased): All liars will have their part in the lake of fire (Revelation 21:8). This verse may sound harsh, but quote it anyway. It's God's Word, and it is quick and powerful. Also quote 1 Corinthians 6:9-10: "Do not be deceived. Neither fornicators, nor idolaters, nor adulterers, nor homosexuals, nor sodomites, nor thieves, nor covetous, nor drunkards, … will inherit the kingdom of God." This covers the first, second, seventh, eighth, and tenth commandments. It also covers the fifth, because someone who proves to be a lying thief has dishonored his parents' name. All you are wanting to do at this point is to awaken the person to the standard of God's Law and to their desperate state before the Judge of the universe.

Show genuine concern for their plight. Try to ensure that all of your hearers (other teenagers) are listening and let them know that they too have to face God. Say, "I don't want you to go to hell. You don't want to go to hell, and God doesn't want you to go to hell. Do you know what He did so that you wouldn't have to go there?" Then take them to the Cross of Calvary, stressing their urgent need to repent, because they may not be here tomorrow.

➤ One night in July 2002, I spoke with two young brothers—Kevin, 16, and Adam, 12—at our camp. My wife, Chelsea, spoke with them for an hour about the gospel, then she came outside and asked me to give them my testimony, because Kevin's questions were so similar to my own as a teenager.

We three talked for two-and-a-half hours. Kevin and Adam were so sure of themselves, so knowledgeable about religion, life, justice, etc. They had every question you could think of, and they were good and smart questions. I started by being a good listener and kept my mouth shut and ears open. I commended them on their questions and praised them for being real thinkers. Kevin had good intuition about truth. He said, "Why doesn't God just put something within us so that we will know what is true?" I told him about his conscience (the word *conscience* means "with knowledge") and his own spirit that will testify with God's Spirit that Jesus' words are true. I shelved other questions until later (about the Bible, evolution, etc.), but they never came up again.

I asked Kevin if he considered himself to be a good person. He said yes. We went through most of the Ten Commandments and the consequences of sin according to God's Word. I used many analogies: If someone raped and murdered his mom, the man would deserve judgment; the sheep standing on green grass looks clean until it snows, etc. Kevin and Adam threw in some divertive questions, but I tried my best to stay on course for the next half hour. Adam eventually got cold and went inside. Kevin and I sat and talked for another forty-five minutes. I repeatedly talked about his guilt and the consequences of sin in hell until I felt he understood. He said, "God is angry?" I told him that He was, because "God is angry with the wicked every day" (Psalm 7:11). When I felt that Kevin's mouth was shut up under the Law and he knew he was guilty, I moved on to the Cross and God's mercy (giving the analogy of the guilty criminal whose fine has been paid).

Adam came back and listened to me talk to Kevin. I gave them my testimony and explained how I felt different after I had asked God to forgive and change me. Adam said, "It sounds like you felt almost like you were *born* again." I could hardly believe the words he chose to use. I couldn't have asked for a more beautiful confirmation and encouragement from the Lord—he was getting it! We then talked about why Jesus is the only way to be saved (the parachute given by the captain, Jewish sacrifices being a picture of Jesus' sacrifice). We talked about the difference between believing in Jesus and being born again. We talked about the horrible offense of rejecting God's Son when He is available to all people everywhere. (I gave him the parable of the vineyard owner, Jesus' words, etc.) I stressed the importance of the blood of Christ, the Resurrection, and that good works will never work. We talked about a good tree producing good fruit, not fruit producing a good tree.

Kevin said things like, "I never understood why Jesus died on the cross until tonight." "So Jesus is our parachute!" Then he said, "You can't understand God until you understand why Jesus died on the cross."

Kevin asked if I ever sin. I explained the difference between running into sin and falling into sin. I also used the analogy of crocodile-infested waters to describe my desire to honor my Father's wishes.

Adam then said, "I'm getting a tingly feeling all over my body right now." He started to show signs of tenderness of heart. Kevin said he did too and that he felt that way whenever he is around someone he knows God is with. Adam said with tears in his eyes, "This is a big night for me. I want to go write in my journal about this whole experience. This is a turning point for me, even if I am so young."

I told them the whole gospel, went over the Law and the Cross again, and they both seemed to understand why Jesus is the only way to heaven. It made sense and was no longer offensive to them. I asked Kevin if he thought he could die tonight. He said yes, and we talked about the importance of getting his heart right with God. I told him that if he died in his sins, he was an enemy of God— that God's wrath was upon him and that he would perish under His judgment. He must turn from his sin once and for all and put his faith in Jesus Christ alone to save him. I turned and applied it all to Adam also. I asked if I could pray for them both. They said yes. I prayed, and then asked them if anything I said offended them. They shook their heads no. I told them my motivation was that I want them to accept God's offer of love and forgiveness and escape the wrath to come.

They mentioned how Kevin had almost not come there that night and how thankful they were to be having this talk with me. I told them it is because God loves them and wants them to know the truth. When I shared about the Ethiopian eunuch to whom God sent a messenger, Adam said, "Just like you being here right now!" I also reminded them not to let this night pass, but to mark it in their minds and hearts and let it be a new beginning, a new start, a new direction in their lives. I hugged them both and told them I loved them. They said good night and went into their rooms; I sat down and prayed for their salvation.

Two days later, Adam told me he'd been up all night thinking about what we had discussed. So had his brother. Then he said, "I want to reject all my sin and put my faith in God." He told me he wanted to be born again. I sat next to him and watched as he prayed. Almost immediately, he told me that he really loved his family and wanted to share the gospel with them as soon as possible. —KC

Your Role in Witnessing

Take great confidence that you don't have to convince a sinner of the reality of Judgment Day. That is the work of the Holy Spirit. John 16:8 says that the Holy Spirit "will convict the world of sin, and of righteousness, and of judgment." The mind of the unsaved cannot understand the judgment of God: "The wicked in his proud countenance does not seek God; God is in none of his thoughts.... *Your judgments are far above, out of his sight*" (Psalm 10:4-5, emphasis added). The word used for *convict* in John 16:8 also means "to convince." Only the Holy Spirit can *convict* a sinner about his sin and *convince* him of judgment. We can't do that. All we can do is plant the seed of truth. When the sinner repents and trusts the Savior, it is then that the Holy Spirit dwells within him and seals him (John 14:17; Ephesians 1:13).

Neither is it our job to convince someone of the deity of Jesus. When Peter identified Jesus as the Son of God, He said, "Blessed are you, Simon Bar-Jonah, for flesh and blood has not revealed this to you, but My Father who is in heaven" (Matthew 16:17). It is God who reveals that great truth, so let Him do that task.

Forsaking the use of the Law in evangelism has made many in the Church think that apologetics is our great weapon in the battle for the salvation of the world. One could make a convincing case for that thought in this "age of enlightenment," when issues such as evolution and atheism have made these times unique in history. However, arguments come from the sinner's *intellect*. The ungodly mind is like a brick wall; it has been built to keep God out. It is at *enmity* with Him. It refuses to bow to the Law of God, "because the carnal mind is enmity against God; for it is not subject to the law of God, nor indeed can be" (Romans 8:7). The human mind lays up arguments against God, so if you stay in that area you can expect a vicious battle. It is the mind that the Bible cites as the place of hostility: "And you, who once were alienated and *enemies in your mind* by wicked works, yet now He has reconciled" (Colossians 1:21, emphasis added). This wall of antagonism is hard and immovable, so make a habit of going around it. Learn to speak directly to the conscience (this is good news—it means we can be effective in our Christian witness without having to learn how to pronounce *Australopithecus afarensis* or to define the fossil record). When you address the conscience, other things become nonissues. The conscience is that part of human nature that isn't an enemy of God. The conscience is God's ally. It doesn't speak against the Law of God; it speaks for it. It is the work of the Law written on the heart, "bearing witness" (Romans 2:15). The conscience *testifies* for God. It is the trustworthy witness who points out the guilty party in the courtroom. It presents evidence of the Law's transgression. Because of what it does, we should make room for it to speak as quickly as possible. If we want to win our case, we must bring out our star witness and put it on the stand to give it voice. We want to stop the mouth of the criminal, and that's what the lawful use of the Law does (Romans 3:19). It condemns the guilty and drives him to give up his defense, so that he will be forced to look solely to the judge for mercy.

> ➤ Please don't skim over the preceding paragraphs. They speak of something so important that it should be written across the sky. If you understand the biblical principle of appealing to a person's conscience through the Moral Law of God, it will revolutionize the way you share your faith. —KC

How wonderful it is, when talking with someone about the things of God, not to be thrown into panic when the person responds, "I'm a Roman Catholic." Before I understood the use of the Law I would think, "Horrors! Now I'm going to have to deal with transubstantiation, Mariology, papal infallibility, the mass, etc." Not so now. I simply say, "Would you consider yourself to be a good person?" I do the same with a Protestant. I do the same with a Muslim, an intellectual, an evolutionist, an atheist, etc. It is simply a matter of moving from the intellect to the conscience. Many Catholics have heard much about Jesus, the Cross, sin, and salvation, but most have never heard the true gospel. Our mandate is to "preach the gospel to every creature" (Mark 16:15), and it is the *gospel* that is the "power of God to salvation" (Romans 1:16). Once the Law is manifest, the usual rational arguments that so often cloud the issue become irrelevant.

Kirk shared the teaching on the use of the Law one morning at a large church in Ohio. A few days later we received an e-mail that shows the power of the Law to prepare the heart for the gospel:

> *I just heard you speak this morning. I'm a Catholic—have been all my life. I can't even begin to tell you how much your message affected me. I've been quite speechless all day long, and I'm rarely quiet. It's been a good quiet because I am so humbled all of a sudden. I want to "take the ball and run with it," as you put it. However, I'm confused. You see, I've never been hit that hard in any Catholic service I've ever attended. How do you minister to Catholics? I can tell you that most of them don't want to hear anything unless it's from a priest. I could be wrong and hope that I am . . . but I'm full of questions on what to do next. Everyone needs to hear this message. My life has been changed since this morning. I can't thank you enough. I'm going to end here and start reading the book I purchased this morning! Thanks again and God bless you!*

As mentioned earlier, we are to reason with a sinner using the Law. Never underestimate the power of reasoning about the reality of hell. Learn how to give extreme scenarios that stretch him into a moral dilemma. Say, "Imagine if someone raped your mother or sister, then strangled her to death. Do you think God should punish him?" If the person is reasonable, he will say, "Yes, of course. That makes sense." Then ask, "Do you think He should punish thieves?" Then follow with liars, etc. Tell him that God is perfect, holy, just, and righteous; that He will punish all sin, right down to every idle word, and that His "prison" is a place called hell.

Always take him back to his personal sins. Remember to speak to his conscience ("You know right from wrong. God gave you a conscience," etc.). Some people teach of a temporary hell (purgatory), or of annihilation (the belief that the soul ceases to exist after death). The Bible, however, speaks of conscious, *eternal* punishment. If he thinks that is harsh, tell him that it is. If we think eternal punishment is horrific, what should we do about it? Shake our fists at God? When such foolish thoughts enter our minds, we must go to the foot of the cross and meditate on the great love God has for us—that He was in Christ reconciling the world to Himself. Then, we must turn any horror into concern, and plead with sinners to flee from the wrath to come.

C. S. Lewis seemed to sum up the terrors of hell when he said, "There is no doctrine which I would more willingly remove from Christianity than the doctrine of hell, if it lay in my power. But it has the full support of Scripture and, especially, of our Lord's own words; it has always been held by the Christian Church, and it has the support of reason."

That's why the Law is so wonderful. It gives hell rationality, and thereby gives access to a heart that was once closed. I found this to be the case just after the September 11, 2001, terrorist attacks on New York City. It's not every day that you see, live on television, three thousand people go to their deaths in a matter of seconds. The experience made people around the world realize both their vulnerability and their mortality.

A Unique Witnessing Opportunity

It was in that climate that I found myself speaking to hundreds of unsaved university students. I have often said that one good session of open-air preaching can reach more people in thirty minutes than the average church reaches in one year. There are a few drawbacks, though. It's difficult to get, and then hold, a crowd. Often hecklers create confusion. However, I think I may have found something that can reach more people in thirty minutes than many good open-air preaching sessions.

In August 2001, I called a large university in my home city (Christchurch, New Zealand) and spoke to the president of the Students' Association. I said that I would be visiting in October and would give any atheist an honorarium of $100 to speak for twenty-five minutes on "Why There Is No God." It would be a "debate," but without arguing. I would go first for twenty-five minutes, simply presenting my case for God's existence, and then my opponent would present his case and get $100 for his time.

He said it would be interesting, but doubted if many would show up as it was in the middle of exams. I said that I would like to try it anyway. A short time later I was informed that a resident professor of philosophy had agreed to the debate.

Here is the text of the student president's promotional letter:

As exams are now with us, many students will be praying for a miracle. But is anybody listening? UCSA is proud to present the title fight to decide the heavyweight theory of the world.

In the dark corner, hailing from UC's Philosophy Department and weighing in on the side of atheism—Dr. Paul Studtman.

In the corner bathed in an ambient glow, the author of How to Make an Atheist Backslide,* *and weighing in on the side of God Almighty— Ray Comfort.*

At stake is a genuine offer from Ray Comfort of $US250,000 for anybody who can provide scientific evidence for the theory of evolution. For that sort of money Turi Hollis, the university chaplain, has been digging around in his "not for public disclosure" files.

This meeting will not be broadcast on any network and is exclusive to: Shelley Common Room (upstairs at UCSA) at 1 p.m., Wednesday, October 24.

I arrived in the hall on that date at 12:40 p.m. and found about a dozen people. At 12:45 there were about one hundred. At 1:00 the room was packed with hundreds of students, sitting on the floor, crammed into the doorways, and even packed down the halls. No doubt they wanted to see a Christian get eaten alive by a professor of philosophy.

* Now titled *God Doesn't Believe in Atheists* (Bridge-Logos Publishers).

I spoke for twenty-five minutes. The outline for God's existence was: (1) the evidence of creation; (2) the evidence of the Bible; and (3) the evidence of the conscience. When it came to the evidence of the conscience, I explained that if someone wasn't a Christian, his conscience was deadened, and I was going to resurrect it by going through the Ten Commandments. I explained that it wasn't going to be a pleasant experience—it was like looking into the mirror first thing in the morning (not a pretty sight)—but that it was most necessary in order to present my case, so I asked them to be patient with me. That gave me license to go through each of the Ten Commandments, then into Judgment Day, the Cross, faith, and repentance.

The professor then shared his thoughts. His words were so big and his sentences so long that it was easy to forget the subject on which he began the sentence. Frankly, it was hard to stay awake. Then he had to leave after he finished speaking—which left me with hundreds of unsaved students asking questions such as "Who made God?" (one of my favorites).

During the presentation, I explained that evolution was unscientific and that there was no proof for the theory. I then told them to go to www.wayofthemaster.com and collect Dr. Kent Hovind's $250,000 offer—if they could provide any scientific evidence for evolution. During the question time a student said, "I would like to know if anyone *does* have scientific evidence for evolution." There was a deafening silence as everyone waited for someone to say there was evidence. No one said a thing, so we went on to the next question.

One older man (perhaps a professor) sarcastically asked if I believed in aliens. I told him that I did, and that California was having a problem with them coming across the border from Mexico. Everyone laughed, and he sat down.

I thanked them for listening. They gave rousing applause. Every one of the 250 tracts I brought was taken from the table. Most of them were our skeptics' mouth-stopping tract, "Science Confirms the Bible." The professor was pleased with his one hundred dollars, and I was ecstatic.

This is something that anyone can do. It is much easier than open-air preaching. There are no hecklers, the crowd is already there ... and no one will beat you up. This is an unprecedented opportunity. Don't let fear stop you.

Remember, you don't have to debate or even have a question-and-answer time—just pray, present your evidence, and make tracts available. Make sure that you speak first so that you won't be tempted to answer your opponent's objections and get distracted from your mandate. That mandate is simply to present the gospel—which is "the power of God to salvation."

Let me close with a quote by George MacLeod of Scotland:

> I simply argue that the cross should be raised at the center of the market-place as well as on the steeple of the church. I am recovering the claim that Jesus was not crucified in a cathedral between two candles, but on a cross between two thieves; on the town's garbage heap; at a crossroad, so cosmopolitan they had to write His title in Hebrew and Latin and Greek . . . at the kind of a place where cynics talk smut, and thieves curse, and soldiers gamble. Because that is where He died. And that is what He died for. And that is what He died about. That is where church-men ought to be and what church-men ought to be about.

A few months before our friend Bill Bright went to be with the Lord he said (referring to the modern church), "We need a bombshell dropped onto the Laodicean church of today." I am convinced that the use of the Law in evangelism is that bombshell. Please, take a few moments to read the testimonies on the next several pages to see the potential of this teaching to bring about genuine revival.

Thank you for being open-minded and allowing me to share my heart with you. May God continue to bless you and grant you your heart's deepest desires as you delight yourself in Him.

APPENDIX: TESTIMONIES

When we follow in the way of the Master and use the Law to bring the knowledge of sin, it is sure to affect our witness. The following testimonies relate how individuals have been affected by learning this biblical principle.

o o o o o

I believe I became a Christian in 1997, at the age of thirty-seven. I *thought* I was a Christian for thirty-two years, but in truth I believe I was a false convert. I responded to the very *first* invitation that I ever heard to receive Jesus Christ as Savior at Vacation Bible School during the summer of 1965. I remember *running* from the back of the church to meet up front with someone (apparently I was already a back-pew sitter!). I went to a room with a very kindly lady and I vaguely recall her going through some Scriptures. She led me in a sinner's prayer and probably assured me that if I "really meant" what I prayed, I could be assured that I was saved for eternity. For the next thirty-two years, if anyone asked me if I was a Christian, I would state positively that I was.

Tragically, no one ever told me to reflect my life in light of God's holiness during those years. During the few times growing up that I *did* doubt my salvation, friends and family would assure me that I was saved. No one seemed to base this upon Biblical indicators of salvation, but upon the fact that I "prayed a prayer" when I was five years old.

I always thought of myself, and was thought of by others, as basically a "good person." I was fairly "innocent" too, at least when I compared myself to others. I was considered a very "positive" person—about situations, about other people, and about *myself*. When I *did* have an occasional twinge of guilt about some wrongdoing or offending others, it was brief and shallow.

My wife and I were attending a solid Baptist church in 1997. By God's grace someone gave me a copy of "Hell's Best Kept Secret." He asked me to listen and tell him what I thought of it. After I heard the tape I realized, for the first time, that I was *not* "basically a good person." I responded to God's command to *examine myself*, whether I was in the faith (2 Corinthians 13:5). "Reprobate!" seemed to be the reply. I finally saw that I was wicked and undone in the eyes of a thrice-holy God. I cried on and off for days and acknowledged to God: "I'm not a good person! I'm not a good person! I'm a liar and a thief and a murderer and an adulterer. I've broken every single one of Your commandments my whole life—*no wonder* I deserve to go to hell!" My whole view of myself was crushed. The "good" person that I thought I was for those thirty-two years was actually very wicked and deceived when I finally compared myself to God's standard.

I grew up during the "God loves you and has a wonderful plan for your life" era. I loved myself plenty already. My family loved me (and so did my girlfriends), and I thought my plan for life was pretty great. God wasn't really a major part of my life picture. I *definitely* didn't love Him with all my heart, soul, mind, and strength. Not only did "Hell's Best Kept Secret" cause me to realize that I wasn't saved, it helped me realize that the full gospel of Jesus Christ is *not* being preached today.*

○ ○ ○ ○ ○

I was one of those who thought that preaching "Christ crucified" alone [without the use of the Law] was the way to go as far as winning souls was concerned. Boy, was I wrong. I have told people about Jesus many times in

---

* Robert Alan Holm, the gentleman who sent this first testimonial, called our ministry in October 2002 and asked if he could visit us. He told me that he was a great-, great-, great-grandson of Charles Spurgeon. I was skeptical until he showed me comprehensive documentation that proved he was indeed related to the great preacher. What a blessing—that God would use this teaching to save a descendent of the Prince of Preachers. Mr. Holm has a Web site (www.cyclonegraphics.com/ holmministry) where you can learn more about his ministry.

my life and have led many in the "sinner's prayer," and then afterwards I would ask them, "If you died right now, where would you go?" Many of them would answer, "Heaven," and I would say, "That's right." What I did was help to create false converts who are now convinced that there is no way they could go to hell. I have really messed up. I never again want to be that type of hindrance to the body of Christ, or to those who are lost and going to hell. You have truly helped to change my whole understanding of salvation and soul winning.

○ ○ ○ ○ ○

Whew! This is a very "meaty" book! It is not something to read lightly. After reading the quote about Kirk's own reaction to the truths of this book, I can certainly echo his sentiment! While the concept of personal repentance is not new to me or my witness, this book is a powerful affirmation of the urgency for including the Law in the gospel presentation, so that it can do the work that it was created to do. I wonder if we (the modern evangelical church, in general) do not omit the Law in our witness out of a misplaced sense of compassion, i.e., that we can spare the sinner the anguish of person-ally interacting with the Law as a condemned person. What that compas-sion overlooks is the fact that this is exactly what we need to do. I think so far the most powerful analogy in this book for the works of the Law and grace is the needle (which must be sharp and strong) and the thread, which is silken and follows the needle in after it has opened the way.

○ ○ ○ ○ ○

I've always had a hard time witnessing to people—knowing how to approach someone and what to say. Kirk's story about witnessing at the golf course brought a new light to my heart. Everyone knows the Ten Command-ments, but I would never have thought to use them to witness to anybody. That story was so touching and uplifting. To know that you can use a tool like the Ten Commandments to lead someone to the Lord is just amazing. I've been browsing through your Web site and I can't believe all the things I have read so far. I am an assistant youth leader. I'm just starting out, but this site has taught me so much more about how to witness, among other things, that I really feel will be beneficial to bring to my youth.

o   o   o   o   o

I just have to tell you how thankful I am for your ministry. It is causing a revo-lution in my life. Yesterday I watched the new video on your site, "How to Break the Ice." Today I visited a nearby skateboard park and had a great con-versation with four skaters. I went through the Law with them, and talked about judgment, etc. Even though we had fun, it was easy to see conviction come over them. I couldn't believe my ears when one of them suddenly folded his hands, as if his friends weren't there, and began to pray for forgiveness! Wow. After evangelizing for thirteen years, in street meetings and door-to-door, *with no fruit at all,* to see teens have true conviction and pray from their hearts because they know they are sinners . . . well, this is not a normal experi-ence for me, to say the least. It's like heaven has come to earth (and it has).

o   o   o   o   o

In all honesty I have been hiding in the safety zone of the church for the last five years. I have always believed that my big destiny was to teach, and I have been perfectly comfortable doing that until I heard "Hell's Best Kept Secret." *Congratulations*—you and the Lord have blown me right out of my comfort zone! If I don't do something with this fire inside me it will burn out. . . . I want to bring people into the kingdom of God.

o   o   o   o   o

I have started to use your method of going through the Ten Command-ments one by one and showing how we have all broken each one and are under the death penalty. Last night a lady came under the conviction of the Holy Spirit and gave her life to the Lord. She said that she had never seen the depth of her sin like that before—and she was weeping that she had grieved God. She said that she could not wait but needed to commit her life there and then. Praise God for His truth and for people like you who have redi-rected us back to the core of the gospel message. I have never been afraid of speaking on sin and hell before, but this is first time that I have actually used the Ten Commandments in such a way.

o   o   o   o   o

My wife and I both listened to the tape "Hell's Best Kept Secret," and we believe you are right on with your teaching. I have also been reading [your book].... This is one of those life-defining moments for me.... It's a great book because it makes everything clear and destroys my excuses. How can we not preach the Law and the consequences of sin? I'll give this book to all my youth pastor friends and anyone else who can read! Thank you for your insight and boldness to stand in the face of sixty years of modern evangelism and its diluted message.

o   o   o   o   o

I was so surprised to see Kirk Cameron at a funeral. When he got up to speak and started talking about the Ten Commandments, I thought, "Oh, he's just going to be superficial; how sad." Then he started being direct, and he made me think about my life. It seemed like everyone in the room disappeared and I was totally focused on his message. I was blessed by it and I can't get it off my mind.

o   o   o   o   o

Mr. Cameron, I heard you speak in Knoxville, and I have never had the gospel preached to me in the way you did. You made a great impact on my life which I will always remember. Thank you for your dedication and your love for the Master. Because of your message, I have rededicated my life to Christ, and both my wife and I are going to live our lives as we should, and live for Him and praise His name. Hopefully I can take a little of what you said and spread it to someone else. I am only a vessel and I want the Lord to use me in any way possible. Again, I just wanted to thank you for your obedience to what God has called you to. Yesterday I had the privilege of leading three folks to the Lord. I talked to two sisters (in their early twenties), and I took them through the Law first and then grace. Their father overheard and came in, and all three bowed their hearts to the Master! I have led more people to the Lord in the last forty days than I did in all of last year. Knowing what to teach and how to present it gives me confidence. I'm not trying to beg people to take Jesus—no, after they see how utterly sinful they really are, they want Him, really want Him.

o   o   o   o   o

For a long time I allowed myself to fall into the "soft" gospel approach—witnessing without preaching the reason why sinners will go to hell. There are so many subtle reasons to "soften the blow" to make it "seeker-sensitive," but it cheats those I witness to. Your tape has changed my perspective and my outlook on sin as more serious, which drives a greater burden for witnessing.

○ ○ ○ ○ ○

I wanted to tell Kirk Cameron that I was so impressed with his lesson last night. I was at the First Baptist Church of Concord in Knoxville, Tennessee, and was just amazed. I have been a Christian for ten years and have always struggled with witnessing. I have always had a desire to witness, but have usually failed. I love this approach and I will be learning as much about it as I can so that I can share the good news and reach people.

○ ○ ○ ○ ○

About two months ago I gave your book to a friend of mine who is a pastor. Since he has read the book I have seen a great change in him. I believe your book is crucial for many reasons. It all goes back to Truth vs. "feel good" gospel. And your book has not only caused me and my pastor friend to scream bloody murder over the false gospel that is being presented time and time again, but it has also caused us to check the status quo on all things. It has awakened us to challenge the way our church has operated—seeking "success" instead of excellence, preaching "feel good" messages instead of God's Word and Truth.

○ ○ ○ ○ ○

Just listened to Ray Comfort's message—*it is terrific!* I confessed my sins of omission in not preaching the Law, which at one time I did, but got away from doing. This is revival in my heart! *Thank you, Lord Jesus!*

○ ○ ○ ○ ○

I am forty-two years old and have shared my belief in Christ for almost twenty years, but I have never seen anything as powerful as the teaching I have received from you guys. I have watched young men weep when confronted with their sin against God, and have watched old men literally fall to their knees when they see themselves the way God sees them. (It is incredible—I have never witnessed anything so awesome in my life.) I have seen confessed witches' hearts change. I have seen hundreds of young men and women in juvenile detention cry and squirm under the weight of the Law. I feel that God has given me a new direction in life because of your willingness to obey. Thank you. Praise God for what you are doing, and may His blessing continually be upon you.

o   o   o   o   o

This letter isn't intended to be some "pour your heart out, gushy, tearjerker, crying in the coffee" letter (I do that with my Lord). It is just to say that your book woke me up. I realized while reading that I was taking advantage of the grace Christ had given me. I saw myself before a holy, gracious God, and was found lacking.

o   o   o   o   o

I just got through reading [your book]. It has deeply challenged everything I have ever thought about witnessing to nonbelievers. I have also listened to your tape "Hell's Best Kept Secret" several times, and it has been a blessing to me. I'll be the first to admit that I have tried to bring sinners to salvation with the "God-shaped hole in your heart" style of evangelism. It's interesting that I tried to witness that way, because I knew (my conscience bearing witness) that I myself was a wicked, nasty sinner who was deserving of eternal flames. Yet I would preach "Jesus loves you." I guess I was just a product of modern evangelism. Anyway, I'm grateful for what the Lord has done in your life and how He is using you to reach sinners. In my witnessing now, I make sure to use the Ten Commandments, knowing that the sinner cannot "know sin, but by the Law." However, I'm still not where I need to be in witnessing. I ask that you would pray for boldness for me in witnessing. I have no problem talking to people, it's just that initial contact that I struggle with.

o   o   o   o   o

I have been camp pastor at four youth camps so far this summer and am halfway through. I must say that your tape "Hell's Best Kept Secret" and your book . . . have had a huge impact on my ministry. The messages that I have preached and my dramas are flooded with God's Law, and I have seen so much more brokenness in the decisions this summer than ever before. A church in Louisiana had sent me your tracts for years, and I had gotten your book about a springboard to powerful preaching many years ago, but this has had a *much* bigger impact on my life. I wanted to say thanks for sharing this.

o o o o o

I must admit, I went to the church with great excitement to get to see Kirk Cameron. I was a big fan. Not that I don't like you now, but it's for such a different reason. I was amazed, blown away by what you said. I soaked it all up and am still on fire because of it. I told everyone in the weeks leading up to your appearance that I was going to get to see you, maybe get an autograph. Once I heard you I forgot why I had come in the first place. I even got up to the table to talk to you, and instead of asking for an autograph, I had to tell you that I learned from you. I wasn't interested in you as a star, but as a brother in Christ—let me tell you, that amazes me. I totally got what you were saying! I had a chance to witness to my cousin last week, and I really messed it up and didn't even get a single point out. I was so disappointed in myself, but I am going to study my notes that I took and pray about it, and I will go back to her. I am so excited about this Web site and about the Academy. I plan on learning everything I can and really doing my job as a Christian by spreading the good news. I am so excited—I told everyone I saw about it today. I can't stop thinking and talking about it. I want to thank you for showing me a different way. It just makes so much sense!

o o o o o

I'm a relatively new Christian. Through the loving grace of Christ Jesus, I am saved.

My family owns and operates some of the largest "adult" retail stores in the country. . . . Ashamedly, I rewrote the marketing plan to target women and couples. As a result, the annual gross profits went from $300,000 to over $15 million in six years with the opening of a third store. . . .

After watching *Hell's Best Kept Secret* on a locally broadcast Word Pictures program, it had a profound effect on my life. No other presentation of the truth had such a powerful and piercing effect on me. I had heard "Jesus loves me and has a wonderful plan" a few times in the past. Yet it made no sense.... [Now I can see that] the Law was missing! The Lord touched my heart with his truth and saving grace at that very moment. As a result, I have turned my efforts from furthering the world's cause into advancing the Kingdom of God.

God has forgiven me ... [and] I am no longer part of that business or the porn industry.... As you can imagine, the family relationships are strained at best.

o o o o o

A friend recently directed me to your Web site to listen to "Hell's Best Kept Secret." I was so excited after hearing the message that I downloaded all of your messages available for that purpose and am in the process of listening to them. They have stirred within me the fire to share my faith with others like never before! I accepted Christ thirty years ago, but my passion for evangelism has waxed and waned over the years ... until now. Some of your examples in "How to Have Passion for Souls" were especially striking, and caused me to think about the lost in a new way. This morning, I went running with a group of men. We run three times a week for fellowship and exercise. At thirty-eight, I am the youngest of the group. One of our runners is a fiftyish surgeon of Jewish descent who does not know Christ, and in fact does not know Judaism either. He shared that his eighty-year-old father has a tumor in his kidney that may be cancer. This brilliant, intense surgeon looked me straight in the eyes and said, "What happens to your soul when you die?" I immediately thought of just answering his question and seeing where the conversation went from there, but then I stared back into his eyes for several seconds and saw pain, fear, and uncertainty—things rarely seen in men of his intellect and position until they are face-to-face with death. This stirred within my heart such compassion for him that I explained to him why we are all sinners, using the methods you shared in your sermons regarding the Ten Commandments. We went around the circle and each man admitted that he had, at some time in his life, broken every commandment. (These are prominent men in the community who are disciples of Christ.) Then I explained to him that the penalty for sin is to spend eternity in hell—eternal torment and separation from God. Then I explained that Jesus shed His blood to pay the price for our sins, and that the only way to avoid the penalty of death was to confess our sins to God and ask Jesus to be the Lord and Savior of our lives. This surgeon did not make a commitment to Christ this morning, but I was able to share the gospel of Christ with him out of compassion, on terms he understood, using the Law, which he knew from his Jewish heritage, and various examples from your messages.

o o o o o

I have just been so blessed the last three months to have you disciple me with all of your teachings. I just got back from a youth camp in Louisiana, and I want you to know that I used the "Have you ever told a lie?" scenario with five youths, and all broke down in contrition and repented and put their faith in Jesus.

I just witnessed to my two favorite nephews for two-and-a-half hours. It was a beautiful work of the Lord. They started out proud and full of knowledge, and they ended up humbled, quiet, and thanking me for helping them see for the first time why Jesus died on the cross (they have grown up Catholic). They had tons of initial objections to Christianity and Scripture, but all melted away in the heat of the Law against the conscience and then the story of God on the cross saving them. *Yeehaaa!* I am pumped, and so grateful to God for this opportunity. They are so precious to me. I've been waiting for this conversation for many years! Another example of how nothing but the Law would have worked here. Can you tell I'm excited?

o o o o o

I have been engrossed in your tape series "Hell's Best Kept Secret"* and your book.... I feed on these constantly. I have pastored for more than eight years and these materials are sure answering a lot of questions for me. I am from the Word of Faith camp, so I was attentive to the letter you published in the book. I have certainly seen the abuses of the faith message and have done it myself. But instead of throwing it all away (we must live by faith), I am just reexamining my heart and will use the faith concepts for souls instead of always focusing on my needs, etc. This message definitely needs to invade the Faith camp as well as all other camps.

---

* Now called The Way of the Master tape series.

o o o o o

I want to thank you for doing God's will, because I am now reaping fruit from what I heard you preach. I was searching and I knew something was missing. I knew it was personal evangelism, but I didn't know how to share or even what to share (although I knew it wasn't "Jesus loves you and has a wonderful plan for your life"). I was impressed by what I read. Your teachings allowed the Holy Spirit to set me on fire! I have probably reaped more fruit in the last month than in my whole life.

God transformed my life eighteen months ago. Since then, I have been on fire for God and have seen many family and friends make "decisions" for Christ. My problem is that 50 percent of them are back in the world. . . . I couldn't pinpoint why until I purchased your Way of the Master DVD series and your book. Thank you.

o o o o o

Thank you for sending me the CD of "Hell's Best Kept Secret." I believe . . . the Lord has been trying to let me know this for quite some time. Finally, a lightbulb went off. Wow! I used to think that everyone *knew* they were sinners. No wonder my witnessing wasn't working very well.

o o o o o

On March 1, 2002, after listening to "Hell's Best Kept Secret" for the fourth time, an anointed lightbulb went off in my head. I jumped up and ran around the house yelling, "I understand! I understand!" I ran up to my dad, gave him a hug and said, "Dad, I understand!" His response was, "What?" Until that day, I had never heard of Judgment Day, never used the Law, and didn't even fear God! I had what you would call "an idolatrous idea of God." During the last few months, God has been showing me how to fear Him and the horror of what I've been saved from. Every night and every morning, I feel the length of eternity on my heart.

o o o o o

Your ministry has touched me and my husband so deeply. Never have we burned with passion for God's Word and purposes as we do now after listening to your tape "Hell's Best Kept Secret."

o   o   o   o   o

I have attended church my entire life. I'm twenty-eight, a deacon and youth leader. I have known I am a sinner and accepted Christ as my Savior as a young child, but I always thought I was missing something, and I just couldn't put my finger on it. Once I listened to "Hell's Best Kept Secret," I was blown away. Why hadn't I ever been taught like this before? I examined myself, and my salvation became so much more real. I felt so alive and free and full of joy that I just had to tell everyone I knew. I have been revived and want to seek and save that which is lost. I now hunger and thirst for righteousness and no longer care about the things of the world.

o   o   o   o   o

I guess I would say I am one of those "Word of Faith-ers." ... My spiritual "walls" went up, but my curiosity won out and I began reading. I was almost immediately enthralled. That night I woke up at 3 a.m. thinking about the book. I got up and continued reading. It has consumed my thoughts for the past several days. I feel so convicted that I too have been deceived, slumbering—and still I feel that my heart is somewhat callous, as though I were in a state of shock. I am so grateful for this spiritual awakening. I wish I could give this book to all of my friends (Christian and not), our pastor, and my family. Thank you, thank you, *thank you* for having the courage to speak *the truth* in love. I feel as though a great light has shone on me. Perhaps this message will be responsible for ushering in revival.

NOTES

Preface
1. See "Closing Words of Comfort" in *The Evidence Bible* (Gainesville, Fla.: Bridge-Logos, 2003), 1684.
2. Read the whole story in Ray Comfort, *Out of the Comfort Zone* (Gainesville, Fla.: Bridge-Logos, 2003), 269 pages .

Chapter 1: Dereliction of Duty
1. Bill Bright, *The Coming Revival* (Orlando, Fla.: NewLife Publications, 1995), 65.

Chapter 2: Phenomenal Growth . . . But Where Has It Gone?
1. *U.S. News and World Report,* August 19, 1996.

Chapter 3: The Way out of Problems?
1. I have deliberately avoided naming specific ministries and individuals, because my purpose is simply to point out a problem with the message, not the ministry or minister, most of whom are sincere and earnest in their desire to reach the lost.
2. John Piper, "Kindling for Christian Hedonism," October 20, 1983, http://www.desiringgod.org/library/sermons/83/103083.html.

Chapter 4: A Lifestyle without a Life
1. J. I. Packer's introductory essay in a 1959 edition of *The Death of Death in the Death of Christ* by John Owen (1616–1683). The text of the essay can be found at http://www.covenant-urc.org/literatr/jpiedddc-1.html.

2. http://www.amazon.com/exec/obidos/tg/detail/-/0743222970/
   002-5282311-0608838?v=glance
3. https://watch002.securesites.net/contact/submit.htm
4. www.nirankari.com/literature/utarget/2003/spring_2003/
   article01.htm
5. http://www.wimmauritius.org/quest.html
6. Matthew Henry, *Commentary on the Whole Bible, Genesis to
   Revelation* (Grand Rapids, Mich.: Zondervan, 1961), 1425.
7. Ibid.

Chapter 5: The Purpose of the Law

1. I give away money because it gets people's attention. Jesus
   referred to money in His preaching—He borrowed a coin for a
   sermon illustration, and even had someone retrieve one from the
   mouth of a fish. If the lost don't love God, they do love money.
   Money is often their source of joy. It is their security. When money
   speaks, they listen.

Chapter 6: Our Broken Backbone

1. K. Connie Kang, "Next Stop, the Pearly Gates," *Los Angeles Times,*
   October 24, 2003.
2. *South Florida Sun Sentinel,* March 18, 2003.
3. J. C. Ryle, "Expository Thoughts—Matthew 5:21-37,"
   http://www.iserv.net/~mrbill/exp/mt051320.html.

Chapter 7: What Did Jesus Do?

1. John Wesley, "Sermon 35," http://wesley.nnu.edu/JohnWesley/
   sermons/035.htm.
2. A. W. Pink, "Studies on Saving Faith," http://www.reformed.org/
   books/pink/saving_faith/saving_faith_1_01.html.
3. Bill Bright and John N. Damoose, *Red Sky in the Morning: How You
   Can Help Prevent America's Gathering Storms* (Orlando, Fla.:
   NewLife Publications, 1998), 218.

Chapter 8: Mangled Bodies

1. Jim Cymbala, *Fresh Wind, Fresh Fire* (Grand Rapids, Mich.:
   Zondervan, 1997), 90.
2. Gordon Miller, "Our Surprising Converts," *Reflections,* September/
   October 1999, http://www.carey.ac.nz/leadership/ref11.htm.

Chapter 9: Making Grace Amazing

1. The audio version of "Hell's Best Kept Secret" can be heard free online at www.wayofthemaster.com.

Chapter 10: From What Did They Flee?

1. Bill Bright, *Heaven or Hell* (Orlando, Fla.: NewLife Publications, 2002), 32, 48.
2. Ibid., 37.

Chapter 11: Well Versed

1. www.mikesmalley.com
2. C. H. Spurgeon, "Coming Judgment of the Secrets of Men," July 12, 1885, http://www.spurgeon.org/sermons/1849.htm.
3. Henry Breeden, *Striking Incidents of Saving Grace* (Hampton, Tenn.: Harvey Christian Publishers, n.d.), 188–89. More information is available at http://home.psknet.com/harveycp/biographies.htm.

Chapter 12: The Motive and the Result

1. Charles Spurgeon, *Morning and Evening,* April 11, Morning.

Chapter 13: Experience: The True Test

1. J. C. Ryle, *Holiness* (Cambridge: James Clarke, 1952).
2. For further teaching on how to use the Law to bring the knowledge of sin, see my books *Hell's Best Kept Secret* (New Kensington, Penn.: Whitaker House, 2002) and *How to Win Souls and Influence People* (North Brunswick, N.J.: Bridge-Logos, 1999).
3. John Wesley, "Sermon 34: The Original, Nature, Property, and Use of the Law," http://wesley.nnu.edu/JohnWesley/sermons/034.htm.
4. Robert Flockhart, *The Street Preacher* (n.p.:), 77, 81
5. Jim Cymbala, *Fresh Wind, Fresh Fire* (Grand Rapids, Mich.: Zondervan, 1997), 92.

Chapter 14: The Badge of Authority

1. Seventh United Nations Survey of Crime Trends and Operations of Criminal Justice Systems, covering the period 1998–2000 (United Nations Office on Drugs and Crime, Center for International Crime Prevention)
2. We have an open-air preaching video called "In Season, Out of Season" (showing open-air preaching in Santa Monica, London,

Paris, Amsterdam, New Zealand, and Tokyo) in which you can see Lazarus in action. See www.wayofthemaster.com or call 800-437-1893 for details.

Chapter 16: How to Share Your Faith

1. *The Way of the Master* Foundation Course includes a video that shows how this approach works with dozens of people. See www.wayofthemaster.com for details.
2. If the person to whom you are witnessing seems to be having trouble understanding a spiritual truth, you may find *The Evidence Bible* (Bridge-Logos) very helpful. It is filled with analogies, one hundred of the most commonly asked questions about the Christian faith, and many other helps. You can obtain a copy through our Web site, www.wayofthemaster.com, or your local Christian bookstore.

Chapter 17: Forget about Jonah

1. See *The Evidence Bible* (Bridge-Logos) for answers to one hundred of the most commonly asked questions about the Christian faith. You can obtain a copy through our Web site, www.wayofthemaster.com, or your local Christian bookstore.
2. Andrew Murray, *Spirit of Christ* (Minneapolis: Bethany, 1979).

Chapter 19: An Angry God

1. *U.S. News and World Report,* January 31, 2000.
2. *Washington Post,* January 9, 2000.

Chapter 20: A Burden for the Lost

1. *Dallas Morning News,* June 11, 1994.

Chapter 24: The Finger of God

You can order "101 of the World's Funniest One-Liners" and other tracts on our Web site, www.wayofthemaster.com, or call 800-\7-1893.